MISSION IN THURINGIA
IN THE TIME OF NAZISM

Paul Beschet, S.J.

MISSION IN THURINGIA
IN THE TIME OF NAZISM
(MISSION EN THURINGE
AU TEMPS DU NAZISME)

TRANSLATED BY THEODORE P. FRASER

MARQUETTE
UNIVERSITY
PRESS

LIBRARY OF CONGRESS CATALOGING IN PUBLICATION DATA

Beschet, Paul.
    [Mission en Thuringe. English]
    Mission in Thuringia in the time of Nazism / Paul Beschet, S.J. ; translated by
Theodore Fraser.
    pages cm
    Includes bibliographical references and index.
    ISBN 978-0-87462-095-5 (paperback : alkaline paper) — ISBN 0-87462-095-3
(paperback : alkaline paper)
    1. Beschet, Paul. 2. World War, 1939-1945—Prisoners and prisons, German.
3. World War, 1939-1945—Conscript labor—Germany—Thuringia. 4. World
War, 1939-1945—Personal narratives, French. 5. Young Christian Workers—
Biography. 6. World War, 1939-1945—Religious aspects—Catholic Church.
7. Youth—Political activity—France—History—20th century. 8. Anti-Nazi movement—Germany—Thuringia. 9. French—Germany—Thuringia—History—20th
century. 10. Thuringia (Germany)—History—20th century. I. Title.
    D805.G3B476813 2012
    940.53'1—dc23
                                                                2012034271

Marquette University Press is grateful to Directeur Général Bernard STEPHAN
and to Les Éditions de L'Atelier / Les Éditions Ouvrières,
51-55 rue Hoche, 94200 Ivry-sur-Seine, France,
copyright holder of the original French edition, *Mission en Thuringe au temps du
Nazisme*, for permission to publish this English translation.

Cover photo copyright holder is the
Nederlands Instituut voor Oorlogsdocumentatie (NIOD).
Photo courtesy of the United States Holocaust Memorial Museum Photo Archives.

♾The paper used in this publication meets the minimum requirements of the
American National Standard for Information Sciences—
Permanence of Paper for Printed Library Materials, ANSI Z39.48-1992.

Association of American University Presses

MARQUETTE UNIVERSITY PRESS
MILWAUKEE

The Association of Jesuit University Presses

To my martyred companions,
To their families,
To all those who shared our exile, and to those who remained faith-
ful during the time of our Mission,
I offer this modest and too hurriedly-written account of out story.

Easter, 1946

CONTENTS

AUTHOR'S PREFACE

A committee for the revision of the text helped us to make corrections and add some needed explanations and supplementary material to the 1947 edition. We hope that this recounting of the story, appearing more than 42 years after the first text was published, will be an improvement for today's readers.

Paul Beschet, S.J.
Lyons, November 28th, 1988

AUTHOR'S ACKNOWLEDGEMENTS

We would like to take this opportunity to thank the families and friends who have contributed to the book, and especially Jean and Christiane Millet, Emile Picaud, Auguste Eveno, Julien Van de Wiele, Roger Martins, the Editions Ouvrières, and Joseph Murzeau, S.J., artist.

TRANSLATOR'S PREFACE

My interest in translating Father Paul Beschet's *Mission en Thuringe au temps du Nazisme* was motivated and inspired by my research of the Spiritual Resistance of the French during the Occupation. His powerful travel/journal chronicle, written only a year after his liberation during the death march from the Flossenbürg Concentration Camp, is one of a very few extant works to tell the story of a very important and poignant example of this phenomenon: the plight of the laborers forcibly deported to work in Germany. In it Beschet provides a priceless documentation of of the aims and modus operandi of these Christian militants in their concerted resistance against the Nazi program to reduce these forced labor conscripts to the level of robots who were to be divested of all moral discrimination and religious practice in order become cogs in the Third Reich's extended slave labor force.

In my translation I have attempted to faithfully reproduce the somewhat complex range or modes of language usage presented in this challenging text: the sprightly narrative tone of the voyage in the journal's initial phases, the language of the working-class conscripts, the truncated and Tower-of- Babel like nature of the language spoken by the deportees in the concentrations camps, and the moving, introspective passages of meditation that accompany the realistic reportage of events throughout the work, especially in the segments which narrate the periods spent in the prison and the camps.

Throughout the work I have taken the liberty to append in the endnotes a number of translator's notes to Beschet's original annotations whenever there was a need to elucidate the mention of persons and cultural, historical, or political allusions which might not be known or understood by a non-French reader. All of the translations of the German texts in the text are my own.

TRANSLATOR'S
ACKNOWLEDGEMENTS

Frist of all, I owe a great debt of gratitude to the following who have played an important role as participants in the Spiritual Resistance and who inspired me to dedicate my research to this aspect of the French Resistance: First, Jacqueline Péri d'Alincourt, survivor of Ravensbrück Concentration Camp, who opened the door to my work by personally introducing me to prominent resistance figures and who offered constant encouragement in the last years of her life.; and my gratitude to two other prominent resisters, also surviving deportation in the camps: Geneviève De Gaulle Anthonioz, and Jacques Sommet, S.J., who both gave generously of their time in discussing their experiences and motivations as Christians in the Resistance. Two people whose aid in preparing my translation was of huge importance are Monsignor Charles Molette, the foremost French historian and authority on the activities of the Christian militants operating within the STO in Germany, who instructed me during the many hours of personal consultation he generously provided.; and Renée Keller, for many years Secretary General of the Union Chrétienne des Déportés et Internés, who was always the source of essentiall information as well as the writer of many letters of introduction to important resistance figures; in fact it was she who first made me aware of Father Beschet's text and led me to him, and who in so many ways facilitated my access to libraries and archives in Paris. There are many others who provided valuable assistance and encouragement: Hans Mittelmeyer, translator and editor of the German translation of *Mission en Thuringe* who generously granted permission for the use of the maps from his text that are reproduced here; the Redemptorist Community in Paris, whose facilities I used as my residence in Paris and where I first met and interviewed Father Beschet; the Jesuit Community of La Chauderie in Francheville, whose hospitality I much enjoyed during my consultations with Father Beschet; the Visiting Scholars Program at Brown University at whose facilities I resided while completing my translation; Professor Gretchen Schultz of the Brown Department of French Studies who generously sponsored my stay there; the librarians of the John Hay Library at Brown who made every effort to facilitate my work during the pleasant days I spent in their splendid reading room; Professor Ambroise Kom, Elinor O'Leary Chair in Francophone Studies at Holy Cross College who carefully read my translation and gave invaluable suggestions and comments; William Zwiebel, Professor Emeritus of German at Holy Cross College, whose expertise aided me enormously in preparing the translation of the German documents; Virginia, Hopcroft, Government Documents Librarian at the Bowdoin College Library who gave of her time in aiding me to locate official German documents; Eben Graves who greatly assisted my efforts at the computer; Andrew Tallon and Maureen Kondrick of Marquette University Press for their patience, expertise and unflagging support during the process of publication; finally, Father Beschet for his patient attention and clear responses to my many questions during the many hours of consultation the I spent with him at La Chauderaie, while preparing my translation.

FOREWORD

June 1940—After the Armistice the Nazis, now the occupiers of our country, decide upon the following:

1) The division of France into various zones: one non-occupied and labeled "free," one occupied, and the forbidden or closed zones (in the coastal regions of the North and the East). Because the borders of these areas were completely sealed off, inter-communication among them became virtually impossible.

2) The control of all activities. A law put into effect on August 28th, 1940 made it mandatory for all associations and movements to ask for and obtain authorization to continue to function.

3) The putting into effect of the policy of consolidating all youth organizations into one single organization.

In the opinion of the occupiers, the French should be expected to contribute to the German war effort by being part of it: hence the first call for "volunteers" put out during the period of 1940-1941, which ended in failure.

Then, to provide for its need for workers, in 1942 Germany adopts forceful means to recruit them throughout its occupied territories. In March Fritz Saukel demands 500,000 French laborers. In June the *Relève* ("prisoner exchange program"), instituted by the German authorities—under the cover of the Vichy government—holds out the false promise of repatriation of French prisoners of war in exchange for workers. Then there is enacted the law of September 4th, which formally institutes the *réquisition* ("compulsory conscription") of workers. Younger workers are now rounded up as they leave their factories.

All this does not satisfy the occupier's demands. Germans are being mobilized to be sent to the battlefields of Russia and their places in the factories must be filled. On the 16th of February, 1943, there is put into effect the *Service du Travail Obligatoire* ("Compulsory Work Service") law, the STO, which makes all young men born between January 1st 1920 and December 31st 1922, subject to obligatory labor (and deportation, if sent to Germany).[1]

---

1   The *Service du Travail Obligatoire* (STO), instituted on February 16, 1943 by the Vichy Government, required young men of an age ordinarily making them eligible for military service—those born between 1920 and 1922—to perform

Immediately there is an outpouring of draft notices everywhere. The government had decided to act quickly so that those called up would not have time to disappear, and numerous were the young people torn from their homes and forced to go to German factories. The Nazi political machine was very adept in using threats of reprisal against a family or a brother, who would be sent in the place of the draftee. Very few succeeded in escaping this pernicious edict by camouflaging their identities. In many cases the draft dodgers went off to join the Resistance in the *Maquis* (underground forces).

Risking persecution, the organizations of Catholic Action, and in particular, the *Jeunesse Ouvrière Chrétienne* ("Organization of Young Christian Workers") or the JOC,[2] refused to abide by the stipulations of the law of August 28, 1940. On August 3, 1943 at about 4 o'clock in the afternoon, Gestapo agents arrested three national directors of the JOC. They were subsequently released after the arrest of Abbé Guérin, the founder of the French JOC, who was himself imprisoned at Fresnes until December 22, 1943.

"Wherever there are French workers, there the JOC must be as well," became our slogan. During this time in Germany, Jocists and Scouts took control of the running of welcoming centers, sports, and recreational activities in the labor camps. Aided by clandestine chaplains and seminarians conscripted for the STO, they organized all forms of Catholic Action that had been strictly forbidden and were actively prosecuted by the Nazis. Such activities led to the martyrdom of a number of them.

The Beatification of one from their group, Marcel Callo by Pope John Paul II, on October 4, 1987, provided the occasion for a meeting between the generations and for a moving reunion with one another of former activists who had been engaged in clandestine activities in Germany

---

two years of compulsory labor service. It was generally understood that most of those affected by the law would be sent to Germany—hence the use of the word "deportation" used to describe their situation to the adamant objections of the German and French organizers of this conscription of French workers. It is estimated that some 750,000 (and over 30,000 women) were forced to go to work in Germany from 1942 to the end of the war. (trans. note)

2   An organization established in Belgium in 1927 by Joseph Cardijn, a Belgian priest. Its purpose was to rechristianize young men of the working classes. It rapidly spread to France and other European nations (including Germany), and its French members constituted a large contingent of those drafted under the STO laws enacted in 1943. (trans. note)

of that period—priests, religious, Jocists, and Scouts. Those present at Rome, on the eve of the Beatification, decided to organize in order to:

—honor and transmit the memory of those who, like Marcel Callo, had been arrested by the Gestapo for their Catholic Action and who died as "witnesses for Christ" in Nazi concentration camps.

—actively collaborate through research, sources of information, testimony of witnesses, and documentation for the purpose of initiating the cause of beatification for these young men who had died for their faith.

On September 14th, 1988, Cardinal Decourtray, president of the Conference of the Bishops of France, decided to open the collective cause for "the Martyrs of the Apostolate organized within the very center of the STO operation." Conducted on a national scale, this collective cause involves at present nine priests, two seminarians, four brothers in religious orders, eleven scouts, and seventeen Jocists. These 43[3] martyrs worked, as the survivors have testified, in different

---

3 The number has been updated to 51 formally identified as martyrs who were put to death as a result of their involvement in the "Mission Saint. Paul." The "Mission" comprised those priests, religious, and laypersons engaged in day-to-day work as laborers in Germany who simultaneously carried out their program of mission work and aid for French conscripts deported by slave workers as a result of the Vichy government's national draft program, the *Service du Travail Obligatoire* (STO)—"Obligatory Work Service" put into law on February 16, 1943. The individual members of the group of 51 and their mission in Germany have been the subjects of intensive research by Monsignor Charles Molette who has also studied the broader topic of Catholic/spiritual resistance to the systematic program of Nazification and dechristianisation carried out by Hitler Germany in France and the other occupied countries. Monsignor Molette describes and documents the determined efforts of the Catholic Church to oppose this Nazi objective among French workers through the efforts and sacrifices of militants, both clerical and lay, leading some of the group to the willing acceptance of martyrdom. His works are highly regarded for their impeccable standards of historical research, scholarship and accuracy. All subsequent studies of Spiritual Resistance to Nazi Occupation have relied heavily on the groundwork he has provided. See in particular his definitive study of the movement "Mission Saint Paul" in which Father Beschet and his comrades participated, enduring prison, internment in concentrations camps, the "march of death," and for some, martyrdom: La "*Mission Saint Paul*" *traquée par la Gestapo. Pérsércution et déportation des militants de l'apostat catholique français en Allemagne* ("The Saint Paul Mission, Hunted Down by the Gestapo, and the Persecution and Deportation of the Militants of the French Catholic Apostolate in Germany") Paris: Francois-Xavier de Guibert, 2003. Also an earlier work: "*En Haine de l 'Evangile*" *Victimes du décret de persecution Nazi contre l'apostolat catholique*

areas of Hitler's Germany. The work by Paul Beschet, S.J., *Mission in Thuringia in the Time of Nazism*, edited in 1946 and 1947, is one of the few testimonies written after the war about these apostolic and spiritual activities set in the historical context of the times.

The events dealt with herein have sparked a demand for a new edition of this work, which is presently almost unavailable. Many of the activists and their friends, who lived through the STO captivity, the Resistance, and deportation were eager to have a new edition.

Young adults recently become parents are also more and more interested in this period and certain of its aspects that were more or less unknown or passed over during their own adolescence. Historians, study groups, and numbers of young workers and students are now requesting a new edition because it constitutes a living and authentic testimony of what Christian lay activists, priests, religious, and seminarians accomplished, while firmly bearing witness to their faith and sharing it with others, in their resistance to the Nazi ideology.

It is for these reasons that thirty or so activists, who had been involved in the *Mission in Thuringia in the Time of Nazism* and who came together from the 19th to the 21st of April, 1988 in the Briandais Manor in Missilac en Loire-Atlantique, unanimously decided to prepare a new edition of this work.

May the reading of these pages dealing with the extraordinary adventures of these young people who, by risking their lives, succeeded in providing organizations to safeguard the morals of their comrades and despite the harshest of living conditions, managed to hold fast to and strengthen their own faith, thus providing aid and encouragement to other activists of our own day who are faced with equally serious causes: the economic crisis, " the new classes of the poor," delinquency, lack of respect for life, moral degradation, racism, world hunger and international conflicts. These are pressing problems that demand urgent attention and organized action motivated by concerns for liberty, peace and respect for human rights—worthy commitments for Christians as witnesses of Jesus Christ.

Auguste Eveno
Emile Picaud
Former Directors of Clandestine Catholic Action in the STO
44350 Guérande, October 1988 J

---

français à l'oeuvre parmi les travail leurs requis en Allemagne 1943-1945. ("Out of Hatred for the Gospel," Victims of the Nazi Decree of Persecution Against the French Catholic Apostolate Involved with the Workers Conscripted to Germany, 1943-1945") Paris: Fayard, 1993. (trans. note)

PREFACE

A reading of these pages of modern Christian life calls to mind memories of the primitive Church of the first centuries. We find in them the same living faith that illuminated the catacombs, the same supernatural love of the first witnesses for Jesus Christ, whose blood reddened the Roman arenas.

Here the catacombs are the woods, the streets, the cafes, the *Lagers* ("work camps") of German industrial cities; and the Nazi circuses are the concentration camps scientifically equipped to inflict suffering and refine ways for killing people. Young Christians and especially the Jocists will find in this work (for which we cannot sufficiently thank Paul Beschet) examples in our times of authentic Christian conduct. They will read here how their older brothers, aided by admirable clandestine chaplains, found very natural and appropriate apostolic paths for action, and in union with Christ, drew from within themselves extraordinary virtues which allowed some to become martyrs, and all of them missionaries.

The words of one of them, who died at Mauthausen,[1] make clear their own personal feelings: "I am leaving [for the STO] not as a worker but as a missionary."

This was not mere verbiage because indeed, he and his companions immediately accomplished this role in magnificent ways. Paul Beschet tells us: "I found a half dozen or so leaders who, with impressive style and a highly developed social and religious sensitivity, had already begun to bring others together."

How cogently does this rapid ability to adapt to situations prove the value of the education received by some (the religious) in their novitiate and by others (the lay people) in organizations sponsored by Catholic Action Organizations! One thinks in particular of these young religious who abruptly had to interrupt their studies and leave a welcoming and loving community. They tried and succeeded magnificently in building a new (yet so different) one, yet every bit as closely

---

1   Marcel Callo, Jocist from Rennes, died at Mauthausen on March 19th, 1945 and was beatified in Rome on October 4th, 1987.

knit, supportive, inspiring, and fraternal as what they had left, so as to allow it to raise up an entire mass of unformed young people, susceptible to all manner of moral decadence because of the terribly demoralizing life they were forced to lead.

They all resolved to "return better and in larger numbers."[2] And in fact they did return better and enriched by this sorrowful but authentically Christian experience, with an immense desire to dedicate themselves totally to the reconstruction not only of their country, but even of the entire world.

However, they seem at some point to have experienced a let down, almost all of them, in this afterglow of enthusiasm, because of a host of circumstances, disillusions, and failures which finally discouraged them. They wanted to continue to live this "high powered Christianity" but found they were not able to do so. May they take to heart this reflection Camille Millet made from prison: "We may be 'arrested' but is this any reason for us to stop?"[3]

Permit us to add the following: "Don't be discouraged. Life and truth always win out in the end. Your desire for a 'high-powered religion' is nothing more than the Bible in action. You are carrying out Christ's teachings. You are his apostles and witnesses."

"You are other Christs living in the midst of your brothers. Your victory is assured."

Do we need to add that we recommend these "memoirs" to all those who do not believe in Catholic Action, to all those, priests or laypeople, who have not yet known the priceless experience of significantly changing a milieu from within, and the valuable collaboration that laypeople bring to these special organizations?

We are convinced that the reading of this book should intensify missionary activity in our modern societies, in those very centers where the masses no longer live in a hostile religious environment but one supportive of them.

The mission of charity and light entrusted by Christ to his Church is precisely what these young STO conscripts carried out in Germany. We no doubt need to use different adaptations and employ different methods in continuing to carry it out in our homes, our neighborhoods, and our factories, but we must be animated by the same

---

2   Jocist motto.

3   A play on words: the French verb *arrêter* which can mean both "to stop" and to arrest someone. (trans. note)

audacious faith and willingness to make a total gift of self that these missionaries in Thuringia so well exemplified in their own lives.

Joseph Cardijn[4]
May, 1946

---

4   The founder of the JOC in France.

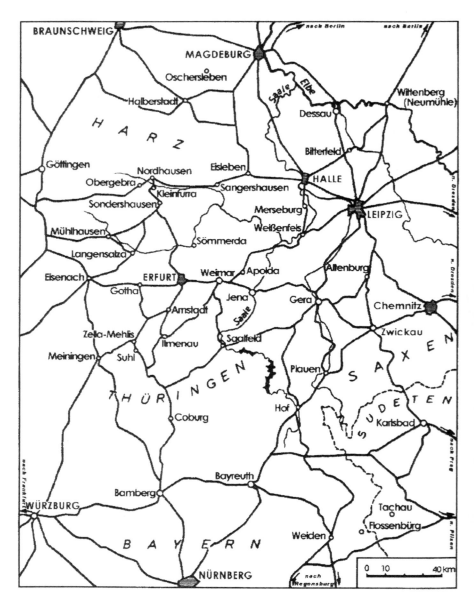

The events of this narrative took place in this area of Germany.

PART I: THE STO

CHAPTER ONE

A STUDY TRIP IN THE LYONS-BROTTEAUX RAILROAD STATION

Saturday, July 31ˢᵗ, 1943—12:15 a.m. An unlit train slowly rolled out of the Brotteaux Station at Lyons, headed toward Dijon. All the travelers crowded up against the windows, not because the view was particularly attractive—it was only the standard décor of the merchandise platforms of a train station receding into the dark of night—but despite its banality, they all seemed to want to fix it in their memory as a kind of symbol. This was a train carrying draftees for the STO—including our own group numbering 1,200 students from the Southwest of France.

Our convoy's departure was the cause of considerable commotion. Sauckel's[1] recruiters could take pride in having called up a large group of students—most of them with diplomas—consisting of seminarians and young religious representing all the orders—a recalcitrant troop not easily controlled. About twenty or so of them had had the crazy idea of bursting into the *Amicale* ("Welcome Center") wearing their cassocks, backpacks, valises in hand, and with their religious superiors at the head of the line. The system almost breaks down. "No funny stuff. Get over there! Enough of that!"

"Calling the group leader, if you please." They discuss the situation for form's sake. Those in charge beg us not to force them to take any action that could harm us. O. K. We won't press the point. We defrock

---

1   Fritz Sauckel, Gauleiter of Thuringia, was named plenipotentiary for the recruitment of foreign labor for the Reich in occupied territories March 21, 1942. (trans. note)

in the midst of the station and walk around for more than an hour with open cassocks exposing trousers and summer short-sleeve shirts. A French inspector for the Red Cross and someone who fully grasps the comic and grotesque aspects of the situation asks: "You mean you people are going too?"

"What do you expect?" we respond. "France is wherever its young people are, especially when they are being called upon to suffer. Don't worry, we intend to be the kind of ambassadors for France that the posters displayed in your Welcome Center propose that we become." There were still some heated disturbances coming from within the group. The *Marseillaise* reverberated throughout the station. Then little by little everything became quiet. No one had any desire to talk. Each would only have said to the others the same things he had heard them say. It was useless to reveal feelings we shared in common. Soothed by the monotonous sound of the train wheels in our darkened train compartment, we slipped from dreams into sleep, the only reaction possible in facing the uncertain but surely difficult days that lay ahead.

We travel three hours and a half and then make a stop at Saint-Germain-au-Mont-D'Or. Since we are simultaneously of considerable value yet insignificant, we are forgotten for hours, parked in a railroad garage and placed under military guard. (These two points of view will constantly be in play—we will be badly treated because we are deeply hated, yet relatively well cared for as potentially productive workers.) At the crack of dawn we pass through Villefranche, then Mâcon. At Chalons we wash up at the station's water fount, splashing a bit of cold water on ourselves to overcome the fatigue of sleeping in the rough. Ten o'clock and we arrive at Dijon. Our first roll call (this won't be the last, and for two years we'll learn what it is like to be penned in, counted, recounted, and our names read off). Some young girls from the German Red Cross offer us a snack and we immediately resume the voyage. This time we really are leaving. We sing the *Marseillaise* and *Le Chant des Adieux*,[2] the railway workers become teary-eyed. We won't get off this train until we pass beyond the German border. I remember an old woman who wept as she watched us leaving and, shaking her handkerchief, cried out: "Cheer up, kids, you'll be back in three months!" (This was the moment of optimism just after the fall of Mussolini when people in the know were certain that Germany

2   A French evening song. (trans. note)

couldn't hold out much longer all by itself!) Under brilliant sunshine the train passes by endless fields of grain ready to be harvested. Now in good humor we share our food in common, in little groups. About one o'clock in the afternoon, we arrive at Besançon in its bombed-out station. We're black with dust and soaking with sweat. We crowd around the only water fount, and the process goes very slowly. The train whistle blows, the group leader shouts himself hoarse, but our men (jokers and philosophers) reply in a bantering tone: "If you're in such a hurry, why don't you just leave without us, we're in no rush. Don't worry, it won't leave without us." But we get back in and the train slowly moves out of the station. Three o'clock, Mobéliard, then Belfort. Three kilometers farther along and still not German territory because we're in Alsace, but the Grand Reich awaits us Customs inspection, rumors circulate—"They're going to frisk us, no books, no notes, no cards, a limit on the amount of French money." But in the end, our passing through customs turns out to be benign and without incident. Goodbye, France! We've come to the end of a calm and still afternoon, during which the children, women, and men of Alsace greeted us as part of the *Relève* ("prisoner relief plan") while in fact we represent something very different from what Hitler (and Laval) had in mind.

At Mulhouse, where we arrive about 6 o'clock in the evening, Jacques Vignon,[3] a young priest draftee, says Mass in the train compartment. We take communion on the rails outside while our friends catch in mid-air the little bottles of beer that the young girls of Alsace are throwing to them from either side of a crosswalk level with the train. Another roll call, another snack—a bit of bread, a taste of classic German sausage, soup and the first payment by the Grand Reich, one and one half marks. (This makes me think of the old woman who, meeting a child in the street, slips him ten cents, saying, "Look here, my boy, buy everything you want and then give the rest back to your Mom!"). A few of us chat with the station master who, though he wears a German uniform, has remained a true Frenchman at heart. He speaks his mind, delighted to be in touch for a few minutes with France. But we are definitely no longer there and are abruptly reminded of this when we hear a translated message over the loud-speaking system telling us that if we cause any disturbance, we'll be severely punished. Many of us lean outside the railroad carriage windows, and the *Marseillaise* resounds triumphantly and impetuously throughout

3 Of the Diocese of Lyon.

the station, as the train moves out. There can be no doubt that the
psychological make up of the French will ever remain a closed world
to the average German and something never understood. At 7 p.m.
we cross the Rhine. Then at Fribourg, the train passes through the
Bade plain, and the excitement we've felt during the course of the day
gradually fades as evening approaches. In silence we view the fields of
growing hop with the Black Forest in the distance. We think about all
the familiar things we're leaving behind as well as our new adventure.
After Offenburg we settle down for the night. Dédé and I share the
space between the two benches on a floor redolent with sweat and
other strong smells. With good will and vertebral agility Pierre, André,
Jo, and Momo find a satisfactory place to stretch out on bags and cases.
Where now are our quiet dormitories with their well-ordered rows of
beds? Other times other places!

Arriving at the Karlsruhe station around midnight, we stop opposite a train of draftees coming back from leave. We greet each other
from both sides of the windows, and the more experienced draftees
shout out to us precise words of advice and comments fortunately not
understood by the natives. When our train moves on once again, we
intone another *Marseillaise* sung at the top of our lungs, which momentarily seems to startle the people in the station. After this brief
intermission we then return to the warmth of our compartments and
try to get back to sleep. We are told that we won't change trains until Nuremberg where a copious meal awaits us. Relying on this, we
abandon ourselves to the workings of Mr. Saukel's marvelously efficient system (or so it is reputed to be). Stuttgart, Sunday, August 1st, 4
o'clock in the morning, a major commotion—everyone has to change
trains because ours, being late, threatens to upset all traffic patterns;
our itinerary has therefore to be changed with the result that we are
obliged to stop at sites where we are not expected and thus have to
hear people say, as we down our cold soup and scraps of food, "Well,
too bad because at such and such a place a magnificent banquet was
kept on hold for you." This I'd really like to believe, but it surely is
strange that splendid things always seemed to be scheduled for places
I couldn't get to. Sauckel might undeniably be a great organizer, but
because everything is so rigidly planned, at the slightest mishap everything goes awry. Meditating upon this and other such lofty matters,
half asleep, we collect shoes, valises, coats, mess kits and other uten-
sils. I doze off, my eyelids drooping in repeated futile attempts to fall

asleep. Some of us are more stoical, like that chemistry student who, barefooted on the tar of the platform, seems to take a manly pleasure in trampling down on German soil. We pass by Avalon, Grailsheim, Ainsbach. The sun continues to shine brightly. At each station we rush to the water fount. Eleven-fifteen, Nuremberg, sacred city of the Nazi regime. A two-hour stop. Major wash up on the platform now transformed into a bathroom before the shocked gaze of the native populace. A wag suggests that we take up a collection to break up the crowd of spectators. As this is going on, Jacques says Mass for us in his compartment. We hear it as we pace up and down on the platform. Another departure, direction of Leipzig. We take the mountain route—Beyreuth, Hof. At one station, other French people get on board. We chat and they tell us about the terrible phosphorus bombing of Hamburg. But what is most remarkable is the general attitude of our group. A train full of draftees? Not on your life, rather one of conquerors who sing, constantly heckle quiet spectators, and prevent other people from boarding by shouting out, "French, this train is for French people only." And the well-disciplined Germans remain calmly on the platform. This train isn't for them. For quite a while now the countryside has been changing: factories, industrial areas, more factories throwing dark and yellow smoke into the skies. All these buildings give off an ominous appearance in the growing darkness.

FROM LEIPZIG TO SONDERHAUSEN

In the dead of night we detrain on one of the 27 platforms in Europe's largest railroad station. The lighting is strictly camouflaged, and we can't see a thing. Jostling with the crowd, we arrive at the Welcome Center—a large, cold and dingy building where we are confined for the night. At midnight a snack—obviously these people have no sense of the time or frequency of meals. Everyone receives a ration of jam—as expected. We bed down wherever we can, men and women pell-mell on the floor which nevertheless seems so comfortable to us, tired as we are. Very early in the morning Jacques risks going out. He comes back with the Eucharist after hearing mass in a neighboring church. Rapid distribution of hosts in the midst of the general hubbub. During the morning, assisted by Jacques, I confer the scout insignia on André Yverneau who has just made his solemn promise. Then we undergo the first work selection: Jacques Vignon is assigned to

Chemnitz,[4] Magne, La Bonnardière and A. d'Oncieu,[5] who are intent on going with him, falsify their designated numbers for waiting in line and thus round out a curious mix of seminarians, Spiritans, Marists, and students of all sorts who go off together. Our first leave takings. "Don't worry, guy. See you again at … the Bastille … Let's get on with it! Hang in there, Jacques. So long, Paul."

Around noon the rest of the group, counted and recounted, is delivered back to the station. People stare at us as if we are strange animals. I recall a conversation with a Czech. We offer him a cigarette and sing the popular Czech song, *Tetché, voda, tetché*. He leaves us feeling in better spirits. A train is departing for Halle with ridiculously few seats left for us. We refuse to go in, and then our group leader is obliged to dislodge all the comfortably ensconced travelers who now have to give up their seats to the *Franzosen* ("the French"). We "occupy" them in high spirits. "So long, come back later for your seats." We travel for a whole hour through terraces cut up into finely cultivated parcels of land and attractive houses all resembling each other, with their identical boxes of red geraniums. One-thirty. Halle. We get off and wait once again. Some keep an eye on our bags and boxes piled up on the station platform. Others take a stroll about as we wait for the wagon to bring our luggage into the camp. We have our first contact with dark beer and observe the cosmopolitan nature of the Reich's population. There are many French all around us, as well as Belgians, Czechs, and Russians, A huge fellow, speaking French with a heavy Belgian accent, relates his odyssey and offers several political observations, which he invariably concludes with the expression: "They're mad, every single one of them!" He drags along in his trail, like a faithful dog, a German station worker who seems to be uniquely in his service. Despite the German's elaborate gestures and objections, the Belgian remains in control. Finally, they disappear into the crowd, one following the other. The cart comes, we load it. Suddenly the huge blond fellow who is the driver asks for a cigarette. Our immediate reaction is to say, "No way, you've got to be kidding."

"He's not a *Chleu*" ("a German") someone says, "he's Russian."

"Oh, that's another story." And cigarettes are offered from all sides.

---

4   Today, Karl-Marx Stadt.

5   Jesuit students from Mongré (Villefranche-en-Beaujolais).

Now we're in the camp: at the selection center for French workers en route from France to Germany where, after registration and a physical examination, they are assigned to factories in the region. It's also a collection center for Russians and Poles who are sick and not able to work. It's here that we get our first view of inhumane treatment. Men, women, children and old people, half naked, and enclosed in shacks behind barbed wire are waiting to be shipped off to other areas. Totally abandoned without virtually any food and kept in disgustingly filthy conditions, they resemble a herd of lost cattle. When our guards aren't watching, we throw them some bread: they hurl themselves on it like a pack of famished animals. Evening arrives—we are given a thick, tasteless soup. Facing the West, we sing *Vieux chalet* before going to sleep in our two-tiered bunk beds.

Next morning the Flemish SS administer physical exams. They tap our skin. The gleaming apparatus, the multiple medical forms we have to fill out, the taking down of our vital statistics—none of these things manage to cover over with an air of respectability what we represent: a meat market of human flesh being prepped for work. Midday—another tasteless and thick soup. Five hours later we get permission to go to town. Accompanied by Maurice, I try out my German. "Where is the Catholic Church?" *Elisabeth Kirche? Ja!* With exaggerated gestures an old man and war veteran gives us directions. Then we persuade a little "Hitler youth" with the offer of a cigarette to show us the way, and he leads us to it, followed by a swarm of kids—blue-eyed, blond locks, strange looking and aggressive, with daggers attached to their belts and their stockings pulled down. In church, communion and friendly greetings from the priest. One of us goes to the organ and we sing with full voice: *Chez nous, soyez Reine.*[6] And in the evening: *Sois fier et sois fidèle, De France douce et belle … Souviens-toi.*[7]

We are beginning to get used to people always shouting: it's well known that a pure-blooded *Chleu* never talks without shouting. They yell out everything they say. "Thank you, hello, what time is it?" (*Danke Schön, Morgan, wie spät?*) You just have to know this. But we have with us Jean, a Jesuit novice and musician-emeritus of swing, who can

---

6   A French hymn often sung by those on pilgrimage (especially to the destination of Lourdes): ("Dear Lady be our Queen"). (trans. note)

7   This song became one of the most popular for French POWs and workers in captivity in Germany: ("Be proud, be faithful, Never forget sweet, beautiful France"). (trans. note)

coax delicious harmonies from a simple harmonica, and when one of these gentlemen begins to yell a command, he accompanies us as we serenade the official with a rendition of *Sur deux notes*.[8] Finally we get ready to go to bed.

Wednesday, August 4th, another work selection. The German priest hasn't been able to tell us if there are some brother Jesuits still in the area; it seems that about twenty of them had left sometime earlier. We'll have to check out their whereabouts later. Jo Boutry, Louis Guéguen, Marcel Laure, André Meynier, Henri Noyelle, Jean Reynaud,[9] several seminarians from the diocese of Vivier, and a large segment of our own group will be leaving us for Saalfeld-am-Saale, in Thuringia. A few will remain in Halle. Yverneau and Jo want to bribe the group leaders with chocolate so that they can stay in this city (Halle). The same German priest has told them that there are several thousand French workers living in the surrounding camps without benefit of a single priest! The group leader hurries our leave takings, saying "Tomorrow, tomorrow." We bid goodbye to each other and sing *Chant des Adieux*. With smiles and jokes we try to cover over our feelings of anguish and humiliation. Those still remaining—about thirty seminarians—regroup. One of them, Ronzon from Lyon—a heavy smoker, hence his nickname—grouses because this time he hadn't been able to slip away in the Dijon railroad station as he managed to do last May. There is a large delegation from Viviers. Then we have Pierre Sournac, a colorful Southerner from Montauban; André Yverneau, diminutive in size and non assuming in appearance, but from a solid peasant background; Jean Carton, André Dupont, Emile Lebrun, your typical Northerner; finally Jacques Lozé, a plain-spoken Parisian originally from Angoulême: these are to be my fellow adventurers. Our destination is Nordhausen. We ask the leader, "Where is this in relation to Saalfeld?"

"A distance of two railroad stops." We look at the map.

---

8   One of the best known songs of the very popular French songster, Charles Trenet. (trans. note)

9   Other Jesuit students from Mongré.

"What a joker, it's over on the other side of Thuringia, more than 150 kilometers away!" We now begin to appreciate the reliability of information given by these people from D.A.F.[10]

Several hours go by before we get the order to depart; as usual, our transport leader profits from the wait to inculcate us with good Nazi philosophy. In the process, he clumsily pulls out all the stops, running the gamut from being amiable, to brutal, then conciliatory. "French women," he says, "are going to be drafted into the STO. Turkey has just recently come over to the side of the Nazis. New secret weapons are being developed." Completing his apostolic labor, he leaves us to begin again the same lucrative task with other convoys just arriving from France, and he puts us in the hands of another very pleasant gentleman who seems somewhat embarrassed to be playing the role of slave trader. When we leave Halle, we are placed in train wagons locked on only one side. These folks really have a sense of irony and, from time to time, must want to make us feel relaxed at their own expense. We travel toward Nordhausen—pass fields of wheat and sugar beets … arrive at 5 p.m. Our leader leaves us at the station and then returns to tell us that the Labor Bureau doesn't want students. We are now posted for Sonderhausen, twenty kilometers further on. We get back in the train; when we pass a mine, André looks at me as if to say, "Is this for us?" Wolkramshausen, Kleinfurra. Still not Sonderhausen. Ah, finally we're here.

A dapper, smiling and pleasant Herr Schaärschmidt, the director of foreign labor for the manufacture of electrical appliances at the firm Brunnquell and Co., meets us at the station and takes us to our quarters 200 meters away. It is a new building, clean, well kept, and our first impressions are indeed positive. For the time being we'll be housed in two square blocks. Herr Brunnquell, Jr., thirty years old and our boss—a handsome, sturdy, polite but rather cold-looking man—asks us what we do for work. Marcel, our interpreter, a dyed in the wool native of Lyons, though now living in Mâcon, replies: "I'm a student!"

"And the others?" queries Brunnquell, pointing at us.

"Theological students."

---

10   *Deutsche Arbeitsfront-D. A. F.* ("German Labor Bureau")—the official German labor union and watch-dog agency overseeing the life and work habits of foreign labor. It had representatives in all the work *Kommandos* and factories where foreign conscripts were assigned. (trans. note)

"Ah, yes," Brunquell replies, smiling. We smile back. He packs us into his truck and drives us to a little *Gasthaus* ("restaurant") three kilometers away, at the entrance of a picturesque forest. We are only served soup but find it very appetizing. Afterwards, we spend the evening relaxing. I go back to my barracks with Jean and we exchange impressions. We're lucky: it's a small factory in a quiet area. Fifteen of us here are *curés*; that's a lot, but we'll spread out. And once we become accustomed to the area, thanks to Hitler, we'll reunite these communities that he himself has torn apart.

CHAPTER TWO

FIRST CONTACTS

On one particular day, they located several militants and, since that time, they have been spending their nights talking with them. This all happened on a Saturday afternoon in August. The POW chaplain had managed to slip away from the prison *Kommando*[1] and while proceeding on the road to the cemetery, he heard our confessions, one after the other, as if they were innocent chats that we quickly and casually struck up with him along the way. Since that time we've only been able to depend upon our German *curé* who, after we arrived, had taken on the task of learning French.

On our return to the city, Pierre Sournac and I would often discreetly accompany the French priest on his way back to his *Kommando*. On weekend afternoons the worker trains punctually deposit on the city streets a crowd, freshly groomed and looking its best, consisting of middle-class people, workers, POWs, foreign workers, and Russian women, their heads covered with large white kerchiefs. Many of these coming in from the surrounding areas are easy to recognize among the passersby because foreigners, and especially French people, are rarely seen in and about Sondershausen. Together with Pierre, we reconnoiter a bit because you never know. When, at the other side of a short road crossing, we come up to a trio in animated conversation, speaking loudly, hands in their pockets, and cigarettes dangling from their mouths—we generally reveal who we are by the way we behave in public—Pierre cries out, "You're French, aren't you?"

"I should hope so, yes indeed!" replies a strapping fellow with large black-rimmed glasses, dark smoothed-down hair and a narrow beard of the same color. He introduces himself: "Jean Ménager, call me Julot, from Guérande. And a pure-bred native at that," he adds, uncovering

---

1 The priest was Abbé Danset, from the diocese of Lille and chaplain of the *Kommando* of French POWs.

the white coat of arms of the red Cross of Malta that he wears embroidered on the pocket of his coat.[2]

"By the way," I ask, "Are you a Jocist?"

"Yes, and I'm looking to have a brief conversation with a chaplain."

"Really, well there's one right behind us."

"And you know him personally?"

"Yes, we're seminarians."

"Hmm, only two of you?"

"No, there are a few more of us—about 15 who've just recently arrived." "Good, wait for me here; no, better still, go directly to the church."

Julot, with his two friends in tow, disappeared to go off to engage the priest for the "brief conversation" they had in mind.

Taking care of some errands as we pass through the city, we head for the *Elisabethkirche*. En route we give vent to our surprise at this chance meeting. Where do they come from? Is it possible that there is a camp nearby? That would be astonishing because no one, neither the German priest nor the POWs, have mentioned anything about this. After going around in circles in this God-forsaken country without finding any apostolic opportunities, we seem to see a door opening before us. With Pierre, we decide somewhat brashly to take the lion by the tail. We'll tell the others that we came upon them by chance and that our meeting was providential.

But upon opening the door of the church we are even more baffled. Inside there are already about 15 young men wearing insignias that leave no doubt about their faith commitment. André Dupont and Jacques join them in the pews. When one of us moves farther back in the nave, a few of them cast cautious glances about. They too need to see to believe. But they are not deceived by the way we conduct ourselves. André Yverneau recites the *Confiteor* too well and genuflects too expertly. They are immediately aware that they are dealing with people who are very practiced in such matters.

About thirty people took communion. Pierre went to find the leader with the thin black beard who was praying in the back of the church; he suggested to him that we join in a common prayer of thanksgiving. For his part Julot had already had similar thoughts, and, while each of us is in silent communion with God, he announces in a strong and clear voice:

---

2   This is the Jocist insignia.

Our friend Louis Palvadeau, president of our section, has just gone
to the hospital at Nordhausen, stricken with a serious illness. In
terrible pain while being transported there, he told me: "I offer my
sufferings for the working class, the JOC, and our Catholic Action
organization in Germany." You should know that he remains in very
critical condition and could leave us at any moment. Lord, you test
us, but always in your own way. Louis's sufferings and the loss that
our Kleinfurra section will undergo through the death of a leader
of his caliber will not have been in vain, because You have just sent
us these older brothers, our unexpected neighbors who will work
with us. Now we'll be less isolated in advancing your cause. For this
we thank You.

The prayer of thanksgiving continued in this vein for a little while longer. Father Kirchberg prayed while watching us from his choir stall.
Then, before leaving, we rose in unison to sing the *Magnificat*.

Outside on the church steps, they introduced themselves with
booming voices. These young men are from Aveyron, Nantes, and the
greater Nantes area. They work about 10 kilometers from here in a
Wehrmacht factory, constructed on an old salt mine. Some of them
handle artillery shells and gun powder 600 meters underground;
others unload trucks and train wagons at ground level; and some carry building materials to the work area. Julot introduces his friends.
Among them is Emile Picaud, Federal Representative from Saint
Nazaire, a tall man, calm, square-shouldered and cut out to be a leader.

Not wishing to waste any more time, we spend the evening in the
Ratskeller—a restaurant in the town hall. A half dozen follow us
there: Julot and Milo, François, Jean, Marcel and Louis.[3]

As is usual on Saturday nights, the *Gastzimmer* of the Ratskeller is
noisy and crowded. Sensing our feeling of being somewhat out of our
element here, our friendly waitress disappears for a moment, then re-
appears, smiling, and seats us in a little room reserved for card players.
We talk for a long time and they tell us about the kinds of activities
they had begun to initiate at Kleinfurra, the camp that Pierre Sournac
would have the opportunity to get to know a few weeks later. Jean

3   Jean Ménager, Emile Picaud, Federal Jocist from Saint Nazaire/ François
    Granier from Millau, Jocist Federal Director from l'Averyon. Jean Laurent,
    Jocist Director from Decazeville. Marcel Peyraud from Nantes, a new ac-
    tivist. Louis Latapie, scout master from Decazeville. This team, that we got
    to know that evening, would work with us during the twenty months that
    would ensue before the Liberation (April 11th, 1945).

speaks about his Protestant friend with whom he has weekly discussions. François reports that he has taken over the sports activities— the soccer team and the swimming program at the Sonderhausen pool. Julot, a man who seems to be able to do everything with undaunted enthusiasm, has, with the aid of a scout,[4] launched a theatrical group and some humorous radio programs, in addition to the many causes and activities he is busily directing to provide for the well being and freedom of the young workers. Marcel teaches catechism to a Navy POW who will soon make his first communion.

As I listen to them speak, I reflect on the fact that only yesterday we were preparing projects and discussing how we might carry them out by going in twos to various other cities because there seemed to be nothing for us to do here. But now a door has surely swung open onto a seemingly ideal field: there are about 150 French people in the immediate vicinity, and that number is doubled if one adds to it a large contingent of Belgians evacuated from a factory in the Ruhr—all of these served by a half-dozen really impressive activists with a solid grasp of social and supernatural realities. And now we will augment their ranks with a good fifteen or more new leaders.

The dining room grows quiet as people gradually get up to leave. The waiter politely asks us to give up our places to card players. We regroup around another table with Pierre who tells the others who we are: young religious who have already been involved in scouting and Catholic Action, whom their superiors have sent to work for the STO for reasons of solidarity and charity. "We've been asked," he says,

> to submit out of obedience and to transcend our deep patriotic feelings in order to come here and serve as missionaries to the masses of workers living in exile and deprived of any spiritual aid. Having come to witness, we have chosen to be here and are committed to play an active role. We're not priests yet, but, as insignificant as we are at this point, we want to work with you with as best we can.

Milo, who hadn't said much up to now, breaks his silence. Glancing about the smoke-filled room, presently empty except for these young men bending towards each other around the table, he clearly feels the need to speak.

> This being the case, we agree to work with you, Peter, Paul, and all your other colleagues at Brunnquell. You'll provide the center for

---

4   André Fargeon, a scout from Millau.

our religious community, to which we'll return again and again to gain new strength. You're Heaven sent and we'll learn a great deal from each other. Now we can finally start achieving the real goals we've set for ourselves in this locale. Don't worry, there's no lack of work to be done. We've already started." Then Milo goes on to give a lengthy description of the Catholic activities that his group carried out in Thuringia during their first months as STO conscripts.

...Our section at Kleinfurra began its work upon our arrival in April 1943. Then we tried to find other Jocists. On Sunday, May 2nd, François and I met two fellows in the restaurant of the Nordhausen railroad station:[5] René Tournemire[6] and Paul Giraud.[7] We agreed upon a common plan of action, and on July 18th we conducted a study day in the woods near Kleinfurra: in attendance were 25 members from four regional affiliations. We dealt with the topic of fidelity to one's fiancée, a very pressing and timely question for people here after three months of deportation. On the same day, René Tournemire linked up with Leipzig for a regional council meeting called by Paul Léon,[8] who had gotten word of our work. René met about 60 regional representatives there who had come clandestinely from all over to receive assignments from Father Clément Cotte.[9] René came back determined to make exploratory contacts for our mission in Kassel (we went there last Sunday with Julot), Erfurt, and Eisenbach. Clément [Cotte] promised him a visit which took place on August 15th at Nordhausen (a wonderful day). Now we're about to inaugurate a study project for all of Saxony and Thuringia under the logo "Come back better and in greater numbers"—a study that will investigate the working conditions of our young STO people, those whom they're in touch with, the conditions under which they work, what they talk about, what they read, what their religious life is like; and our findings will determine the kinds of outreach and other services that Julot and François have been talking about creating.

---

5 Nordhausen is located above Klelinfurra, 25 kilometers from Sonderhausen, on the Kassel-Halle-Berlin line.

6 René Tournemire, Jocist Federal Director from Rodez.

7 Pierre Giraud, Jocist Section Director from Niort.

8 Paul Léon, permanent National Director of JOC, and an STO conscript in charge of all Catholic Action activities for Saxony and Thuringia.

9 From the diocese of Clermont-Ferrand, a volunteer chaplain who came to Leipzig in May of 1943.

When the waiter comes to ask us to settle our bill before closing, we're all of the opinion that, for the time being at least, we could wish for nothing more. We continue our conversation outside until the arrival of the 12:30 train from Erfurt, which will take Julot and his team back to Kleinfurra.

The next day, Sunday, a good number of young people are already in the church before the Mass begins. Among these are most of the people with whom we have already been in touch, as well as some new faces. About forty of us go to communion, along with a few mothers of families, kids in their *Hitlerjugend* outfits, and soldiers in *Feldgrau* uniforms—the usual Sunday congregation.

After Mass, we follow the old country custom of paying visits and normally invite friends back to our barracks. Emile heats up coffee, puts out *pain d'épice*, and throws packages from his inexhaustible supply of Belgian tobacco on the table. Alex, Maurice,[10] and Pipe look for books that people have requested or notes down errands they can do for them in town. So goes the morning. At 12:30 P.M. we're back on the now very familiar train platform. Passing through the gate, Milo cheerfully announces his projects. "I'll be going as planned to Erfurt next Sunday with Tournemire to explore the area, so I won't be back here. You and Pierre can come to Nordhausen on the 12th, when Cotte will be there all day long."

Very early in the morning of the following Sunday, Pierre and I cautiously wend our way to catch the 5:30 train for our very first weekend excursion. There are hardly any empty seats and the compartments are crowded with people carrying guns: soldiers on 48-hour leaves, peaceful looking hunters, veterans in uniform, and *Hitlerjugend* decked out for a day of military exercises. After two stops, the master announces Kleinfurra. A cavalcade approaches, shouting, milling about and joking as sounds of the French language waft through the air. Some forty of our friends assault the old 3rd class wagon, jumping in from the platform, most from the wrong side of the track despite the "forbidden" sign and the station master's frantic blows of the whistle. They crowd into the compartment where people have to let them squeeze in and then listen to them converse long distance over the shoulders of these regular-paying and law-abiding passengers.

At Nordhausen, where we arrived twenty minutes later, a number of them are stopped by the conductor who forces them to pay. Then

10   A. Grattessole and M. Devise, both seminarians from Viviers.

Julot leads everyone through streets still wrapped in sleep. We walk in little groups and arrive at the church. Milo has still not arrived there; and Tournemire, who works at a flour milling plant several meters from the church, is not "at home." But the fellows from Nordhausen and neighboring camps regroup in the cathedral's old, dark but majestic gardens. Here we're bothered for awhile by an intruder speaking French with a heavy German accent. Pretending to be Belgian, he absolutely insists upon knowing when the Mass officiated by a French priest is supposed to be said this morning. Someone must have talked too much, causing news of this event to make the rounds of the city. We definitely have to get rid of this person who is making us all very nervous. Pierre finally takes him aside, asking him his address and writing it down. This must have made a strong impression on the man, because he leaves immediately with his wife in tow.

Clément Cotte was to have come incognito yesterday on the 11 o'clock evening train. Something must have delayed him because he's still not here. Now it's ten o'clock and the last Mass has just begun. The day has not gotten off to a particularly good start.

Then a fellow comes with news from Tournemire who asks us to meet in the cemetery at Louis Palvadeau's grave. We go in small groups. I remain with Julot near the entrance to the graveyard where we wait for Milo and Tournemire to find out what's going on and to relay our suspicions (about the intruder). A few people are coming and going throughout the cemetery, which is a really an attractive garden with tombs spread out behind the shrubs of privet which border the walkways. Then I make out Milo's profile and silhouette in the distance. He is alone and seems pensive, his hair blowing in the wind, hands in his pockets. A little ways behind him, René Tournemire, who is shorter, is talking with someone of his same height. The latter is walking slowly, a thick briefcase in hand, looking tired and quite run-of-the-mill dressed in his every-day suit of nondescript color. With heavy dark rings around his eyes that are encased in very cheap eye-glass frames, he fails to make a very favorable impression. They now approach us. "That's he," says Julot. We introduce ourselves while entering the cemetery. This will have to be quick. Unable to take the express train last evening because of an unexpected meeting,[11] he (Cotte) will have to leave right afterwards.

---

11   He was delayed in fact by a meeting with Yves Rabourdin, chaplain at Gera.

Now all the Jocists are grouped around the grave of their brother, on which has been placed a simple cross. A fine rain has begun to fall, and the atmosphere resembles that of an All Saints Day ceremony, only more somber and without flowers. Milo comes forward to say a few words of farewell, reiterating what he had said a few days before for his fallen comrade who has since returned home. Then he enunciates the unspoken challenge we are all feeling: "Who will now be the next one to fill his place?"

Then Marcel Peyraud, a recently arrived militant, comes forward and calls out to André, the Navy POW whom he then introduces to the entire community as someone who will soon be making his first communion: "You're twenty two years old and, as the child you've wanted once more to become, you're going to receive the same bread that we Jocists are nourished by. Always keep yourself close to Christ and He'll be your strength and your joy." The two men embrace, and Clément who has now joined them, embraces them as well.

Cotte gives the following homily:

> My young friends, my young brothers, I see again reflected in your faces those beautiful souls that I first became acquainted with during my visit of August 15th. Thanks so much for this splendid ceremony in which you are silently participating but which will have such a great and lasting effect. Thanks in the name of Christ, who sees everything, even our most hidden thoughts. All of this will be made clear when we enter the kingdom of Heaven. Emile, you are in charge of a team whose members are living their lives as true Christians. Today you have provided me with the most inspiring moments that I have experienced as a priest ever since my arrival in Germany. All this augurs very well for the future. Now let us go to church to celebrate together what for all of us will be the most meaningful Mass we've ever attended up to this point in our lives. But before we break up, let me give you a message from Paul Léon, our regional director, who couldn't be with us today: Conduct yourselves as if you were living in the time of the catacombs. We're already being watched. It's a good thing to be proud of wearing our insignias, but we must now keep them deep in our pockets. As sheep among wolves, we have to conduct ourselves with the simplicity of doves and the wisdom of serpents.

Eleven-thirty a.m. Now it's stopped raining. The sun-filled nave is crowded with French and Belgian mass-goers. Among their midst is the intruder of a few hours ago. Clément goes up to the altar. After the beginning of the dialogue, a leader intones the song *"Jeunesse, debout, entends l'appel suprême d'un monde qui meurt ..."* ("Young people, arise, hear the death knell of a dying world"). As the brothers rise, the church resounds with the words of this hymn which some 150 ardent young men sing at the top of their lungs. Clément turns around and comes to the communion table. He is no longer just anybody. His grey suit has disappeared beneath a white stole and chasuble. His words, which I can still remember, were like those from the catechesis taught by the early church.

> Be Catholics, build your lives on the rock. Believe in Christ alone who was born, lived, and died for us. This belief will motivate everything we do. Dear young men, keep your eyes fixed on Him. May his will always be yours. What a tremendous satisfaction will be ours if we possess our souls in peace. Be sure to guard this peace, develop it, and the surest way is through apostolic action—authentic and not vain—in engaging in serious kinds of work such as that which Christ has undertaken in redeeming us.

This time it's *Father* Clément Cotte who is talking to us as a priest of that Church which has become the center of lives since that day on which we were wrenched from our homes, our loved ones, and our native country.

As soon as those attending the Mass receive Christ, we go out in small groups to eat in various restaurants. The militants return to the church at 2:30 for a Way of the Cross led by Father Chaudesaigues, chaplain of the Nordhausen *Kommando*, who, thanks to his Red Cross armband, can regularly enter and exit the camp.

Clément is to take the 3:00 express. We leave the church and accompany him, praying and conversing, on our way to the station. "I'm sorry that Paul Léon was not able to come. You could have met him. My plan," Clement continues, "is to make Nordhausen-Kleinfkurra a center of Catholic influence throughout the whole region, under the supervision of Paul and the team at Leipzig, especially now that you've come to give us a hand."

"Yes," I rejoined, "Milo and René Tournemire have already made contact last Sunday with the leaders at Gotha and Weimar, at a meeting organized by Abbé Rabourdin and Paul Marannes,[12] who came to Gotha for this express purpose."

"Indeed, I've recently seen them at Leipzig. But Erfurt remains very isolated and without priests for its 3,000 Frenchmen. We must go there. I hope to be able to visit with you soon. Having changed my address and now being able to work incognito, I should have more freedom in the future to continue my work in the area west of Leipzig. I've left the Eastern region to Perrin who has just arrived there."

"Henri Perrin[13] is with you?"

"Yes, do you know him?

"Certainly, we studied Greek together at Mongré. He came to see us in July before our respective departures for Germany. Since then we've known nothing about his whereabouts."

"He's been visiting the Chemnitz area in the East."

"Where J. Vignon and several of our friends who came here with us here in July are now working?"

"Exactly, and as far away as Wittenberg."

"We have members of our community there whom we know very well." "Some seminarians from Lyons and your own region, I believe."

"Yes, they're also in touch with us." Clément gives me news that whets my appetite. While listening to him I am filled with a mad desire to burn up the miles that separate all of us from one another.

"But how do you manage to travel?"

"… Without papers. I'm already under surveillance and will surely be arrested any one of these days. What does that matter! Now that the communities have been formed and group leaders assigned to them, I can disappear. Until then I'll continue my work. The other day I was interrogated on the train by a policeman who asked me what I was doing there. 'I'm doing my job,' I replied. 'And just what is that?' 'I'm a priest and am on my way to see people I'm responsible for.' With that he let me go." Clément climbed into the express for Leipzig. We were

---

12   Abbé Yves Rabourdin, from the Diocese of Orleans, whose status had been transferred to civilian worker in July; he organized Catholic Action activities with Henri Marannes (Jocist Federal Representative from Paris-West). We'll meet up with them later.

13   Henri Perrin, a Jesuit priest sent clandestinely into Germany as priest-worker to serve as chaplain for French deportés in 1943. He was arrested, imprisoned and then repatriated to France in June of 1944. (trans. note)

never to see each other again. He would learn very soon what a terrible price the Nazi police network would exact from anyone making light of their regulations and restrictions. Later on that evening, under still bright sunshine, the leaders return to their respective camps.

As for me, this day seemed to be a bit like Pentecost. By his calm and courageous manner, Clément had managed to instill in us some of the same kind of concern for the universal church which had inspired the Apostle Paul. From this day onward, our primary concern would be to strengthen our ties with our sister communities through visitations. So we inaugurated our program of Sunday excursions, traveling everywhere, from four to 500 kilometers on each occasion, throughout Thuringia and Saxony. These weekends provided us with the means of fulfilling the precept of charity for all our brothers, as well as offering concrete ways for us to reassure those deeply distressed parents in France who, after having seen their children taken away from them, have continued to do everything in their power not to lose contact with them and to be kept informed of their well being. These trips also afforded me and my companions an opportunity to cement relations with the other centers of Catholic action and to experience on the spot the kind of apostolic work being performed by their district leaders, with whom we shared the same cause in Christ regardless of our location. The camps of Neumühle at Wittenberg and Saalfeld-ober-Saale would mark the furthest extent of our operation.

AT THE NEUMÜHLE CAMP

Wittenberg,[14] the birthplace of the Reformation, whose monuments preserve Luther's memory, is enclosed by a large belt of immense factories which comprises the region's primary economic resource. The Neumühle Camp, built in a sandy pine forest, is located at about a three-quarters-of-an-hour's walking distance to the north from Wittenberg. Among its 1200 inhabitants is a relatively small contingent of 200 Belgian and French men and women, lost among the thousands of workers who operate the immense W.A.S.A.G. ammunitions factory in the area.

The entrance to the camp is made to look like a tourist site with its seductive exterior of lawns, walkways and flowers. However, the first

---

14   Wittenberg-Lutherstadt is on the Halle-Berlin railroad line, on the Elbe River.

cabin, a cantine, exposes the place for what it really is. People come here to buy rations and tobacco and quite a few remain to sip beer. Among these are always to be found some who try to gain the approbation of the regulars around the bar by striving to outdo the next one in offering lewd stories or songs for the general entertainment and thus burnish their reputations as "entertainers."

In the vicinity of the nearby barracks, French women volunteers strut about in shorts, attracting any number of passersby.[15] Have any of them ever resisted the temptation of using their rooms as brothels? A ridiculous sign hanging at the entrance to their quarters officially forbids men from going inside. But the *Lagerführer* ("camp commander") is the first to lay his hands on any woman who initially strikes his fancy, and he will then bestow on her the honor of satisfying his lusts, without, of course, ever allowing them the opportunity to say no. Even so, there can be no doubt that most of these women live a promiscuous lifestyle. If they don't wait for their beaus on their doorstep, they certainly don't lock themselves away in their rooms either; rather, they expose themselves half naked through the open windows. Their suitors often prefer not to follow up invitations for sex in these women's squalid rooms. Very quickly they organize groups and go to spend the entire night in the woods. Such nocturnal traffic has given rise to the following expression, currently very much in vogue among the Germans to explain why a foreign worker has not shown up in time for work: "[He] still taking [a] walk with Mademoiselle!"

The area housing the canteen and the female "panthers," as a veteran of the area called them, also comprises the very busy center for a black market, extending throughout the entire region and used even by the

---

15   Some of the women working in Germany had gone there to be with their husbands or fiancés (and often were prevented from rejoining them despite promises to this effect by the German officials at the selection centers); others had gone to free male POWs—often their brothers—as part of the "Relève" plan; still others went as militants for Catholic Action and to aid the JOC conscripts. The charge of promiscuity has most often been leveled against the women who had *volunteered* to go to Germany as workers before the STO legal statutes had been imposed in 1943. These were generally regarded as women of dubious reputation who had come to Germany to seek adventure or escape from a troublesome or even criminal past. There is no question that some of them had been involved before in prostitution in France. See Vine, Richard. *The Unfree French.* New Haven: Yale, 2005. pp. 167-170. (trans. note)

Germans themselves. There one can buy the rarest and hardest-to-come-by produce: honey, coffee, new clothes, etc. Despite the growing difficulties of procurement that have caused prices to spiral (the cost for a kilo of bread will in a few months time increase from 80 to 200 francs), there will always be buyers, since salaries are relatively high and there are very few other places at which to spend money.

A little farther on, one finds something even worse: a building called the *Champs-Elysées* which houses the seediest kinds of illegal trafficking—for example, non-distilled alcohol stolen from the factory that more often than not has fatal consequences for the consumer. The occupants of this compound operate with a kind of tight-knit Mafia mentality that defies the imagination.

The German administrative offices: secretariat, kitchen, infirmary located nearby, look somewhat respectable from the outside. But whoever enters them leaves disgusted at the sight of so many injustices, bullying of people, and shocking examples of immorality. While continually fooling around with the nurses, doctors dismiss with a single sleight-of-hand the people who come to be treated for accidents incurred in the workplace, and they only seem happy to break out from their routine to perform abortions.

The rest of the camp presents nothing much out of the ordinary: rows of identical, low-roofed barracks in which men penned up in groups of twenties drag out their lives as slaves, dying of boredom and embittered by suffering. Here the law of the wolf pack prevails. You have to defend yourself against robbers who will take advantage every time you let down your guard.

Just about all of these men will return to France ... but in what kind of shape? Some will have suffered from under this yoke without having understood anything. Others will come back totally demoralized, and still others will have lost whatever degree of health they may have had.

However, a limpid stream has somehow managed to break through to the surface. Whoever has sown has not done so in vain. Even in this soil, where couch grass grows so coarse and thick, some grains of wheat have sprouted. Julien,[16] a Jocist militant, has superbly organized his compound and there is a constant flow of clients (of another kind) into the "Hotel of the Three Ducks." Here many services are provided

---

16 Julien Van de Wiele, Jocist Federal Representative from Roubaix-Tourcoing.

for people, and there is also a lending library. A new community is gradually taking shape. Paul Léon has come from Bitterfeld, and he has thirty Jocists working with him here at present. Study conferences and retreats, led by Clément Cotte and Louis Rolland, who has come from Leipzig, are held in the woods. Julien has become the camp's right-hand-man and serves as representative to the French Delegation at Halle. He is able to travel and thus can visit the Jocist centers of the region. He was overcome with joy on that day in July, when the most remote camp in the region—recently visited by André Yverneau, Jean Carton, and myself—became "a rectory" for a new community consisting of Jesuit students arriving from Mongré and seminarians from the Lyons Diocese (who had left for Germany on the 16th of that month). Yet from the very beginning, this group has not ventured out very far from home because of a very understandable instinct for self preservation.

More and more songs of a different kind can now be heard rising from the pine groves. Boisterous pantomimes acted out at the end of air raids, which first have a disturbing effect, end up being accepted by the spectators as an effective means of faithfully parodying the conditions under which they are forced to live. The militants manage to "swipe" from the factory the where-with-all to make candles from pure paraffin. And they have outfitted a meeting place that has really taken shape. Others come to check it out, go inside, then want to stay. Gradually the day-to-day factory life, with its commonly shared risks and burdens, is making it easier to establish contacts with the others. With its reputation as an open and hospitable site ever on the increase, the community center is slowly extending itself beyond its borders, revealing the presence of a stronger kind of love which silently causes this thick dough to rise. Under the direction of Paul Watrelot,[17] the "rectory" has been organized as a chaplaincy to aid the Jocists. Having spent a certain period of time living among them as their guest, I now can well appreciate what a tremendous boon their presence represents for the entire community.

Aren't they (the militants) identical to what the Son of God consented to be while sawing wood during his first eighteen years: that is, a representative of love amidst these Galileans who were ignorant of his message and even of what He really was? Not revealing anything of his identity at this time, but acting out of secret charity, He would

---

17   A Jesuit student from Mongré.

later on, without their still not having understood much more about Him, be most willing to give up his life for them. This day represented a triumph for those believing in an invisible force. Others may smile in disbelief, but what power can possibly prevail against those who are bound together in love?

THE COMMUNITY AT SAALFELD

On Saturday, the 23rd of October, André Yverneau, André Dupont, and I travel south to Saalfeld. The trip goes without a hitch, and we find that the team from which we had been separated at the selection center in Halle last July to be in very good shape. Our arrival had caused a sensation in this little city, so attractive in its provincial setting against the dark rise of Thuringian forests. About one thousand French people live here. Our first contacts elicit a very friendly response and make us feel that operating here shouldn't be so difficult. Straight off, they ask us to organize a Welcome Center for workers. Henri Noyelle takes charge of the secretarial duties and Jean Reynaud of recreation. We enjoy a huge success. Most of them are astonished to meet priests who know how to supervise boxing matches and are very familiar with popular songs from the music hall.

Maurice Lefebvre has reassigned several district leaders: among them, the interpreter, who is a scout, and Louis, a Jocist from the North.[18] So overcome was the latter on the day of our arrival that he insisted on carrying all of our backpacks. The community had organized itself around a German priest, Father Link, a magnificent example of a Christian. Very early on he had actively opposed the government, had even spent some time in a concentration camp, and now enjoys great prestige among Catholics and others for the impressive serenity that he constantly displays. Using great discretion, he is currently guiding the community as it embarks on its new life. As things have to move quickly, Maurice organizes a meeting for all French Catholics in church after Mass on Sundays. On the agenda are hymns, directed mediation, and silent prayer. Seven families from Lorraine, who had been deported here for acts of resistance, are now part of the group. Ardent patriots and fervent Christians, they have immediately adopted the seminarians. How wonderful for these young men to find themselves in a home-like environment after so many long weeks of

18   Louis Pierre, a Jocist from Saint-Amand-les-Eaux.

factory work! The mamas from Lorraine take on the task of feeding them often, stuffing them with bread and jam and baking cakes for them. At each feast, the group is enlarged and there are new faces to be seen seated around the table. In the various factories in the town, teams are formed to bring together the various outreach groups working within the association.

The campaign to persuade the men to live as fully committed Christians continues in high gear here on the banks of the Saal. Everyone seems to have already been caught up in the spirit of things when Henri Maranne and Abbé Rabourdin arrive from Gera (their arrival had been announced on Sunday) to conduct an intensive all-day training session. After communal prayers and Mass at the parish church that we attend along with the regular church goers, we spend the rest of the time in animated discussions while Maurice takes his leaders to meet with Marannes.

The men are very impressed with Maranne's cool style. His speech conveys the powerful inner grace from which he drives his strength. "Yes, my young friends, we are living out a great adventure in which we are to follow Christ even more closely than ever. This is the moment to sanctify ourselves and others!" Speaking as someone who has already given witness for his faith, he explains to his listeners that kind of mission he had cut out for himself. Departing as an STO worker in November of 1942, he had willingly taken the place of a young father with a family, his comrade from the workplace, who had been drafted for the *Relève*. Once arrived at Gera, he began to learn German and Russian so as to become a volunteer interpreter and organized a number of militant Jocists. One Sunday he met Yves, the chaplain of the POW camp, and persuaded him to change status and become a civilian worker.[19] From that time on, they both promoted Catholic life in the Gera region. They conducted a rally in the woods and, at its end, composed a group message signed by everyone, which was sent to Canon Cardijn. Then they embarked on apostolic visits throughout all of Thuringia: Hermsdorf, Weida, Plauen, Gotha, Weimar, and Efurt.

---

19 POWs could change their status and become "civilian workers." In doing so, however, they would no longer be protected by the Articles of the Geneva Convention and hence would become more vulnerable to Nazi discipline and persecution. A number of POW priests took this opportunity to serve as members of a clandestine chaplaincy under the authority of the French bishops, which was created to assist STO conscripts in Germany.

All of this did not go smoothly, and they often encountered dangerous situations along the way. Louis Bacle, Maranne's right-hand-man, was picked up upon returning from one of these visits. "But," continues Henri, surrounded by an audience captivated by his plain but compelling air of authority, "three days in prison and a fine of 70 marks isn't too much to pay. And at least that money won't be stolen. He (Bacle) risked everything, and you have to do the same. There are no two ways about it. We have to be part of Christ's action of redemption and live among the masses; and to do that we have to be where they are. It's as simple as that."

Just as he was leaving, Henri relayed his instructions to the leaders.[20] From this time on, Saalfeld would swarm with activities while still keeping in close touch with Gera. At the end of the session, everyone said that they had profited enormously from the workshop and they left feeling that their day could not have been better spent.

Did the Saalfeld station master suspect that, at the very gates of his city, a fervent community is rising up in prayer to Christ present in their midst? I don't believe that back in the days of the early Church the places of prayer at the gates of the cities would have been the scenes of any more fervent devotion than what we had witnessed here today.

As our exploratory excursions throughout the area become increasingly recognized and supported by the major district leaders throughout Thuringia and Saxony, we are now at the point of being able to focus our efforts where we think our activities will be the most effective. André Yverneau and his two seminarian assistants[21] are to be in charge of Erfurt, in accordance with Clément Cotte's recommendations, since Pierre and I have been assigned to give a hand to the Klelinfurra directors. Jacques Lozé will provide contact by visits or mail with all the seminarians and priests, whether isolated or living in communities. The discreet and efficient Emile Lebrun will have his charity put to a hard test with his task of finding places for impromptu meetings, creating an appropriate environment for the men living in the compounds, and being responsible for the daily functioning of the mission: providing the necessary materials, doing errands in town for

---

20   Louis Pierre, the two Tarral brothers, Jocists from Millau, Rahmond Garde, a scout from Marseilles, Marcel Zeender, René Landry, a POW transferred as civilian worker, and René Chave, a seminarian from the Diocese of Viviers.

21   Jean Goin and Maurice Devise, seminarians from the diocese of Viviers.

those unable to go there, organizing vigils and feast days, and putting up guests or, travelers passing through, or returning again. For some time now, he has been dedicating his Sundays to the French workers living in the city whose only hope for entertainment is the invitation extended to all of them to drop into the "Your Home at Brunnquell Barracks." There you can smoke, eat, sing, find books, and more importantly, meet up with savvy and friendly guys who will write your letters for you, keep you up to date on things, and, by talking with you, help you to stand your life as a beast of burden.

THE BISHOP OF ERFURT

We then had to take on the most challenging area: Erfurt, a large community of 180,000 inhabitants 60 kilometers from Sonderhausen. A young STO priest[22] recently arrived from France is said to be living in nearby Sommerda along with several seminarians. Early on the morning of November 14th, André Yverneau and Jean Carton leave from the Sonderhausen station to take a flying trip there. Upon their arrival, as they begin their search, they happen upon a barracks housing French STO women volunteers. The place is a pigsty. Even so André asks everyone, "Where does Louis Maga live?"

"No one by that name here." Laughter breaks out. Finally, in the midst of the hubbub in this large dormitory of some 150 women, they find Father Louis in the middle of a group of young men.

Among them are two fellows from Erfurt who have come to spend the day with him. One of them, short, a handsome face, with dark slightly curling hair and looking very confident introduces himself. "Camille Millet, 173, Route Stratégique, Ivry Paname (Paris). Section President of Central Ivry. And this is my brother Jocist, Michel Vacherot, from Boissy-Saint Léger, who works with me. And you and your friends?"

"We're seminarians from Sonderhausen."

"Great. We've been waiting for you ever since Emile Picaud visited us and promised us your support. Let's have something to eat and then we'll get to know each other. We'll take the train to Erfurt together and you can take the night train back home later this evening."

While lunching with Louis, the four of them get caught up on what is happening here. Although Sommerda is only a short distance from

---

22   Louis Maga, from the Lyons Diocese.

Erfurt, Louis can go there only rarely because he has been under surveillance since the day he changed his status (from POW to "civilian worker"). And on several occasions, his mail has been intercepted and sent to the Gestapo at Weimar by the *Lagerführer*. "O.K, so as not to add to the problem, we'll come on Sunday as planned," André responds. "We've already done several hundred kilometers without permission and without any problem."

"Agreed," says Camille and he continues:

> I'm the only one for some 4,000 French people in this large city. Just imagine, I arrived here on the 23rd of December, 1942, to spend Christmas—the only Frenchman around, living in the home of a gardener who normally only hires Italians to work for him. Not knowing a word of German and unfamiliar with the city, it took me many weeks to search out a few brothers. Michel only came to join me in July. Now we've become our own family and have succeeded in making some contacts with the rest of the area. Since then we've hosted several clandestine meetings at our place.

After leaving Louis and then returning to Erfurt, Camille and Michel cordially welcome André and Jean into their "home": a mansard-roofed room over the barn of their florist-employer's house. "Here's the cross I made out two pieces of wood on the day I arrived, and over there is the library," Camille tells us, pointing to a wooden-plank shelf holding thirty or so books sent from Paris by the Rodhain Chaplaincy Office.

> Quite a few end up never being returned but that means that they're being passed around. And over here is a photo of my fiancée Michelle. We got engaged just before I left, and I'm the one who got her involved in JOC. And, André, it's in this very room that Catholic Action got its start in the area, on the 5th of September, to be exact. Since he was present, Emile must have told you about it. The event occurred three weeks ago when Louis came up from Sommerda to say Mass. There were about 60 guys in this room and my boss didn't know that anything was going on. From time to time I looked out of the attic window to see if there were any troublemakers lurking in the vicinity. At present I'm organizing six groups which include all of the militants from the major work camps in the city. And the leaders of each of the groups have been meeting here regularly every Saturday evening. They're all former federal representatives, but …

"What's the matter, have they let you down?"

"They think that they're still in France and seem unaware that this is a special mission. They don't have genuine feeling for the mass of workers and avoid being in contact with them because they find they are too difficult to deal with. And I'm just a simple sectional leader."

Michel cuts in saying: "Perhaps that's why your boss who, contrary to what you said earlier, knows perfectly well what's going on, always jokingly refers to you as 'the Bishop of Erfurt'"; and he ends this comment by suggesting that they that they go down to prepare their supper in the worker's canteen.

The four enter a small room located at the far end of the building's courtyard. They sit down at a table to share a light but nourishing soup which Camille prepares without a let up in his conversation. At that particular moment André witnessed a little scene which helped him to round out his impressions about this Camille person whom he had been getting to know for the past few hours.

The door opens suddenly and a fellow enters: "Hello Joseph!"

"Hello, Camille, hello everybody."

"Hey, two new ones?"

"Yes, Jesuits, or if you prefer, people from the 'sem.!!!"

"He's not very much in the know about these things," explains Camille, "and he was converted not long ago when he went on a snail hunt."

"You don't know what I'm talking about, do you?"

"No."

"O.K. Joseph, tell him," insists Camille, while stirring pasta that is already cooking nicely.

"Well, I work for a baker," Joseph begins, sitting down and taking out a few white rolls from his duffle bag as he speaks.

> One Sunday in May, when I was dying of boredom, I went out to hunt snails in the thickets near the woods in the area. I was amazed to see suddenly emerging from a path a group of Frenchmen who were *singing!* (Imagine, Frenchmen singing!) Saying "Hello," to them, I continued to go about my business; I still hadn't found one snail when they invited me to come over. I hesitated. "Come with us." Camille is the one who spoke. I didn't resist and left my snails behind. They sang the whole evening long and upon leaving, I gave them my address. All the next week back at my bakery, I constantly relived my afternoon with them. For people so isolated and alone like us, to be so joyful, as we certainly were, was indeed

extraordinary. I went back several times to see them and they were always the same. So I asked to become a member of their team. "Of course, Camille replied," "Come with us and, you'll see, you'll be even happier. But on one condition: No dirty stories." Ever since then I've learned a lot just watching him in action. One night I told him how much I've always liked bees and that when I was back in France I used to spend a lot of my time watching them. "Fine," he said, "we're going to act just like them. Read this and you'll see; we'll talk about it when we're together." "Yes, that's right," said Camille, interrupting him and obviously feeling that the story had gone on long enough. "Snails were his path to the Bible; that's it in a nutshell. Now he belongs to our group and approaches guys even on the trains to ask whether they know anything about the JOC, which is a pretty risky thing to do!"

André and Jean now know the kind of person they're dealing with. They spend the evening planning future projects and agree that they will have to gradually raise the consciousness of the masses of workers scattered in more than 30 camps. But to do this, they'll have to rely on the leaders who must themselves be radically reenergized.

The first shock wave was transmitted the following Sunday when André and Emile returned to Erfurt to participate in an all-day meeting, not only of delegates from Erfurt, but of directors from all the principal cities south of Thuringia. In attendance were budding Christian communities from more than eleven cities.[23] After taking communion, the representatives from each district reported on their own particular problems, failures and successes, and audacious dreams for the future. They exchanged ideas for projects and offered advice, all the while becoming more aware that they were not alone in the struggle. Though they had been inexperienced up to now in working with others beyond their local borders, they were determined to reorganize and operate as one so as to offer better support and a new life for their brothers.

André Yverneau, who had originally intended to go to China, was now finding a new mission field to cultivate every Sunday. Thus God

---

23   From Gera, Yves Rabourdin and Henri Marrannes; Weimar, Marcel Carrier; Saalfeld, René Landry; Gotha, Abbé Lecoq, André Vallée; Eisenach, Fathers Dubois-Matta and Louis Pourtois; Suhl, Jean Haméon; Zella-Mehlis, Marcel Callo; at Apolda, Meningen, etc. At this meeting, Cardinal Suhard's protest regarding the arrest of Abbé Guérin (French National Director of JOC) was read, as was the response to it sent by the Head of the Gestapo in Paris.

was not absent in our midst and continued to intervene. So we took this as a sign that the narrower path we thought we had chosen in leaving on this mission was in fact leading us toward the major goals we had set for ourselves early on.

During these first days we had often expressed disappointment that our group seemed too shut off from the others and that we were living in a too-comfortable situation. But our spiritual director, who had proceeded us in leaving France for the mission field, urged us, in a message which he sent, to be more patient: "... There will surely be," he wrote,

> difficult periods that we've foreseen and prepared for. I sincerely believe that the life of heroism that I expect you to fulfill isn't simply an illusory idea on my part, but something that is bound to happen. This will be all the more marvelous since I know that your having gone there was motivated by Christ so that He could use you to carry out the will of the Holy Spirit. You should reread Saint Paul and the *Acts of the Apostles*—similar events still unwritten will come to pass through God's grace. We continue, in fear and hope, to pray for you. The present period of calm that you're experiencing cannot last for long. Remain united, very united. Avoid being separated from each other. The future may well bring you unexpected suffering which you must be willing to share as one. Take courage for you are proceeding on a well-lit path at the end of which can be seen against the horizon the figure of a newly redeemed France. Christ Jesus is leading your group, He who is the way, the truth and the light. Though far away from you, we are determined to share in you suffering and charity. Be assured that your work will gradually grow in importance where you are. One day you'll see that you've become very much needed. He who is strong in faith is also aware of his true worth....[24]

These words, read by us in the context of what was going on in our daily lives and written only a month ago, gave us new insight and stronger incentive to deal with our situation at this particular time. And indeed, on the 25th of November, vigil of the feast of the Jesuit saint, John Berchmans, Pierre Sournac is forced to leave us, the victim of an underhanded move on the part of our boss. Wanting to intimidate the *Pastoren* ("priests"), Brunnquell decided to transfer one of

---

24   Letter from Father François Charmot, Father Superior of the Jesuit Seiminary at Mongré.

us to the munitions factory at Kleinfurra (located at the bottom of
a mine). You'll really have to work there, he seemed to insinuating.
Pierre (Sournac) and I, so we were told, were both leading candidates,
and he was the one finally selected. Herr Schaarschmidt informed
him of this as if it were a promotion of some kind. He was being sent,
the latter maintained, to fill a job as secretary for the Head of Security
in that particular factory. And because the labor commission of our
own factory had declared him to be ineligible for hard physical work
(which Brunnquell was eager for him to do), he was actually assigned,
once in his new location, to a gardening crew, and he spent the winter
in the cellar sorting potatoes and rutabagas for the camp canteen.

Yet thanks to this job, Pierre was able to develop close ties with
Émile and the entire Christian community at Kleinfurra. Sharing the
same way of life, they had all become tough and seasoned "workers."
Now Pierre also had plenty of time—during the evenings and vigils—
to strengthen the faith of the leaders by making them aware of the
spiritual dimensions to be found in so much of what they were doing
in their daily routine in the work place—things they had instinctively
understood within themselves but which up to now they had not been
able to express with others nor sufficiently reflect upon so as to create
a community truly united in Christ. From this point on, Pierre will
only leave his "parish" to accompany its members when they go to pray
in the other churches in the communities surrounding Sonderhausen
and Nordhausen.

At this very moment there is a storm brewing. The regional council
meeting scheduled for the 5th of December at Leipzig is put off until
the 12th. Paul Léon sends a message warning us "to cease all communication with Leipzig. G(estapo) is on our case. Clément and Henri are
about to enter the hospital.[25] A persecution is something none of us
wants, but we have to realize that it could very easily happen."

Nevertheless, Pierre and Emile do not put off their plans for going to Leipzig on the 12th. Just having boarded the train after leaving
work, Milo opens his mail and finds in it this counter command from

---

25   That is, to be sent to prison.

Jacques Etevenon:[26] "No need to throw ourselves into the wolf's jaws. Henri Perrin is out of operation since December 2nd."[27]

Although written on the 5th, the letter had been delayed in the mail by an air attack which took place at Leipzig on the night of the 4th. Without hesitating for a second, Milo and Pierre disembark from the train at Sonderhausen where they take communion and inform the community of Henri's arrest. They then take the night train to Nordhausen to get in touch with me.

We've now clarified what our mission is to be. We have to act as priests and, to the extent possible, fill the shoes of those who can no longer actively minister within the Christian communities, which were being revitalized by them up to now through regular visitation. That's why I took the initiative to travel incognito to Nordhausen on Sunday, December 10th so as to be once again with this large contingent of militants, in whose midst Pierre and I had passed virtually unnoticed on that now far-distant day of September 12th.

A SUNDAY IN ADVENT

Arriving there alone—and remembering the first solitary steps I had taken in this impersonal city—I start to live out real-life situations that I've been imagining. Quite rapidly I get my bearings and must look as if I were from the neighborhood, because some lost soul comes to ask me how to get to Kasselerstrasse. I'm able to give an evasive reply in a German so correct as to amaze myself. The surest way to locate someone and to find out where "the others" are is to head for the church. And it's also a way of gaining focus and strengthening your resolve. Once inside l find myself alone, under the dark arches behind a pillar in the back of the church. While standing there, I reflect:

> All things considered, You certainly are inaccessible in this your temple! Why has this tent that You have raised up in the midst of men grown hard and petrified to the point of becoming something like a museum room, whose only activities occur during the hours posted at its entrance? Perhaps the moneychangers's booths and the shops in front of the entrance to the Temple in Jerusalem

---

26   A Scout Master who left as a volunteer with the Jesuit priest Henri Perrin to organize Catholic Action and work with scout troops in Leipzig.

27   See Henri Perrin's *Journal d'un pretre-ouvrier en Allemagne*, subsequently published in English as *Priest-Workman in Germany* (New York: Sheed and Ward, 1947). (trans. note)

were better places at which to be because you'd at least find people there to speak with, even though from time to time they'd have to be thrown out?

My time spent alone with Him is suddenly interrupted when the door opens and a young man, looking jaunty in his sheep skin jacket and scarf, his hair well groomed, comes in. He seems to hesitate as if looking for someone whom he can't seem to find. He genuflects and then goes out. I also leave and follow him at a considerable distance. I whistle the scout signal, but he seems not to recognize it. Then I call out to him, and as he turns around, we come face to face. Point blank I ask him, "Are you from here?"

"Yes."

"What brought you to church?"

"I had the chance," he says hesitatingly, "to come this evening before my night shift begins at Montagna." He tells me bits and pieces about himself while we're walking. He's been here since September and has worked twelve hours a day for two weeks without stopping. It's all a dog's life, from living in the barracks to working the machines. You can't go to Mass because your work schedule makes this impossible. Since he's from Lyons, we exchange comments about our city. He has "buddies" here with whom I can spend the night. Fellow *Lyonnais* help each other.

As we're proceeding down the main road leading to Montagna, a young German woman in very fashionable attire comes over to talk to us in her language. I understand what she is saying and take a few steps backward. My companion makes excuses to me for both of them, and they then exchange a few words. It seems that they've had some kind of misunderstanding and both agree to get together at a later time.

"Do you know her?" I ask somewhat inquisitively, when he has rejoined me.

"Yes, she's really great and is a secretary at the factory. She did my laundry, then taught me German when I said I wanted to learn it. Before this I was all alone and now I have someone to take care of me in this prison. Without her I wouldn't have a clean place in which to live, or a reason to put on a tie and act as if I were a real human being."

He wasn't the only one. There were thousands like him, rootless, looking for love and attaching themselves to the first smile or gesture in their direction because, for many long months, they've only known the brutal pounding of machines, more unrelenting than the weapon-ry of their conquerors. And these young men were certainly not born to hate but to love.

Now while walking with him up the Kasselerstrasse to Montagna, I think of the masses of men who are begging for a bit of love yet seem content with scraps cast to the dogs. "Lord, I understand why You were more pleased with mercy than with burnt offerings. The person who is needful offers us the greatest treasure: the chance to give … we hold this talent in the palm of our hands and must not cover it up!"

Montagna is an immense work camp whose barracks extend along-side a tank factory that formerly manufactured agricultural machines. There are fewer French women working here than at Neumühle, and more Russians, Poles, European families, and an especially large num-ber of Italian prisoners of war, who look like skeletons. The fellow from Lyons introduced me to the men in his living area in the bar-racks: the Lyons contingent or, "the old maids" as malicious tongues have dubbed them. We quickly establish a cordial rapport: exchanging names and references to sections of the city that have a familiar ring to them for people like us coming from the same place. Although they live in very crowded conditions, I've already been provided my mat-tress for the night, and blankets, towels, soap and other things which I need to wash up. There is even a snack waiting for me that they've pre-pared from the rations they've received in packages sent from home. My friend tells me to be patient while these young upper-class types dress up. They've maintained the habit of going out in the evening— with pressed trousers, tie, eau de cologne. All of this resembles some kind of liturgical rite that they observe because it gives them status. They ritualize everything—from offering their cigarettes to ordering their meals, which they take together mostly in silence. Obviously, they're out of their element here socially.

We spend the early part of the evening in their Welcome Center that has just opened its quarters in a large café: a relaxed, end-of-the week atmosphere, swing music, gypsy violins, drinks, jellied mussels. POWs who have now become civilian workers, are in the majority. Many go from group to group, shaking hands. The timid or anti-social keep their distance in a far corner. Who can tell me how to locate the ones I seek among these exuberant drinkers, sitting around smoke-filled tables or others, leaning against the bar, looking lost, and holding an empty beer glass between their fingers.

One of them stands out from the rest; something about him makes him appear out of place in the middle of all this racket. When a friend comes to snap him out of his reverie, I can hear their conversation from where I am standing. They are talking about recruiting actors for the Christmas show but complain that they are always given the same excuse by the others of having too heavy a work schedule at Montagna. And it seems that the ones who were supposed to come this evening once again did not show up. When they leave each other, the one standing at the bar goes over to linger with the group positioned near the entrance of the building. Before I go out, I hear him ask a new arrival: "Mourlot, what time are you going to Mass tomorrow?"

"Ten o'clock."

"Then don't wait for me because I'm going to the one at 8:00."

I emerge from the bar in better spirits. After a short but restful night, the next morning I run into Mourlot in the washroom; when I tell him, while shaving, that I am en route to Nordhausen and need to hear Mass as soon as possible, he offers to accompany me to the one being said at 8:00.

On the way there, we are somewhat guarded in what we say to each other. I find out that there had been talk about some Jocists having been in Montagna around Easter time, but nothing has been heard of them since then; there also has been a rumor that one of them had been connected with the black market and had had some nasty run ins with the police and the *Lagerführer*.

As we arrive, I see Tournemire pacing back and forth in front of the church. I tell myself that there must be some reason why he's waiting there. Then I see that he is giving handshakes to a number of those who are entering. We pass in front of him. No handshake for my companion, whom he apparently does not know, nor for me whom he hasn't recognized.

The church is packed—a veritable assembly of all of Europe. *Es ist Advent!* ("It's Advent")—this coming together of those waiting in exile, who walk in darkness. The priest ends his sermon imploring God, in the name of all his people: "Come, Lord! Do not delay any longer, deliver your people from all their tribulations!" When I receive communion, I'm surprised to see Pierre approaching the altar in the same line as I. He is followed by Touremire and two others, one of whom is the person that I heard talking last night in the bar about recruiting actors for the Christmas skits.

As we exit church, Emile is the first to approach me; and handing me a note from Jacques Etevenon, he explains, "We've come to fill you in on everything and join forces with you. We'll be working together all day." René Tournemire, who has now finally recognized me, formally introduces me to his two acolytes in Montagna: Pierre Giraud and Paul Vitel.[28] "Yes, I've finally learned that you really do exist." I share with them the details of my excursion of yesterday and the things that I had observed last evening. They seem quite interested in what I have to say.

Afterwards we have a four-hour meeting in a *Gasthaus* in town. Emile gives a report of the activities being carried out throughout the entire region, and Pierre Giraud and Paul Vitel describe the spiritual morass in which they feel their camp seems to be entangled. More optimistic in his review of what is transpiring in the other camps in the city, René Touremire cites the work carried out in the Salza camp, which has taken on the the administration of the Welcome Center. We quickly draw up plans for a working agenda. The priests who are in prison have to be replaced and the time has now come for the laity to take up the slack. The German clergy will be asked to offer, as a minimum, a church in which we can pray, and where, for a short time, at a discreet hour on Saturday evenings, confessions can be heard and communion distributed. Those militants who are lapsed in the practice of their faith are to be taken in hand through personal contact. Finally, a suitable environment has to be established for Christmas: this entails hosting and preparing *réveillons* in the living quarters of the barracks, around the *crèches* that the chaplains have sent from France, avoiding excessive drinking, especially during the singing of the *Minuit Chrétiens*, which should be followed by a moment of silence; also, if possible, packages should be prepared and given to those who won't receive any. Christmas traditions should of course be observed—have a *Père Noël*, write letters to families signed by all the guys in the respective living areas.

We have to make our militants aware of the existence of our Christian community and fire them up with the desire to minister to the masses with whom they are living. As Christians, we must feel ourselves responsible for all these, our homeless and exploited brother workers, who cling to the least sign of friendship tendered them. For

---

28   Pierre Giraud, director from Niort and Paul Vitel, his friend and a Jocist Federal Director from Saint-Brieuc.

many this Christmas will only reinforce the sorrow they feel about being absent from loved ones, and of being so isolated; or it may trigger their desperate impulse to give in to some kind of cowardly escape. So it becomes our job to take charge of this exiled humanity and to have them participate with us in the powerful flow of charity emanating from our Father, who sent his Son into the world to deliver every human being from bondage.

CHRISTMAS IN EXILE

We see Christmas trees appearing in the factories, homes, churches and the camps, and on each Sunday in Advent, candles are lit one by one on the huge fir tree hanging in the nave of the church. The work force will be given only two and a half days to celebrate *Weihnachten* ("Christmas Eve"). Every barracks in the French camps will offer a copious *réveillon*, made possible by packages from France and provisions from the black market obtained by trafficking with the *Chleus*. The Welcome Centers and each *Kommando* have organized shows and artistic events attended by large audiences. This is a time to relax, be happy, let yourself go and kick over the traces. The body must finally have its say, especially when it has been bullied for such a long time.

But here and there, on evenings before this one, groups united in Christian friendship, have already succeeded in extending their own joy beyond the confines of their particular camp or barracks so as to now include in their ranks others, neighbors living in close proximity but who had previously been apart. Won over by the way these Christians treat each other, today they share fellowship with them. On this special night, Christian charity will be further manifested to everyone in this human backwater through the examples of communities such as these which have already come together in Christian friendship and concern for one another.

Rubbing elbows together around an old fireplace, in a barracks now transformed to look more like a country living room, these young sons of France and of the Church intone once again the ancient hymns of their homeland. Afterwards, one of them tells his story of a Christmas past; and several put on their own original skits. Then someone gets up to read a poem he has written for the occasion, "A Ballad for Christmas Time." Recited under the very shadow of the ammunitions factory just across the way, its text seems to have captured the feeling of just about everyone in camp:

"It's about to snow, a heavy mist is falling.
Hear the sad call of the wind in the pines.
Old Man Christmas, let my song take wing through grey skies,
As I sing the lament of souls in prison.
"Yes, I've been given the chance to help us forget our woes,
And God knows we've had days we'd like to forget.
But now we're all here together, friends seated
Around an old blazing hearth on this frigid December night.

"If we've nothing particular in mind,
If all we can do is sit here shoulder to shoulder,
Must we be as sad and cheerless as the River Elbe
Or suffer on this night from winter's chill?

"No, my friends, let's get on with good cheer;
We have our youth on tap, and for one happy evening
Let the world be ours! Because Christmas is everywhere
For all who have the spirit to celebrate it."[29]

There were also morning and evening Christmas Masses said in pine-scented churches[30] to which people came singing *Les anges dans nos campagnes* ("Angels We Have Heard on High") or *Les marches des rois* ("We Three Kings"). Men of good will were converging upon the entire area to participate in this mystery of light and joy. On entering the church, the only light one sees is coming from the six altar candles that have just been lit. Escorted by a dozen altar boys, one of whom carries a large illuminated star, the priest advances to Christ's crib and begins to read the biblical passages. The crowd interrupts him, softly singing in chorus the *Stille Nacht, heilige Nacht* ("Silent Night, Holy Night"). The lights go on above the choir and the crib. The priest intones some more verses in a louder voice and the worshipers, this time accompanied by the softly-playing organ, continue their singing *of Stille Nacht* in a church that is now all aglow.

"Today, a great light has shown over a peoples living in a country in darkness."

---

29   Written by Jacques Magnan, who was converted to Christ and then took part in the Mission of France (French Worker Priest Movement).

30   As an example, the parish church of Preteritz, near Wittenberg, where the priest was always helpful and open to us, as well as many other members of the German Catholic clergy, at the express displeasure of their Nazi rulers.

Christmas inaugurated a new period for us: we were now decisively engaged in the battle for humanity presently being waged in this country to which we had consented to go. We had become Christ's instruments through our commitment to these masses of men and women for whose sake we had gone into exile.

I now understand, in fact, how the whole action of the Incarnation starts with Exile. Before the reading of the Beatitudes in the Sermon on the Mount, there was the return to Nazareth—before the crucifixion on Golgotha, the night in Caiphus's prison cell, and before the morning of the new day, the burial in the tomb.

Lord, since the worker will be treated in the same way as his master, have you set aside similar stages for us along our way?

CHAPTER THREE

PREPARING FOR THE MISSION

Now we must decide upon which activities we will use to launch our program for the coming year. The DAF has decided to give the workers a forty-eight hour leave, and we have taken these two days off to hold intensive meetings with the directors from Nordhausen and Kleinfurra. Pierre Giraud and Paul Vitel have come to join me at Sonderhausen on the morning of January 1st. After Mass, we retire to a safe place and spend the day getting caught up with what each of us is doing and taking this opportunity to pray together. We review the results of Christmas activities at Nordhausen and the camp at Montagna: Christians were able to identify themselves and unite thanks to these events. And the militants had succeeded in gaining the sympathies of the workers and in gaining a discreet but significant presence among them by having themselves appointed to the organizational commit-tees sponsored by the DAF in the various camps. We also take stock of the morale of the men in working in the field. Both Paul and Pierre admit that they're worn out and feel they're running around in circles, getting nowhere. Sabotaging or neglecting their work, which they're expected to do as slave laborers, still offends their professional dignity as workers, and the "after-all-you've-got-to-live-for" attitude is gradually eating away at their Christian principles. They are very deeply troubled by such matters and of course we too share their anguish in our own situation because, "if the salt loses its savor …." The lifestyle led by the masses of workers is obviously wearing them down as well. It's up to us to revitalize them, and we start by trying to make them appreciate the true worth of the life they're being forced to lead. This isn't so hard to do; I only need to read them a few letters from among the many that have come to me from all parts of Germany during these past few days—the same procedure used by the Apostles during the early days of the Church to rekindle the courage of those confessing the faith. So we'll use this method as well.

I first select several from among them which echo in many ways all the things that we saw going on here at Christmastime; the last one that I read comes from Wuppertal-Barmen, a large industrial city in the Ruhr:

> From many points of view I find this an ideal kind of life that I would have given a lot to live when I was your age. There is, in fact, no better form of direct social involvement. And through it you will discover aspects of the life of Christ the Worker, that are all too often unknown or ignored. I frequently remind myself that daily work, as insipid as it may be, is in itself a labor of redemption; and one does not have to go any further beyond it to save the world. In fact, our very presence here is to a great extent sacramental in nature, provided we know how to make it reflect the Divine. During the time he lived among the Touaregs, Father Foucauld did nothing more than "be present" for Christ and transform himself to become more and more like Him. Without this our lives have no real meaning. I often liken these poor workers with whom I live to draught horses who have been dragged from their farms to be harnessed elsewhere. They continue to pull their loads with little or no understanding. For you, for us (listening attentively, Peter and Paul are now getting the message) it's another matter. Like the Apostle Peter, we've left behind our comfortable boat to begin to walk on the waters, and we'll only manage not to sink if we obstinately keep our eyes fixed on Him, without looking for anything more. And this, a wonderful way to view the future.
>
> "Enrich yourselves as much as you can through this experience and rejoice in the Lord and the perfect joy of St. Francis ...." The letter ends with the following: "Soon I expect to go on my 'retreat,'[1] as Perrin has done. But that's not important: the Apostle Paul also experienced all of this. I wish you a very Happy New Year, not only as the year of your return but also as one offering you the opportunity to more effectively sacrifice yourselves in order to form a clos-

---

1   "Retreat" here means imprisonment and Victor Dillard is alluding to Henri Perrin's arrest and imprisonment and expresses what he thinks may well happen to him. Dillard would himself be arrested for his apostolic work and sent to Dachau. Before this he had volunteered to come clandestinely to Germany where he would act as chaplain at Wuppertal, camouflaging his identity and working as an electrician in the factories there, while ministering to the JOC conscripts.

er union with Christ. Do I need to say keep up the good work?"
signed, Victor Dillard.

"Who is he?" they ask.

"He's a Jesuit well known in France as a chaplain for young people and for his involvement in the social and religious spheres. He
has been serving clandestinely as a worker priest since the month of
October and expects from one day to the next to share Henri Perrin's
fate."

While munching on our provisions we comment in depth on biblical verses drawn from the Christmas liturgy. The men get the point
in the readings and understand clearly how we too are actually participating with Christ in his exile, because, like Him, we're here to do the
will of the Father.

In late afternoon the militants from Kleinfurra: Milo, Julot and
François, along with Pierre, meet us in the Ratskeller. They've been patiently unloading freight cars all day long and and are famished. When
we've finished the meal, it is Milo's turn to fill us in about their activities. It appears that things have been going downhill for some time.
In his camp, the apostolic fire is on the wane and is even in danger
of being extinguished because of a lack of support and commitment.
To give them incentive I introduce them to Guy Larigaudie and tell
them what he was like as a young man, his great works of charity, and
exemplary spiritual life, and for about an hour we read together passages from his book *Etoile au grand large*.[2] Here in concrete terms we
find described the kind of militant that the present situation demands:
someone who is strong, charismatic, and open and amenable to grace.

Since we've been living and working side by side in the same area,
Pierre and I now consider ourselves to be excellent partners. During
the course of the long hours spent working together in the factory
and in our extended conversations on trains and in cafés, we've been
able to share and refine our spiritual objectives. One simple glance at
each other tonight suffices to convince us that the time is now ripe to
suggest to our friends various ways and means to prepare themselves
for the future. First and foremost, they need to develop a deep spiritual life by using a methodical approach to achieve union with God
(they are not intimidated by the use of the word "method" because
as apprentice workers they have been trained in the use of "methods"

2   *Nez de cuir* ("Leather Nose"). (trans. note)

to learn their craft)—a spiritual life that is nourished by reading and transformed into action through concrete, realistic works apostolic in nature that will benefit the mass of workers.

Then we rapidly outline the essential elements of a missionary program:

1. In general terms, to aid the workers to develop through growth and intensification of their own personal spiritual life a clear understanding of their present situation and how to cope with it, and also, to make them think about how what they are doing here will impact on their future lives as husbands and fathers.

For directors: the practice of daily applied readings, meditated upon if possible, from the *Acts of the Apostles*; saying the rosary; preparation for the Easter retreat, which will take place during Holy Week and conducted using the format of the Spiritual Exercises of St. Ignatius Loyola.

For Militants: daily applied reading (on one's own or in a group led by a leader) from the Bible (starting with Saint Luke), and the recitation of one or two decades of the rosary; participation in "recollections" during which each one is to formulate his own personal spiritual program.

2. Service for Others—by developing a deepening sense of responsibility for the "mission," to be realized especially during the Easter period. This should be based on a study of the working and living conditions of the men and women; a project should be initiated to locate the most vulnerable and deprived residents in the camps; finally, our permanent objective must remain that of keeping all the services for the mission functioning as effectively as possible.

This over-all program, directed and coordinated by Pierre at Kleinfurra, will be presented and fine-tuned during the course of "recollections" and in the course of the trips that we're all going to make throughout the region during the trimester, particularly at Erfurt and Nordhausen.

The yeast is ready: we only have to mix it with the dough. Our group is to break up at midnight. The Kleinfurra people will go back to their camp while I proceed to Nordhausen with Pierre Giraud and Paul Vitel. After three hours of sleep and morning Mass, we have a meeting with all the major group leaders. We have another session in a *Gasthaus* where we present the plans decided upon last evening. From this point on, we can now quietly and efficiently operate at a number of locations every Sunday.

❊❊❊

We first have to prepare to deal with very small audiences—a half dozen at the most because the workers' schedules don't allow for any larger number. No matter, this is perhaps all to the good because it will allow for more discussion among fewer participants. Moreover, the places where we can meet don't allow for any larger groups. At present we have no place of our own and can't meet outside in the winter. So we'll go into churches, cafés, or underground shelters. A little later, on Sunday afternoons we'll be able to use the reading room in the Welcome Center's library. And of course, we should avoid appearing in groups, even in the streets.

The men have been notified by letter during the week and are to meet either at the train or in the church. How well I remember the times I waited at the factory as our shift was coming out at the end of work. Quite a few men were so completely exhausted after a 72-hour work week[3] and would never have had the strength to go if they hadn't seen us waiting there for them. We'd then return to the barracks to wash up and get dressed "to go out."

Meetings always begin on Saturday evening or Sunday morning with the men going to confession to a German priest or to a *Kommando* chaplain, camouflaged and hiding behind a pillar at the back of the church. Then communion and thanksgiving. The two questions proposed for the present day's discussion are: How can each one better spend the work day in union with Christ, and what deeper meaning should we all find in our being here?

In a little *Gasthaus*, the eight or so Frenchmen eating their lunch and drinking what appears to be some kind of pale fruit juice around a table must seem an extremely garrulous group to the restaurant's quiet, regular patrons. One of them in particular never seems to stop his endless chatter which he continuously animates with lively gestures. But why should that be surprising since he's from the *Midi* ("the South of France")! A thin-faced man with deep-set blue eyes rimmed with dark circles and dark hair plastered straight down, he was just the other day taken by someone to be a *zazou* ('zoot suiter of the early

---

3   At Montagna during this period the majority of workers had to put in 168 hours in one stretch (day or night), in a period of two weeks with only one Sunday off a month. One can imagine the toll that this took.

Forties') because of his very fashionable beige jacket, bell bottom trousers and black pumps. Constantly glancing around the room while engaged in lively conversation, he seems to be neglecting his meal. But
appearances are deceiving (the habit doesn't make the monk).

In reality Pierre, the *Méridional* ("Southerner"), has been talking at
length about prayer and gives this response to a remark coming from
someone around the table:

> You're complaining about not being able to find Christ during the
> course of the day? Then take it hour by hour. When you wake up
> say a simple hello to God, as to a friend that you've known for a
> long time. A few words are enough to offer up. Give yourself a
> good wash, don't dawdle over breakfast, then off to work. You can
> connect your morning offering to an act you repeat every day: for
> example, when you slide your timecard into the counter, or when
> you press the button to start up your machine. At the beginning
> when the foreman and workers are still half awake, this could be the
> right moment to converse with Christ about everything or nothing,
> about Him or us, or about a passage from the Bible that you've read
> the night before. You feel his presence within you, you survey the
> scene around you and seize upon the message you have drawn from
> it. Then you can make up your own personal and concrete resolu-
> tion (the "see, judge, and act" formula that you know so well)![4] More
> simply make yourself a spectator of what is going on—as if you're
> watching from the sidelines. The essential thing is that you converse
> with Christ as you would with a good friend, an older brother. If the
> work becomes more intense and if your buddies talk trash, so what.
> When it becomes quiet again you can always get back with Him
> because He is always there working with us.
>
> Then about 9 o'clock comes the break, time to relax with your
> comrades. Afterwards, when the work is going full speed and there
> is more than one team on the floor, you can try to start up conver-
> sations. You will also be united with Christ at this time, because
> He's to be found among them, and it's about Him that you should
> be talking with the others. Before you get your soup at noon, try
> to take a short break with the Lord and review your morning. In
> the afternoon, as you feel more and more tired, you shouldn't try
> to compose any complicated prayers. Your body movements are
> enough, pray with your lips or your arms. Now's the time to say the

---

4   Allusion to the Jociste code or criteria used in promoting Jocist ideals and
    assessing methods of action: *voir, juger,* and *agir.* ("see," "judge," and "act").
    (trans. note)

rosary. When evening comes, if you can find the time, read a little while after supper—something from the Bible, a Jocist book, or religious text; before you fall asleep have a few final words with Christ for the intentions of all the ones you love here or back in France, then a passing—in-review of the events of the day just spent—and that should be enough.

There then follow comments and personal observations. As the session breaks up, they'll now leave feeling strengthened to do the best that they can. At the end of the morning, we go into the church cloister. Under its vault, we take "our exam," as each one lays out his plan of action following the lines of conversation we've just been having.

During the afternoon, the reading room in the Welcome Center library provides a warm welcome. Here we can talk more freely, lay out our papers and take notes. Our discussion revolves around the question of what meaning we should give to our presence here in Germany.

It was during the course of this long afternoon session that I got to appreciate the strength of the Christian leaven that Paul the Apostle caused to rise to such a great effect wherever he went. When we tell these young people who have been beaten down from under the yoke of political and material oppression about the grandeur of their true vocation, they immediately come to life.

Those who are strangers—who come from the outside, as do we who constantly encounter the signs and labels, *nur für die Ausländer* ("not for foreigners")—were called by Saint Paul "the people of the kingdom of God." Deprived of their right to have a city of their own and forced to live without hope in immense multinational camps, where they are housed in these rotting wooden barracks and in dormitories with their bug-infested mattresses, these men are nevertheless closer to knowing that love of Christ "that surpasses all understanding." This passage from the Letter of Paul to the Ephesians wrenches us out from our condition as slaves and makes us aware of what is our true mission. The words from Saint John of the Cross—"Where there is an absence of love, bring your own to it, and you will harvest love in abundance"—which have long been present in my mind now have become a constant topic of mediation for me during the course of so many days of seemingly never-ending trials. The notion that we are victims of a cruel fate only partially describes our situation. Let those around us disbelieve it all they want, but what remains absolutely true is that we have chosen this condition of being slave laborers freely and out of charity. Moreover, there is another hand, a divine one that has been placed over our own and which is holding the tools we're being forced to use.

But we have to rein in our enthusiasm and come down to earth at the end of our discussion. Spiritually renewed and no longer confused or taken in by the lies they are fed through propaganda and what they hear on the radio, these men should now be able to act on their own as independent agents bringing light to those around them.

We reread the message that Cardinal Saliège[5] had sent out to Scouts and Rovers of the Toulouse area who were preparing to leave for STO. I include it here because it has certainly been a great source of inspiration and information not only for those to whom it was addressed when it first appeared, but also for the very many as well who have since taken it to heart!

"My Dear Friends,

> "You are leaving for Germany. Are you going willingly or are you being forced to go? I don't have to know one way or the other. We can submit to a law without accepting it inwardly. But the fact is that you're leaving. What advice can I give you? This first and foremost: Be witnesses for Christ and France.

> "As humiliated as France is at present, fiercely maintain hope. Our cause was a just one and we can never repeat this enough. If through our own fault we have lost the war, the righteousness of our cause remains beyond reproach. Bring to that foreign soil the qualities of your own country. Never forget that you are missionaries. Say, 'I'm going to be an example of what a Frenchman should be—someone full of life, loyal, ingenious, a good friend, a keen observer, who does not let himself be taken in by appearances but is able to discern what really lies behind them.'

> "You are going to a country that possesses a special beauty and grandeur of its own.

---

5   Cardinal Jules Géraud Saliège of Toulouse soon became prominent during the Occupation as the most outspoken member of the Catholic hierarchy and the one who early on had taken a decisive and public stand against the rounding up of Jews in France, deploring the cruel treatment they were suffering at the hands of the French police and German authorities. Even before the Occupation he had also been a severe and outspoken critic of Nazism and its pernicious philosophy of racism. While he did not preach civil disobedience on the part of those drafted into the STO, he was very concerned about the moral and spiritual well-being of the workers forced to go to Germany, as this letter so clearly indicates. (trans. note)

The Germans are a great people and we must not underestimate their good qualities. But we also have to recognize their own enormous shortcomings. They have structured things on a grand, even colossal scale. They've made good use of material things: seen in their factories, refectories, kitchens and showers, all of them spotless. This is all to the good, and we need to have more things like this in our own region of the *Midi*. Workers and their bosses enjoy a cordial rapport, and this relationship is extended on a broader, man-to-man level in their society as a whole, also a very positive thing.

"Yet look more closely and you'll see that behind these enviable and appealing appearances there is something very definitely lacking—certainly not knowledge, but what in simple terms can be called spiritual values. The result is the triumph of technology and convenience imposed by brute force.

"Observe the situation more closely: The Germans believe that they are a chosen people whose mission it is, by reason of blood, to rule over the entire world, and they sacrifice everything to this end. Whoever cannot serve in this mission must disappear because he/she is a useless commodity. The German people see themselves as a kingly race, superior to all the others, the modern day Israel. They have subordinated everything to the victory and triumph of this ultimate ideal. In the midst of such collective pride, you will represent the French concept of life—a humane idea which holds that every human being counts, that people have individual rights and that all men are brothers. Throughout its entire history, France has flourished as a shining beacon proclaiming brotherly love. Any French person who refused to recognize every man as his brother would be seen as betraying his citizenship. And I offer an old French word that sums up very well how you should live while working there, that is, as *gentlemen*.

"As witnesses for Christ, you will find that He has many enemies in Germany. They will have none of His teachings of charity, pity, and mercy. They won't accept the suffering and humiliated Christ of the Passion, a Christ who conceals his strength and ultimate victory under the cover of apparent weakness and defeat. They want to revise all of this. If Germans had had humble, peace-loving and merciful leaders, this war would not have taken place. But their real qualities have been contaminated by a mystique of force and violence which has led to disaster. Their pride has undone them. By instinctively reacting against all of this, you'll regain your French sense of honor and will accept suffering with dignity, without whining or complaining. As witnesses for Christ you will be good, friendly, useful and charitable towards everyone, regardless of race, whom you'll meet in your work place.

"You'll demonstrate by example that a Christian never avoids brotherly service to others, is cheerful, even when feeling sad on the inside, gives encouragement, inspires confidence, and always and everywhere expresses hope.

"On July 1902 Charles de Foucauld adopted for himself the following goal: 'I want to accustom all Christians, Muslims, Jews, and non-believers to regard me as their brother, their universal Brother.' This is a very French and very Christian teaching. I'm sure you'll agree that your acceptance of this will redound to the greater glory of France and Christ.

"Be careful. You're going to a country where sexual morality is less stringently observed than in France. Do they want to make of our young people a new breed of men? Do they intend to eradicate in them a love of their country, destroy the strength derived from chastity, and make them incapable of having children when once back in France? I honestly do not know. Some things are done that aren't ever talked about, and vice-versa. You'll find out when you get there.

"Remain strong, loyal and resolute in your faith. If you do this, you won't be duped or made a victim by anything or anyone. Let nothing happen that might bring about disharmony or break up the spiritual unity that you share with each other. We possess this unity through Christ, and no distance, no matter how great, can separate souls bonded together in charity.

"I am sure that you've understood what I've said: you are going on a mission and I delegate to you the task of conducting this mission for France and for Christianity.

"Through your efforts, may France be esteemed and respected, through you may Christ be adored! Let me give you one counsel that sums up everything that you need to know: Wherever you may be, always conduct yourselves as Catholic Scouts who represent France! Receive my blessing as you depart. How much happier shall I be when I bless you upon your return."[6]

Other documents similar to this that we have also found especially valuable in providing matter for meditation and of real importance in

---

6   Cardina Saliège's message was communicated by Father Paul Doncoeur, national chaplain of the Boy Scouts of France, on that very day when our group left for the STO.

helping us to better understand the reasons for our mission among young French people in this country are, to mention a few:

> The Encyclical Letter promulgated by Pope Pius XI in 1937, *Mit Brennender Sorge* ("With ardent concern") in which he castigates the enormous errors in the Nazi ideology, messages from the Chaplaincy for Prisoners of War and Conscripts in the STO, under the direction of Father Rhodain, the text of Fathers Godin and Daniel, *France, pays de mission?* ("France, a Missionary Country?") which had just been printed and copies of which had been sent to us from the Rodhain Chaplaincy Office in Paris.

We spent the rest of the evening going again and again through mail received from other colleagues and militants from all over Germany— letters recounting Christian witness by those actively involved and, of particular interest, the following one from Victor Dillard:

> "… In the immense city of Wuppertal, whose boundaries seem to extend without limits, I've found no one, not even one seminarian or militant. It's a vast ocean. But that's a good thing—to walk on its surface you need this kind of openness. Up to the present the deep waters here don't seem to be favorable for any miraculous catch, hence I am put more in mind of Nazareth than the Lake. So I'm finding out many things during this stint of manual labor (to which He gave some thirty years of his life). In fact, if He were to come back today, he'd be a mechanic or something like that. In doing his work He would have had the same love for his tools that he had had for the wood which he knew so much about: trees, the fig tree, the boat, the cross! Materials possess their own dynamic kind of life which only those who work with them can appreciate. Machines have their own personalities, idiosyncrasies, rhythms, fidelities and irregularities. The worker is able to commune with them, to appreciate and control them, like someone who is training a horse, and he actually feels them come alive. I'm even aware that for some, such contact with their tools or machines even produces a kind of intoxication. What dignity we find in the skilled worker who really *knows* how to solder, to turn a lathe, to adjust tools! He's now a very different person from what he is at home. Here he reigns supreme as master of all that he surveys. I understand that there is a mystique attached to matter, which is not necessarily materialistic in nature. It only becomes such when cut off from its spiritual roots. But what a revelation does this provide for us who are deeply concerned with the Incarnation, the Eucharist and Humanism. For me this would

seem to provide the means for attaining a marvelous equilibrium. Our Mass attains this perfect point at the moment of consecration when all matter is subsumed in union with Christ. Our redemption has not been achieved through prayer and sacrifice alone, but also through those long periods of working in silence, these many hours of simply being present, this silent contact with matter, and the joy experienced through work that has been well done.

"Pray that in doing their work, the workers shall be exalted and not debased; and that through this monotonous kind of life that you now so patiently bear the world may find salvation.[7] (14-1-44)

"Make a total gift of yourself to your comrades, being careful not to live beyond the reality of your situation; but always try to realize in your work the magnificent dimensions of Christ's incarnation: that He is truly human while at the same time divine. Whenever we deny our own authentic humanity (a condition that is called "angelism") we also veer from the divine plan. The greatest joy that we can give to others is that we become the kind of human beings they have been longing to find. What a challenge this presents for us!

"I'm well aware of the 'superman' phenomenon that you mention. Those who advocate it seem to be everywhere and they force us to face up to the difficult problem of how to adapt our religion to the social problems of our times. It is impossible to be a Christian if one is not also socially committed. The clan mentality is absolutely incompatible with everything that Christianity stands for. This spirit is more prevalent among our French bourgeoisie (for example, the case of the Scouts!) than among the working classes. Hence we have to be unflagging in our preaching about the Christ of the early Christians and relentlessly unmask the Pharisaical ways of so many practicing Catholics, reminding them in and out of season that religion is the business of life, a state of grace, a means of identification in and participation with Christ, and not merely a conventional or juridical code of exterior practices. The observance of our Christian faith is meaningless unless it involves participation, and attending Mass without taking communion is an aberration. We have to repeat these things time and time again.

"A friend of mine from Paris has written to me saying that Christianity does not possess a strong enough mystique to prevent it from falling into sin. I detest the 'pagan' inference attached to this word mystique, but I know what he is getting at and am aware that

---

7   Here we only cite excerpts from letters from Father Dillard that we had been receiving regularly since the 1st of January, 1944.

many share his opinion! If our religion is not living and lived, our actions are absurd and our faith is vain! In short, it is non-existent.

"This is all very important because what is at stake here is nothing less than the spiritual future of our country. From our vantage point, we are well aware of an enormous revolution that is presently tearing the world apart. Military battles convey only illusionary significance when placed in the context of the battle of ideas. This revolution will surely have repercussions in the spiritual, personal, and social dimensions of our own lives. Christ has come to this earth to bring fire, that is, revolution. And it is our duty as Christians to become revolutionaries for ourselves and for others. (26-1-44)

"… A great deal of time and patience are required if one is to understand and really be familiar with this milieu of French workers in which we are living—a milieu that is deceptive in appearance, egotistical, pagan, and heartless to the extreme; yet when our disgust seems complete, we are suddenly confronted with random acts of charity seemingly animated by traditional Christian principles. What do we surmise from this and what kind of hope can we find in it for ourselves? I'm not able to draw any definite conclusions except perhaps that we have to live in very close contact with this social mass, take its pulse, and love it with all our hearts so as to enable it to reconnect itself once again with its Christian roots. For this a revolution needs to occur, first of all, in each one of us. We have to replace those who are in the Church and should not be there with those who instinctively are in union with Christ: the lame, the sick, the paralytic, the beggars. I know the French bourgeoisie too well to expect it to be able to see things from a Christian perspective. The peasant seems to be spoiled by a selfish love for money. The worker remains the most healthy of all of these, or at any rate, the least spoiled. We should dedicate our lives to this class and to the young, because we have to reconstruct the France of the future, what it will become twenty years from now. We have to find a new way to educate our youth, modernize them, educate them from the ground up, and from every point of view. Let's begin now with kids from 10, 12, or 14 years of age. The others are too old and too contaminated by paganism and a general moral *laissez-faire*. What a tremendous job awaits us when we'll be back in France! Let's try to enrich ourselves through all these contacts that we'll never again have the opportunity to experience during the rest of our lives." (18-1-44)

From workshop sessions like these held throughout the area on Sundays, the militants emerge upbeat, their energies revitalized and ready to be directly involved in all aspects of our mission work.

THE LEIPZIG MEETING

January 30th—En route to Leipzig by way of Erfurt. Emile Picaud came to Sonderhausen yesterday to inform me that we should all attend a regional council meeting organized by Paul Léon at Leipzig. I get a Czech friend to purchase round trip tickets. We're prepared for anything. To be more on the safe side, we'll take two others along with us to Erfurt, where we'll spend the night. We're travelling without a permit, but we received communion at 4:00 in the afternoon and begin the trip with Christ, our hope and strength. We take few papers with us, except for a brief memorandum listing the activities and projects that we want to inform the others about. No bérets—short hair, German style—I take along very little to eat.

When we get off at Erfurt, Camille and Michel, who have been waiting for us at the station, bring us to their place. We do honors to the excellent beans prepared by Inès, the Italian cook who is always ready to assist Camille in his projects, and then spend the evening in the workers canteen. Joseph, the snail militant, arrives with several district leaders in tow. Camille presents a summary of the work he and André Yverneau have accomplished since November. Christmas ushered in for them as well a new beginning as regards projects that their militants have since taken in hand. The sick are now regularly visited in hospitals, the dying are attended to, and the dead receive decent burial.

Camille has remarkable tenacity. He manages to perform his activities magnificently despite the worsening of living conditions here: a twelve-hour work day has now been imposed in the factory, there is very little food, air raid alerts and bombings occur constantly, the camps are closed off at 11 o'clock at night, and several of the district leaders seem dispirited and overcome by inertia. He has had to go badger these totally exhausted men, virtually having to tear them from their mattresses where they are dozing off and patiently take over by himself work that has been neglected or even understandably interrupted because of unfortunate turns of events. The members of his group agree that though Catholic action is still holding its own here, the attention which the militants give to cultivating their spiritual life and to frequent reception of the Eucharist leaves much to be desired.

We suggest that the same remedies which had been effective in the other camps be implemented here. Milo outlines the objectives that André has just presented in the retreats held in February and March: a deeper understanding of the *New Testament* through daily readings, the organization of one's entire life with Christ in the factory and camp, and taking the initiative in an apostolic sense to prepare the men for the celebration of the Pascal season.

Camille agrees: "Let me be the first to start this off. Give me a *New Testament*, Paul, and Michel and I will read from it everyday. If it's O.K. we'll start with Saint Luke." The evening ends with a long discussion, during which we communicate with Christ, Bibles in hand. Since we have to take the 3:50 morning express, we have to get some sleep. No one will be around to wake us up. No matter, our guardian angels will see to that.

Milo shakes me awake at 3 o'clock and we abruptly leave Camille. He has already resolved to go find the chaplain at the Ursulines Cathedral in order to arrange for his group to receive communion and go to confession there at some discreet time one evening each week. He's anxious to wrap this up before he goes on leave back home. When he'll come back from Paris, he promises to take along with him a portable altar valise and some more books for the library. We commission him with a few errands to be conducted at the Rodhain Chaplaincy Office there. As we depart, he is looking forward to the joyful prospect of embracing, for what will be the last time, his mother, fiancée, and other members of his family who, despite strenuous efforts on their part, will have failed to persuade him to remain with them and not go back to continue his work among his brothers, for whom he now feels completely responsible.

Milo and I thread our way through the deserted streets to the railroad station. After a three-quarters-of-an-hour wait on the platform across the street from the police station, we are sped away in the Paris express. Half asleep and holding rosaries thrust deep in our pockets, we enjoy a peaceful and uneventful trip on this SNCF coach.

The huge Leipizig station, where we arrive at 6:30, seems to have changed very little from last July, except for its large glass window that has been pulverized into slivers as a result of an air attack carried out on December 4th. After consulting schedules and obtaining the necessary supplementary tickets (and mouthing a convincing "Heil Hitler" as they are handed to us), we go out into the still, dark morning. Under the cover of a public toilet, we use the light of our matches to decipher Paul Léon's map: "No. 30, at the end of 11 Wahren. On the right, your back to the station. From 8:30 on, Paul L." After reconnoitering a few minutes, we jump on a tramway marked "Line 11 Wahren Station" and ride through a totally demolished section of the city just becoming visible in the light of the early morning.

I don't know if the Deacon Philip (Acts 8-26), when he once set out on a deserted road leading from Jerusalem to Gaza without benefit of anymore detailed directions than ours, had to cool his heels while waiting for his Ethiopian minister as long as we did, standing three hours in Wharen Place, on empty stomachs and freezing feet. Trams keep arriving one after the other, each one depressingly absent of any face that might be of interest to us.

A clock strikes 10:00. Still no sign of our friends in the area. We're already beginning to revise our schedule: We'll go to Gohlisertrasse, to the Werkheim-Concordia Camp to find Jacques Etevenon and get caught up on the most recent news about Henri Perrin, which was our second reason for taking this trip.

We were just boarding the tram when someone speaks to me. I turn around, "Excuse me, do you have a light?" The fellow comes up to me extending his cigarette. I get a glimpse of the badge he is wearing and uncover my scout cross concealed on the reverse side of my coat.

"Hello, I guess we're friends; we were ready to give up."

"I've been suspecting for a good five minutes, as I watched from my corner, that you possibly, but definitely your pal with his little cardboard suitcase, might both have just come straight from the Rodhain Chaplaincy Office." (Carrying this valise anywhere in public was always dangerous, but this time at least, it had worked to our benefit.)

"Will we see Cotte, also Etevenon?"

"Maybe," replies our friend, a Federal Jocist representative from Belgium who has also been summoned to the meeting.

"Is there a chance we can hear Mass?"

"Yes, follow me; there's one's being said nearby just as we speak."

We pass through a little garden and enter into a modern-style chapel that is very crowded. The priest is reading the Epistle. "Everything's fine," the Belgian whispers, "they're all here." I have plenty of time during the sermon to pick out certain very French-looking faces. After thanksgiving, the same Belgian leader steers us to a small room in the back—a few chairs and tables laden with books and French magazines—they're certainly taking quite a risk having a meeting place like this!

The person in charge is a young man, broad-shouldered, very well dressed in civilian clothes. My first impression upon entering is that he is probably a priest because of the calm and collected way he has of welcoming people. But I couldn't have been more mistaken. He is wearing a Scout Cross and extends his left hand to greet us. It's Jacques Etevenon. "And what about Henri (Perrin)?"

"Still nothing new; we'll talk about him after a bit. Now let's get to work." Several regional leaders are in attendance and among them: Roger Martins, Director at Bitterfeld;[8] Ligori Doumayrou, a POW transferred as civilian worker, formerly at Rawa-Ruska, now Director at Zwichau; and Sabran, a scout from the area near Dessau. Paul Léon and Auguste Eveno[9] were not able to get here. Jacques will direct the meeting assisted by Louis Rolland, the priest who has just finished saying Mass a few minutes ago. Clément Cotte, who is under surveillance in his camp, has also not been able to come.

It's noon. Even though we're famished—we've been fasting since last evening—we still feel the need to go on talking. Each of us gives a report on the Catholic and social activities being undertaken in his own district. Milo speaks in his own turn explaining our retreat procedures for groups of six or eight participants organized in teams, whose leaders (a priest, seminarian, or layperson) are in close personal contact with the regional directors. In their turn these people form other teams of militants by meeting with people one-on-one and by initiating challenging conversations, because the work-camp lifestyle makes it very difficult to get people to meet together in groups. Those contacted in such ways will themselves then be in touch with others for whom they feel responsible. Success in all of this relies heavily upon a tight-knit program of spiritual formation extending from top to bottom (from leaders, to team leaders and then down to individuals). Elsewhere, very important work is being accomplished through the social organizations. We are pursuing the policy of infiltrating the Welcome Centers and other recreational organizations that had been

---

8   Jocist militant from Roubaix-Tourcoign, Director at Bitterfeld, Saxony, where were also located a team of militants and Father Louis Doumain, an STO conscript from the Viviers Diocese, and "one of the fifty one" to die in the concentration camps.

9   Jocist Federal Representative from Nantes who was in charge of Halle.

put in place before we arrived. We also have to make every effort possible to become members of the important administrative committees
that are responsible for the running of the camps. And of course, the
extent to which we are involved in matters of social concern must continue to be regarded as the ultimate test to determine how well we are
living our lives as Christians.

Roger Martins points out that at Bitterfeld, all the camps provide
representatives who take spot checks of those exiting the church after
Sunday Masses. Sunday meetings are coming along very well. A kind
of informational relay system has been put in place to circulate directives sent out by Paul Léon. Henri Perrin and Jacques have directed
retreats in the area. One such gathering has been held at Neumühle
with members of Julien's team; and some of his friends have expressed
their intention of joining the JOC. Louis and Jacques tell us about the
contacts they've made with the German priests at Leipzig.

After a short walk in the garden, we regroup around Louis, the only
clandestine priest still able to circulate freely in Leipzig, for a study
session on the Mystical Body. Jacques concludes it with a reading from
Mauriac's *Message aux Jeunes* ("Message to Young People"). Finally
we spend a brief time reading from the Gospels. We need to discover
Christ the human being, whom the Bible readings so clearly delineate
and thus develop with Him a kind of friendship that will help us to
bear up under this life of exile and separation from our loved ones.

Jacques Etevenon proposes that we read from John, Chp. 4, the conversation between Jesus and the Samaritan woman. Roger reads the
part of the woman, Jacques that of Christ, and I narrate the text. We
read slowly, without commenting, stopping in places for meditation
and silent prayer to the Holy Spirit. At this moment, we fully realize how very worthwhile have been the four hundred kilometers we've
traveled and all the rest that we've had to endure in order to be here
this weekend.

As we leave, Ligori delivers a beautiful prayer based on John 4/42:
"Now we believe no longer because of what you told us; we have
heard him ourselves and we know that he is indeed the Saviour of
the world."—an exemplary text inspiring the militant to conduct himself in this same spirit of self sacrifice and meekness of heart in his
task of bringing others to Christ. Finally we end the session with the
prayer, "Our Lady, create in each of us a tender and compassionate

heart, loving without asking anything in return; and may we find joy in becoming forgetful of ourselves in the presence of your Divine Son."

Until evening, on the train, in the streets, and amidst the ruins and the crowds, we continue these prayer-conversations. As we enter the railroad station, night is setting over the skeletal remains of the devastated buildings. Roger and Ligori have already left. Jacques speaks to me at length, finally giving me complete details of Henri Perrin's arrest while an occasional passerby trains his flashlight on the two of us.

Inside the station I leave to Jacques the task of relaying the details of the enriching experience we've had this day in a brief written report he will send by mail to our superior, Father Charmot. The 29th of January was two days ago. How very well Saint Francis de Sales took care of us on his feast day!

FIRST WARNINGS

From this point on our activities are regulated by the large volume of mail received from Leipzig (Jacques will send more than twenty rapid but detailed notes in a period of two months). Could the *Reichspost* ("German Postal System") ever have imagined the immense assistance it was providing for Catholic Action? The first message arrived on Feb. 2, 1944:

> "Hello! I received your note of January 1st.[10] Isn't it wonderful to see how our prayer groups and welcome activities are growing? Let's hope that Henri Marannes can come to spend a day with us soon.[11] He was seen by one of ours last Friday; his head had been shaved but his hair was growing back. No other news. I'm told that some of our other colleagues have been sent back to France. Do you know Marcel Carrier? He's at Westsarbeitlager, near Weimar? Replying to a note I don't remember having sent him, he provides news from his area. If by chance you see him, tell him about our conversation of the 30th.[12] On the 25th of March, the *Route de France* (the Boy

---

10   More precisely, a note sent on Feb. 1st, in which Milo and I informed him of our safe return to Sonderhausn.

11   This expresses the hope that Henri Perrin would soon be set free.

12   An industrial center 15 miles to the south of Halle where there was an active community of Rover Scouts. Among them were Bernard Perrin of Lyons, who would die in the Mauthausen camp. The clandestine chaplain from Mersburg, Pascal Vergez from the Lourdes Diocese, would also be executed by the Nazis.

Scouts of France) is organizing a day of unity and friendship for the workers here. Let's try to give it some publicity. I spent all day yesterday at Schkopau-Merseburg, also a lively center. They tell me there are problems at Halle.—Jacques."[13]

I received this second note from him on the following day:

Leipzig, Feb. 8th, 1944

"Hello

Since you told me that Chemnitz[14] is eager to disclose news about itself, can I ask you to take responsibility for sharing and communicating all subsequent information sent from there with your friends? Yesterday I received a very long letter from Henri [Marannes] who could join us any day now, because the doctors who examined him couldn't find that he had anything wrong with him but kept him there to be on the safe side. He often goes out to work in the city. Since he's no longer contagious (from tuberculosis), we can write to him. It's remarkable how well he's been able to use his convalescence, not only for his own benefit, but for others as well. He shares his packages with eight other people and is expending great energy in learning German and faithfully assisting at Mass. He prays constantly. Everything is fine here. I learned that [Henri] Perrin, the priest from our camp, had been imprisoned because someone denounced him for his political and religious activities and for having organized social groups here. His answers to these charges must have satisfied them.

Best to you, Jacques."

We feel very much united in spirit with him—and with all the others as well—who having already borne witness and are now being forced to watch from the sidelines, deserve our deepest thanks. But we were dealt a terrible blow upon receiving this brief note dated Feb. 17th:

"Hello! Clément Cotte has been seriously ill for several days. The moral shock of his arrest must have been too much for him. It's a terribly sad situation. Fondly, Jacques."

I kept this information in my pocket all day while working in the factory. At church in the evening, during our prayers of thanksgiving, I read it to all the members of the community who were present.

13   André, Pierre and I were to give a "day of recollection" there, but we finally could not attend because of the new police measures that had recently been put into effect to limit the movement of the seminarians.

14   Jacques was in continuous contact with the Chemnitz community.

Cotte, who has accepted martyrdom in mind and body. The priest at
Sonderhausen was also crushed by the news. The militants, still vivid-
ly remembering those moving days of August 15th and September 15th
are deeply appreciative of the enormous degree to which he has sacri-
ficed himself for the mission and offer up their prayers for him. Victor
Dillard's profound charity is revealed in the few simple lines that he
wrote us: "Father Cotte of Leipzig is one of my dearest friends. What
you've told me about his condition horrifies me. Please send further
details."[15] In the same letter, Dillard appends a short description re-
suming his own situation at this time:

> "As for me, I'm still experiencing all-round failure because of what
> I see as my inability to know how to adapt. I've had to learn every-
> thing from scratch. But we know how to take our licks. Fortunately
> this is one of the greatest blessings we could ever have received. But
> we now ought finally to have our feet on the ground. Every day I
> find myself in the same poisonous situation—under surveillance,
> hounded yet without anything of importance happening. But this
> is excellent medicine for people who don't want to set down roots.
> We have to accept to live this way. But this should also cause us
> great joy. Poverty, after all, is nothing more than this daily uprooting
> that allows us to place ourselves again and again in the hands of our
> Father. We must refuse to take any easy way out. Goodbye, my dear
> Paul. How I'd love to be there with all of you. But better not to even
> think about this. Do you suppose that you'll be leaving soon? I've
> heard nothing definite about seminarians being repatriated—per-
> haps just another rumor?"

Indeed Jean Carton, André Dupont, and Jacques Lozé, who were
still traveling about a great deal, did manage to glean a few scraps
of information during their weekend spent among the communities
at Saalfeld, Magdebour, and Chemnitz, to the effect that the STO
seminarians would soon be given the opportunity to return to France,
if they so wished, and could finish out their work term there while
pursuing their studies—a favor so unexpected as to raise considerable
suspicion and doubt.

But events keep rushing headlong and what we see happening
around us begins to justify the apprehensions that we've had regarding the real motives of the DAF and the Party. Jacques Etevenon from
Leipzig informs me on the 6th of March that "the *sacerdos* (priest)

---

15   A little later we would receive more reassuring news.

at Chemnitz is in the same situation as Henri Perrin," and that last Saturday he witnessed a dozen or so of his young colleagues (from the STO) being sent back to France.

At Neumühle, Magdebourg, Oschersleben, Saalfeld, and even Vienna, all of our brothers have been alerted to the fact that they are now under special scrutiny. They're being registered; permissions for home leave are being severely restricted, and in some cases, workers have to make special application to be eligible to receive one. Most feel that they are living in a kind of limbo. At the end of the afternoon of March 9th, the factory interpreter comes to inform me that Brunnquell is requesting a list of all seminarians working for him. This has to be in response to a direct order for registration recently sent by the Nordhausen *Arbeitsamt* ("Foreign Workers Office"). In the days that follow, several, after receiving permission to be repatriated, have agreed to abandon the mission and have come back from exile.

I'd pay dearly to burn up the many kilometers separating me from the person (Father Charmot), who is probably already experiencing great joy at once again seeing those of us who have already returned.[16] He must also be fully aware of the struggle each of us feels raging within himself, as well as our desire to share our moral dilemmas with him and hear what he might have to say to help us resolve them. But we too have to face the possibility of our own imminent departure. Our last scheduled retreats are over. Christian teams have been sent out to Nordhausen, Erfurt, and other camps in the area. Preparations for Easter are in full swing. We've adopted for our own use the precise recommendations that Jacques proposed at the Leipzig meeting: that everyone be responsible for bringing three fellows to the communion table; that we all go to communion at least once a week, and that each one of us set some kind of personal goal for ourselves.

But already André and I have had to cancel our attendance at the triple retreat (for seminarians, leaders, and militants) planned for Halle. I rejoin Milo at Kleinfurra on Saturday, March 11th, and find that he and his team are ready for any new trial. If we're forced out of the operation through obedience or arrest, they'll be able to keep things going. We spend the evening deciding on what our objectives should be. Night is already falling. Because I feel that our situation resonates

---

16   The "they" in this reference are the Jesuit seminarians from Chemnitz, who, having left Germany on March 4th, had already arrived back at Mongré.

so greatly with what is narrated in the *Acts of the Apostles*, I ask that we reread again Saint Paul's leave taking with the elders of the Church of Ephesus (Acts. 20/17-38).

Next morning after Mass, said by a refugee priest from Cologne, I leave Kleinfurra to spend my Sunday afternoon with militants from Nordhausen. There I meet a POW seminarian, a real live wire who has just transferred as civilian worker. Because he lives in the *Kommando* adjacent to Nordhhausen, he'll be able to take in hand the training of the leaders. In the evening, the team[17] meets with me in René Tournemire's room. His landlady, Madame Roegner, lets us have the full run of her house. Each one promises before all those present to take full responsibility for his brothers. I find no better words upon which to leave (nor any that could give me more joy) than those included in a letter, dated the 28th of March, which I had received just yesterday from Father Charmot:

> "You are messengers of love and bearers of the Divine fire. Even more, you bear in earthen vessels (how little that matters) the blood of Jesus Christ. These drops of Christ's blood, concealed in the Sacrament, are the seeds for your spiritual mission which you make manifest by your words and deeds. You'll witness wonderful things in the times to come which will make others regret not having chosen to be your traveling companions—you and the scouts whom you are accompanying—and which will prompt others to sing more than one Magnificat in your honor. Hurry and finish up your work before the time comes for your return. The Holy Spirit is living within you. Thus you must renounce your own personal concerns; *but*, you've already found the door that leads out from the prison of the self on the very day that you entered into a country that wanted to hold you prisoners within its borders, but which instead opened you up to the world. I hope you can see how much I strive to be guided in my own life by the same ideals that have motivated you in yours. May this Easter bring you many consolations!"

When I finished reading, one fellow said, "I've never received a letter like this from anyone, except maybe my mother."

Once more united and encouraged in spirit, Pierre, André, Jean, Jacques, André Dupont, Emile Lebrun, and the others understand

---

17   People from Montagna: Pierre Giraud, Paul Vitel and Robert Bertolero (a scout from Saint Avertin, Indre-et-Loire); from Mabag, Garnier, Jocist from Rennes; from Salza, Gresley, Jocist from Paramé, etc.

why we can now apply the words of the Apostle Paul to our own present situation as well: "Watch and wait, guys," I say, "and don't forget all
these months during which we've been working with you with willing
hands and eager hearts. Yes, we *seminos*, or apprentice *curés*, as you like
to call us, have been trying all along to show you how much more joy
there is giving than in receiving."

Getting back at dawn and after having completed a whole day's work
in the factory, I wrote the following long letter to Father Charmot:

"Very Dear Father,

Am coming back from work at dawn this morning. No sleep,
have been talking a lot, so many graces received, the ones best appreciated being the simplest. Excuse the lack of coherence in what
I'm going to write. I received your letter the day before yesterday
and Pierre read it as well, as we were walking through a passageway
between two train platforms. Events here are coming to a head. By
now you must have had plenty of opportunities to welcome back
those of our brothers who were forced to return from Germany.
But from our vantage point, this is how we feel about leaving, were
it left solely up to us. From what I am about to say, you'll be able
to understand how firmly our hearts are attached to the work we're
doing here—like couch grass clinging to the soil.

"Our obligation to go to Germany was not based on political coercion but on motives of charity sanctioned by our vow of
obedience. We ourselves will not leave this country of our mission
voluntarily merely because, as would now seem to be the case, the
political reasons for forcing us to come here are no longer binding
(for whatever exceptional reasons or underhanded motives). Only
a manifest sign from God, made clear by the turns of events or the
invoking of our vow of obedience, will persuade us to take the road
back. And mustn't we not also take into account the opinions of our
fellow workers who, for whatever reasons, even if they be false or
mistaken, will surely take us for cowards or pawns, should we depart? Sent as leaven for the flour, we cannot leave during these most
crucial moments. Operating as God's seed is how we must regard
our apostolate here. So our vocation in this country consists in our
striving to become saints so as to prevent the masses from perishing.
Thanks to our efforts, a small number have already returned to the
faith. But what about all the others? How will they know how to
call upon Him in whom they have not believed? How will they believe if no one speaks to them of Him? And who will speak if no one
is sent? The Church is that chain of human beings who, throughout

the centuries, has acted as other Christs in the face of all manner of adversity. We ourselves must not break it at this particularly griev- ous point in time and place. Here we are serving as pastors. We have great faith and that is why God will see us through. If we're forced to abandon this mission, we'll leave, though with hearts more laden with suffering than when we first arrived. We'll return, with the look upon our faces of people who have dreamt an indescribable dream that they can never forget. I hope you'll also see us as bear- ing the marks which God places upon those who have responded to his grace. One needs to have great faith when even God seems, at least on the surface, to be complicit with the forces that would destroy a work that is progressing beyond any reasonable hope that we might have had for its success. This ordeal of having to work here against forces beyond our control goes on and on. It's a bitter trial but one that we've accepted. While awaiting word, we'll con- tinue to work as hard as we can. Let me pass on to you the latest message sent by Henri Perrin which has just been received today by our friend Jacques. 'We should now have even fewer regrets than ever for having come. What we're doing may seem of little value, and yet it is engraved in letters of fire on Christ's body. We must play a role in the *Réleve*; and the battle is only beginning. God's will be done. We're prepared for anything. Pray and have prayers said for us. Preparations for Easter are moving ahead everywhere …'"

Easter was indeed fast approaching, bringing with it a spirit of renew- al. Pierre managed to obtain a respite of two weeks during which he would spend in his camp's infirmary. Amidst the relative calm revail- ing there, he prepared—writing them up in long-hand meditations based on the Exercises of Saint Ignatius for the leaders at Kleinfurra, at their expressed request. Erfurt and Nordhausen would also hold their Easter retreat using for their format prepared points for med- itation that would be sent them every day. The barracks where the Brunnquell *Pastoren* lived, recently transformed into a mailing center for important packages and letters, now has the look of a secretariat where volunteer scribes replace the function of typewriters when there is a need to make multiple copies of directives, Gospel tracts, and se- ries of directed meditations. We regularly "snitch" paper for the secre- tariat whenever there is a delivery of tobacco here, because we aren't allowed to enter the shops for stationery materials in town. As regards mail sent within Germany, we've stopped posting anything from the factory so as not to raise suspicions. We use the post office, railroad station, and other sites for whatever we send in the mail.

News from the outside continues to give cause for alarm. Father Bousquet has just been arrested and very badly manhandled in Berlin. Jacques Vignon has again been imprisoned and is under lock and key in Chemnitz. The group at Neumühle is still in limbo, and the seminarians are expecting to leave from one day to the next, just when they're beginning to harvest the fruits of their winter's labor. As it turns out, they'll still be there at Easter to celebrate this feast with their support groups; and on the day before they will leave, one of them, André Meynier, assisted by his brothers, will present for baptism René, who has been won over by the spirit of charity he has witnessed and experienced by living among them.[18]

From Saalfeld we learn that the names of the seminarians living there have been red-penciled on the DAF lists and classified as "inassimilable." Moreover, the Welcome Center at Weimar has sent a circular notice to all the leaders in Thuringia, enjoining them not to allow any Jocist activities from this point on, and forbidding them to accept any Jocists in their bureaucracy or as members of their administrative committees. Word is already getting around about arrests that have been carried out in the South; and last Sunday, Jean Goin and Maurice de Vise were trailed and harassed by a policeman on their way back from Erfurt. Camille has been warned by his boss to take precautions and be on his guard.

Weighing these pieces of news in my mind, I keep putting off my reply to Marcel Carrier's invitation to join him on an excursion to Weimar for April 3rd until I receive a fat envelope from Leipzig containing Henri Perrin's prison journal, which he had written on scraps of paper of all sizes and colors. Jacques Etevenson sent this to me along with the brief note: "Carrier has asked me to come see him at Weimar on April 3rd. I'm supposed to be working on that Sunday, but I think that I can make it. I'll drop everything and get to Weimar late Saturday afternoon. I really would like to see you one more time

---

18   Paul Watrelot and his team would leave the camp at Neumühle in good hands when they departed: Jacques Magan, Julien Van de Wiel and Eugène Lemoine, Jocist Federal Representative from Saint-Brieuc and head of camp organization at Schleicher. From this point on, they would team up with the *Scouts routiers* (Rover Scouts).

before you leave."[19] My mind is now made up and I send my reply to Marcel: "Yes, I'll be there, weather permitting."

* * *

EASTER IN THURINGIA

Palm Sunday turned out to be a really magnificent day, real Easter weather with everything in bloom. André Yverneau is coming and we'll go back by way of Erfurt. Everything went well, aside from the bugs that we had to pick from our mattresses for the three or four hours of sleep that we were hoping to get at Marcel Carrier's camp. We took our meal at a table facing the head officer of the Gestapo in Weimar's largest restaurant. Marcel had recognized him waiting next to us for a free table because the place was packed. But Jacques, unflappable as ever, opined that "chatting" quietly in full view was the best thing we could do to avoid being noticed. Afterwards we hold a training session with Marcel's team of militants in his room; we—Jacques, André and I—take the time, map in hand, to make an inventory of how our groups are operating respectively in all the cities of Saxony and Thuringia where they are located. Marcel gives us a report on his travels through the South: he has visited all the cities there, one by one on each Sunday since his arrival in Weimar in July of 1943. At Christmas time, he even went as far as Coburg. He has developed especially good relations with Schmalkalden, from which Jean Tinturier and two other seminarians[20] move about effectively in the neighboring areas: Suhl, Zella-Mehlis, etc., where they organize retreats and clandestine rallies.

Marcel is all fired up—a little too much so in the opinion of Brother Felicien, his roommate, guardian angel, and a member of the Spiritan Order who keeps saying: "This is all going to end badly. Marcel moves around too much and writes to too many people." Henri Marannes, who joined us early in the morning on his way from Gera, completes our review of the areas with news from his own section. He shares Brother Felicien's concerns: "I've calmed down a great deal myself since

---

19   Given the fact that our departure was still somewhat of an open question, we could be leaving at any time in the near future.

20   Louis Kuehn and François Donati, all three were seminarians from Paris.

October. We've granted a great deal of autonomy to our communities. Moreover, Yves[21] has been interrogated on several occasions after we've returned from our trips and now no longer goes out. I myself hesitated before coming here. From now on we'll have to carry out our activities on location."

Jacques sums up the situation in his habitually wise manner: "In any case, they're certainly on to us. Yesterday I went to Gestapo Headquarters to see if I could get any information about what they're planning to do with Henri [Perrin]. While there, I was told that they can lock us up whenever they want, with or without valid evidence. Let's continue to be on the safe side without engaging in too many clandestine activities, and let's cut down on the volume of letters we send out."

Before taking leave of each other, we sign an innocuous card that Jacques addresses to Paul Léon, informing him of the results of our "outing." We also leave a number of New Testaments with Marcel who is out of them: he too had become aware of a good many things during the course of this day.

Because the communities stay in touch with each other principally by communication among their respective leaders, Marcel proposes that a rally be held at Arnstadt on April 23rd for the district leaders in Southern Thuringia. I'll be present as a liason for those coming from Northern Thuringia, who are to meet in Nordhausen on May 7th. On that day I hope to get together there with André Parsy from Eisleben, Marc Julia from Göttingen,[22] and Jean Galtier,[23] recently escaped from Berlin, whom Jean Carton had just met during an excursion to Mülhausen. The pastor at Nordhausen will let us borrow the crypt of his church. As a result of all of this, Clément Cotte's great dream of uniting all the communities to the West of Leipzig will finally be realized. Although maintaining much of their autonomy, the militants will be able to maneuver without raising too much suspicion, at the slightest signal given by Paul Léon or Jacques Etevenon.

---

21 Yves Rabourdin, clandestine chaplain from Gera.

22 The first was a Jocist Federal Director from Roubaix, the second a *scout routier* (Rover Scout).

23 A Jesuit POW who agreed to be transferred as civilian worker. He had already done excellent work in Berlin.

André and I went back via Erfurt. I could now consider completed the work that we had set out accomplish when we last passed through here at the end of January, and the results of our efforts had surpassed even our most ambitious hopes. And hadn't André revealed to me, during our train ride back, that Camille had become so overwhelmed by the manifest workings of grace in the hearts of so many of his brothers that he was now seriously considering a vocation to the priesthood? Could he have had some inkling of what was to come?

Absorbed in conversation all the way to our destination, we had at the same time to keep a watchful eye on the door on the movements of a damn policeman who, in diligently making his rounds, was systematically checking out the occupants of every passenger compartment. We managed to allay whatever suspicions he might have had about us by overwhelming him with exaggerated formulas of politeness we used in dealing with him.

We didn't publicize our Easter activities in any way: not in sermons, nor through advertisements nor with any press coverage. Even though quietly observed, Easter in Thuringia nevertheless turned out to be a splendid event. I think that Father Victor Dillard would have greatly approved, he who when I had consulted with him about our plans for the Easter season, had had this to say:

> I believe more and more in the need to develop an authentically Christian way of living. I abominate that kind of cut-rate religion that has been in vogue for such a long time in France: stylized first communions, pagan marriages officiated in the churches, hypocritical funeral services, etc. Any religion that is not incarnated, that is to say, lived through the flesh in full participation with others, and which does not demand personal commitment does not deserve to be called a religion. We have to link together in the minds of the French these two concepts: 1) the real meaning of religion and, 2) the obligation each of us has to train our will, that's to say, the idea of sacrificing oneself. Without grasping the meaning of these ideas, there is no way we can understand or minister to the masses. At the approach of Easter I fear that glossing over essential truths such as these would make a hypocrisy out of the celebration of this great feast. Simply stated, we must constantly seek out men and try to provide them with an in-depth spiritual formation. I'll sign off before I fall asleep.[24]

---

24   The note is dated March 27th, 1944.

In fact, some militants profited from the three-day layoff[25] to lead their friends back to the Church. A lengthy campaign based on friendship finally resulted in long lines of those wanting to see a priest, were he a chaplain in khaki concealed in the back of the church, or a priest positioned behind barbed wires, a worker priest or a volunteer arriving clandestinely at an agreed-upon meeting place in public parks, or a German priest in his confessional, so very welcoming but often looking so very uncomfortable holding in his hand and consulting the questionnaire written in German and French and designed to facilitate the confession of French POWs and workers to German priests that the Rodhain Chaplaincy Office in Paris had prepared and sent into Germany.

Despite everything, Easter also turned out to be a joyous feast here at Sonderhausen. The little church was filled with French and Belgians, arriving on foot or by bicycle, some coming from a very great distance and many arriving well in advance of the 8:00 and 10:00 o'clock Masses. They had to crowd into the side chapels to give enough room to the German worshippers. Seeing so many French workers in the congregation, Father Kirchberg had remained at the back of the nave after the first Mass. When the last of the Germans had left the church, we once again filled in the pews. Coming over to us the priest suggested, "Let all these young people sing. It's Easter after all. Let's take the risk." And sing they did with great gusto, after Milo, Julot and the Klelinfurra leaders led them in their prayers of thanksgiving.

During the entire week after Easter, the mail provided us with a veritable treasure trove of graces, narrating how, in so many daring and clever ways, a significant number of the workers were persuaded to come back to Christ and describing as well the joy felt by those responsible for bringing this about. And, Father Dillard, isn't this just what you were alluding to in your last letter when you wrote:

"Dear Paul, This Monday of Holy Week finally finds me free to converse a little with you. I've been wanting to do this for such a long time, but with 11-15 hours at work each day, plus an hour for each trip back and forth to the factory and time needed for saying daily Mass, I find that there are very few moments left. But let me just say that Providence certainly works in indirect ways. I drove a screwdriver into my hand the other day and have been dispensed from work for the rest of Holy Week, all of which has allowed me

---

25   In Germany, Good Friday is a legal holiday from work.

to move around more and tend to my parish. What a terrific stroke of luck! This Easter has thus turned out to be more beautiful for me than I could ever have imagined. Indeed, if one even needs to say it, Christ was absolutely right: We must always keep on plowing, seeding, and cultivating the ground around the sterile fig tree and never cease insisting that living the Christian way of life in the state of grace must be accompanied by the systematic training of our individual wills. Anyone who has not understood these things has, in my opinion, understood nothing whatsoever. Moreover, we must add to these a third condition—the absolute necessity for Christians to make a commitment before they can achieve any really authentic union with Christ; and because we possess no certainty at all about our future from day to day, we must therefore abandon ourselves completely to Providence."

Our joy at celebrating the risen Christ and seeing the rebirth of Christianity among the workers did not completely allay the anguish we were feeling deep within ourselves. We were still depending upon the bureaucratic whims of a boss who wants at all costs to keep us here, so that the wheels of the war industry continue to turn in this factory and he won't have to be called up to go to the front; we, on the other hand, want to stay in order to finish the work that has been begun.

❋❋❋

ON THE EVE OF OUR DEPARTURE

This morning, April 19th, contrary to custom, I receive little mail, only two postcards and a letter. The first card, from Leipzig, is still another message from Jacques who writes:

"Hello, Thanks for your card of April 4th. I'm urging Paul Léon to call a meeting for May. I neglected to tell you how I really feel about him when we talked the other Sunday. I think it's a better idea that Paul should serve as our regional director. As I see it, he has more time than I to write and reflect; and (though not a completely decisive factor), since the majority of our guys are Jocists, there would be a smoother and more direct means of communication with him in charge. But the essential thing is to help him as best we can to put in place the kind of Catholic front that he has been the first to want to enlarge and unify. My best to André. I'll soon have letters from Henri

Marannes. Have I told you that Clément (Cotte) is back with him again?"[26]

The second card from Wuppertal is the last message I would ever receive from Father Dillard: He writes:

"April 14th, Dear Paul, I have just written to Jacques Etevenon and I will keep in contact with him. Life is still pretty calm here, but I'm becoming more and more engrossed in my work. Spent three hours this morning with Henri Perrin's young friends, but have heard nothing definite. It's not out of the question that I might be forced to go back to France. I leave it to God's grace. He's done a fine job managing things up to the present and will surely continue to do so. Best wishes for Easter ! Victor D."[27]

Then there is a letter from Father Charmot who writes faithfully on the 28th day of each month:

"... I think that Our Lord intends for you to give very significant witness, and I believe that you've already responded very well to what He has expected from you regarding this, the first stage of your mission. Following the example of our Blessed Mother, you should subject yourself totally to his will which, though it has surprises in store will lead us through unforeseen paths to heights we cannot even measure. What we know for certain is that we've not come to the end of those sufferings reserved for France and, in particular, for its young people who will have to bear the heaviest part of the burden of their country's humiliations. Only the young are capable of raising the souls of the French to the exalted heights to which they are called through their vocation as citizens. But this raising of consciences won't be achieved without a fierce struggle. There is a magnificent match to be won here pitting the reign of Christ against the powers of evil. The demons can

---

26   Arrested on April 4th, 1944, Clément Cotte would not be sent back to France but would be deported to Dachau on July 22nd. There he would find Victor Dillard, S.J., Msgr. Piguet, his bishop from Clermont-Ferrand, and many other priests and laymen. He would survive the camps and return to France in an extremely debilitated state.

27   Arrested on April 22nd, Victor Dillard would remain in the Barmen prison in Wupperrtal until Nov. 27th. Taken the next day to Dachau, he would die there on January 12th in a state of total physical exhaustion, after having been operated on for a leg amputation by his friend, the skilled medical surgeon, Doctor Suire.

be vanquished only by martyrs and saints willing to spill their own blood …."

When writing this, was he aware of how prophetic these words of his would become?

PART II: PRISON

CHAPTER FOUR

WITH THE GESTAPO

INSPECTOR WINCKLER'S DRAGNET

Wednesday, April 19th, 1944. Glockman's workshop has been closed down for several days. *Kein material*! ("No material")! André Dupont and Jean Caron have been working on the presses. Alex Pipe and the others are doing odd jobs in the factory's other workshops. As for me, I've been helping a worker place squares of fibro-cement on the floor of the *Bureau Technique*. At three in the afternoon the radio announces that Soviet troops have taken Tarnopol. With a good deal of pleasure I ask my co-worker to explain the strategy for retreat that the *Wehrmacht* has been employing on the Eastern Front. He voices skepticism about it and punctuates his exposé with the expression "this shitty war" (*Schiese Kreig*), which he accompanies with the ritualistic gesture of dropping the right hand down from his shoulder to his belt. At about 5:15, just before quitting time, as is my daily custom, I thread my way through the workshop and rush back to the barracks for my mail. I have a package but am too much in a hurry to open it. I have only enough time to deliver a message from Cambronne to Pépé, our old *Lagerführer*, who wanted to have us empty out a silo of potatoes. I quickly shave, put on respectable trousers, and accompany the ever-punctual Emile Lebrun on the way to church—evening communion and thanksgiving, ending with psalm *In manus tuas*. Alex goes out first and then reenters to whisper in my ear that Pépé is waiting for me outside. It must be about the potato silo, I thought to myself. It's not going to run away. Let him wait for a minute.

Just as I emerge I see him waiting on the sidewalk, flanked by a heavily mustached man whom I recognize as the Police Inspector of Sonderhausen, and another person wearing light Knickobocker trousers, all three of them standing next to a car parked in one corner of the square. "*Das ist Beschet*" ("That's Beschet"), Pépé says, pointing me out to the other two. I know what's happening even before they show me their badges. Pretending not to understand, when they ask me to come with them, I say in German that I'll be right back, quickly turning on my heels. I reenter the church and inform André in a low voice of my imminent arrest, while at the same time emptying the contents of my wallet in his hands. A minute later I come out and get into the car. Through the car window I can see at a distance André Yverneau who has also just come out and is observing my forced departure from where he is standing at the entry to the church. I wave goodbye as he watches me being sped away.

We stop in front of the police station, located right next to our favorite restaurant, the Ratskeller. The police lieutenant meets us, flanked by his *Schupos*. They search me with meager results—only a pen, knife from the Brunnquell Co. and my watch and wallet. They use some unimportant card or other to check on my identity. They also don't seem to have had better results searching my cupboard in the barracks. My friends back there must have quickly done what was necessary, or so I imagine by observing that the briefcase, into which the inspector is slipping several papers and photos from my wallet, holds nothing else. As they conclude, the *Schupo* who is asking me to sign the deposit slip for my things, says: "Tomorrow morning, return." He then takes me to a cell and lets me keep a light on for about five minutes, enough time to make out a mattress, two blankets, and the toilet.

Now here I am in jail. Seven o'clock in the evening. It's all so stupid and predictable. I should have foreseen all of this, yet I am here without even a crust of bread in my pocket, something absolutely contrary to my usual habits. One's initial feelings are certainly far from heroic. Gradually you become conscious of the awful weight of an unknown that you're forced to accept. The setting changes, but the struggle that you feel churning within you only grows more intense. I'm so tired I could drop. We've had so little opportunity for such a long time to get any sleep. Like a well-behaved child, I doze off while saying my rosary.

This business will probably be resolved before anyone knows anything about it back in France: those whom I love won't have had the time to worry about me.

Thursday morning: up at 6 o'clock. I have to wait for the 7:00 a.m. train to Erfurt. Last evening I was able to decipher where I am to be sent by glancing over the inspector's shoulders at a document he was holding and on which were written their travel orders for me. We wait for a long time near the windows of the police station. I watch the prisoners from the Brummquel Co. go by. No one turns around; they won't be able to see me leave for Erfurt. At the agreed upon time, another *Schupo* takes me away without handcuffs. A pleasant old man, he simply shows me that the one hand that he has placed in his briefcase is holding an unholstered revolver. "Do you understand, Mister?"

"Yes," I say, nodding my head. I must have gained his confidence because he lets me move about on the platform. But there is no one there who might be able to recognize me.

We go into a train compartment where passengers are sitting quietly. "For once I'm traveling legally," I thought, placing my feet on the floor of the wagon. The *Schupo* takes the place across from me. We smoke, I pray and am very hungry. Slowly we wind through the chilly April countryside. But there is this difference between myself and those around me: I'm not going where I want to. Gradually I accustom myself to this half-grey shade of color, like an impenetrable and all-intrusive fog that, from this moment on, will adhere to all (and even the most insignificant) actions of my life. I have been set aside by something more powerful than myself. Even so, my mind wanders in an unknown future that it would like to control and my heart still beats in unison with those with whom I was living just yesterday. I yawn; the *Schupo* understands and shares half his breakfast with me. I try to butter him up and am allowed to go to the WC where I dispose of the Jocist photo of Pierre Giraud, which I had just found in one of my pockets. The old man promises me that he'll inform my friends in the barracks when he gets off duty. But will he? Not wanting to depend solely on this, I prepare in my mind some kind of concise sentence to say to the first intelligent-looking Frenchman I might happen to encounter upon arriving at Erfurt. No such luck. I find no one. The city is decked out for Hitler's birthday. After a tram ride we arrive at the *Staatpolizei* ("Police Headquarters"). We go up to the fourth floor and enter the office of an SS inspector who searches me, putting

everything he finds under lock and key. An air raid—and I remain
in a corridor for two hours. Another two hours later, when it finally ends—at noon—the inspector sends me down to the courtyard to
wash his car. I seize the opportunity to save a clean rag that I'll be able
to use as a handkerchief. He returns after a while, this time in uniform
and not alone. I turn to see smiling at me Camille, in his work clothes,
his sack on his back and holding a chapel valise. I get up showing no
emotion and open the car door so that he can get in. Meeting him here
allows me to no longer have the slightest doubt about why I have been
arrested. As a result, I feel better knowing that it was not for the reasons I had surmised earlier: that Brunnquell might have arranged my
arrest as a maneuver to intimidate once again the *Student* (students)
and the *Priester* (priests). But now that I know the real reasons for it, I
feel calm in an odd sort of way. This makes it all worthwhile.

"*Los herein*" ("Get in"). The SS inspector wrenches me from my
musings and pushes me into the back of the car next to Camille. He
sits directly in front of us and focuses the driver's mirror to keep us in
his sight. While we are passing through Erfurt, I take advantage of the
rumbling of the car motor to exchange a few words. "Are you O.K.?"

"Yes."

"When?"

"Yesterday at 6 P.M." Camille indicates his chapel valise. "Couldn't
hide it."

"Michel?"

"No."

"Marcel Carrier?"

"Don't know.

"*Ruhe, menschen*" ("Quiet, men")! The SS officer has very good hearing. Our car proceeds to Gotha. It's now one o'clock in the afternoon
and I'm yawning because I'm so hungry. Camille hands me a crust of
bread and I whisper a few more words: "We don't know each other."

"Right. Understood."

"We don't know André either."

"Agreed."

At Gotha the car comes to a stop in a narrow street alongside the
Gestapo headquarters. We climb to the 7th floor where a mechanically
automated door opens before us. I see Henri Marannes, in handcuffs,
at the end of the corridor. We gaze at each other. Silence.

"You are Catholics?"

"Yes."

"What goddamn trash!"

"Chrissake, can't you be quiet? Sit still on this bench and shut up." The person speaking to us in this tone and with such a strong accent introduces himself as an Alsatian, address Place Pigalle, and the interpreter for these gentlemen. Camille, in a very working-class-Parisian accent, retorts: "173, Route Stratégique, Ivry-Centre, Panam (Paris) and don't try to put anything over on me, Mister!" Astonished, the other shuts up and moves away. Maybe we'll be able exchange a few words. Henri gives me a sign that I don't quite understand. "You'd better say nothing. He's been badly beaten," says my neighbor seated on the same bench to my left.

"So you're also French," I say, carefully looking him over. I notice his worn out shoes, his greasy, filthy work pants and off-white shirt open at the collar under a tattered jacket, his unkempt dark hair, delicate features and eyeglasses that jar with his over-all appearance. "What are you doing here?" I ask.

"I'm a priest."

"So am I, or more precisely, a Jesuit. What's your name?"

"Jean Tinturier."

"O, so that's who are! We were supposed to get together Sunday at Arnstadt, with Carrier."

"No use now, we're all here together, and Carrier among the first to arrive."

"Who and how many?"

"I don't know exactly; I've just come." We continue a furtive conversation, intermittently interrupted with periods of silence.

About 3 o'clock the door at the end of the hall opens again. Inspector Wincklers, a man of medium build, wearing a dark blue suit, square shouldered, full blooded face and with the confident swagger of one who is master of all he surveys, makes his entrance, followed by the Alsatian interpreter and a slender blond female secretary. This is Inspector Wincklers, a specialist in religious matters. We rise and tell him our names. He sneers with elegant disdain. I sense that he gets a great deal of pleasure from manipulating everything that is pristine, innocent, and defenseless. He obviously is an expert in knowing how to sully whatever is sacred. When the preliminaries are over, he makes the three of us (Camille, Jean, and myself) go down into a dark and dank cell. As we enter, two shadows suddenly loom up. The door grinds shut and we hear Wincklers's footsteps receding.

"Hello guys!"

"You're French?"

"Are you Jocists?"

"Yes."

"Who are you?"

"Marcel Callo, Federal Representative from Rennes and, in Germany, Director of Catholic Action in Zella-Mehlis."

"And you?"

"René Le Tonquèze, a friend of Jean Haméon and Gilbert. We're from Tours. In Hitlerland, we're in charge of our little hole in the wall around Suhl. Jean has been in prison since January. He had a fight with a policeman who had played a dirty trick on him, and they arrested me in his place. It was to be expected because I took over after him." Then Camille introduces himself and ends his remarks saying: "Listen, friends, what we've done is all to the good because we've done it for Christ."

"I suppose so," René says rather gloomily, "but still."

"Hush, guys!" interrupts Marcel Callo, "Someone's whistled." He rushes to the spy hole and, pushing it open, presses his ear up against it.

"Quiet, it's Marcel Carrier. He's just come down after having being interrogated all last night and before that, all day long on Tuesday. He was arrested at 8 p.m. in his room at camp while tending to his mail."

I warn them that there may be a listening device hidden somewhere in the cell. "Don't worry. We would have already suffered the consequences. This isn't the first time we've had this kind of conversation. Marcel has already told Louis Pourtois about all of this this morning."

"You mean Louis Pourtois from Eisenbach?"

"Oh, but you've yet to know the whole story," René replies with a nervous laugh. "Louis was arrested as we all were yesterday morning. The inspector grilled him all morning long and finally decided that he was dealing with a poor slob of very little importance. So you can see how well we're coping here." Now I'm no longer thinking about a hidden microphone but rather of Eisenbach. So there's also a priest there.[1] How is that he hasn't yet been actively involved?

---

1 Father Dubois-Matra, a Jesuit POW, who became a civilian worker in order to aid Louis Portois and the Jocists located there.

While I'm wondering about this, Callo is acting as a telephone oper-
ator for Carrier who is speaking to him from the neighboring cell. He
transmits our responses to Carrier's questions: "They're three of them:
Jean Tinturier from Schmalkalden, Camille Millet from Erfurt and
Paul Beschet from Sonderhausen ... Yes wait, they're going to speak
with you."

Then there follows a long conversation with Carrier, broken up with
silent pauses because of people coming and going. I finally find out
the circumstances surrounding the arrests of the others. Jean Lecoq,
André Vallé and his brother Roger were denounced. Fernand Morin,
Jocist interpreter for the Gotha camp, who after having been arrested,
interrogated and released, would finally end up in prison with us, suspects that they were turned in by two spies "working" in the *Wagon-
Fabrik* camp, who then disappeared shortly after the arrests.

I was to learn a bit later from Fernand himself how this all began:
"On the first of April," which was

> the Vigil of Palm Sunday, the Gestapo inspectors come into the
> camp about 9:00 a.m. They force me to show them my room. I'm
> covered with sweat because I had already seen men in civilian
> clothes going through the same procedures with some other friends
> whom they had subsequently shipped off to an *Arbeitslager* (disci-
> plinary camp). Then they proceed with the search saying, "This has
> to do with the black market." Still not suspecting the real motives
> for their visit, I begin to calm down. They inspect my mail and my
> books. After this they ask me to go with them to be interrogated in
> the same office where I had often carried on my work as interpreter.
> Once there I am asked to explain certain papers and photos. The
> inspector seems to be following a set of procedures written down
> in great detail in a document to which a list of names has also been
> attached. "So you must know something about the JOC?" he ex-
> claims, as his glance falls upon a Jocist photo that I happen to have
> there. Getting up, he forces me to return to camp with him. Once
> there he searches the Vallée brother's place. He even inspects their
> beds, takes their mail away with him, and then goes to arrest them
> as they're leaving the factory. While they're being taken away, André
> is able to drop his notebook of addresses which a friend manages
> to pick up. During the course of his search, however, the inspec-
> tor found a little notebook of André's containing notes on study
> groups, sites for the retreats, and the names of some of our friends.
> His interrogation went on for a very long time. I remember how

very disturbed Wincklers was when he found a letter from Bishop Mercier, Vicar General of Sées, addressed to Roger Vallée, which contained a copy of the vehement protest made by Cardinal Suhard regarding the operations of Occupation authorities against Catholic Action. I spent the night in camp and had sufficient time to warn Jean Lecoq,[2] who was arrested three days later.

With my ear glued to the spy hole I could hear from a distance Carrier's deep, resounding voice. "Excuse me, Paul, it's all my fault. I wasn't careful enough."

"That's got nothing to do with it. Were you taken in on the evening of the 16th?"

Yes. I was cooking noodles in my room and had just taken out the rest of my mail and other papers that I needed to hide. At that moment the door opened, and in comes the *Lagerführer*, followed by two inspectors who showed their badges. "Which one is Carrier? Where is your locker?" asks the stoutest one of the trio. The interpreter grabs me and throws me into a corner. The fat one tells him to treat me with respect; then he asks me if I know why I am being arrested. I say nothing. "What about your Catholic Action? You are Catholic, aren't you?" "Yes." He smiles, orders me to get dressed and then obsequiously sits me in the back of his car, being careful to roll up the windows so I wouldn't be in a draft, as he explains it; then he complains about Félicien and the others who had followed me to find out what was happening.

"What do they know?"

"That I'm the one in charge."

"Did they beat you?"

"Yes, I was forced to admit to everything that they suspected about me, because they had possession of my mail."

"What does he want to know from us?"

"Just about everything—your politics, organization of the JOC, affinity groups, trips taken, clandestine Masses said, information on possible sabotage. You only need to admit to any connection you've had through me. As for all the rest, you're on your own." For me the "rest" amounted to a large number of places: Sonderhausen, Saalfeld, Kleinfurra, Nordhausen, Wittenberg, Neumühle, Bitterfeld, Leipzig—would all these communities with whom I've been involved

---

2   A priest from the Rennes Diocese, initially a POW, who became a camouflaged civilian worker to help André Vallée and the Jocists at Gotha.

end up losing their leaders? I can see them all now: Milo and Julot, Pierre Giraud, Jacques Etevenon, Paul Léon. Our mutual ties with them would inevitably lead the Gestapo to Henri Perrin and Clément Cotte, who are already in the Praesidium prison in Leipzig. I also think of my brothers whom I might compromise as well: Paul Watrelot at Neühle, Maurice Lefèvre at Saalfeld. "As for the rest, you're on your own." I go farther back in my cell and lean against a thick door of solid iron bars that cuts off the entire cell at one meter from the wall, which is pierced through at the top with an air hole covered over with a thick wired lattice. We talk for a long time into the evening. They didn't bring us soup. Henri Marannes was probably still being interrogated. We prayed for him—and for Wincklers, who surely had to be mistreating him. Camille lays down boards, blankets and jackets on the stone floor. Night has fallen. They doze off while I remain awake.

About 11:30 I hear the sounds of footsteps—keys in the lock, voices, a door opens and closes with a grinding of bolts. "Is it you, Henri? Well, did they beat you?"

"It doesn't look good for you; I was forced to tell them that I saw you at Weimar on April 2nd."

"They're interested in the clandestine Masses?"

"Yes, but I placed the responsibility for them onto Lecoq's shoulders, and only he knows about the things that were said at Camille's place in Erfurt."

"And what about Yves?"[3]

"He's of no interest to them, and he also knows that he is being watched by the Gestapo in Gera. The inspector is furious because the JOC has continued its activities in France after the Occupation. He whipped me like a dog because he wanted to make me say that Quiclet[4] and the Chaplaincy office had given us orders to enter into communications with Resistance movements in Germany. I denied it."

"And Saalfeld?"

---

3   Yves Rabourdin, clandestine chaplain at Gera.

4   Georges Quiclet was one of the founders of the French JOC and worked in Rodhain Chaplaincy Office in Paris. The Gestapo alleged that the French Catholic hierarchy plotted to infiltrate the ranks of the German workers and turn them against the Nazi regime by actively organizing and using JOC militants who went to Germany as their agents. There is absolutely no evidence to support this allegation of conspiracy by the JOC against the Nazi government. (trans. note)

"It's no longer an issue. But be careful! I saw mail from Leipzig, cards from Jacques, and Wincklers knows about Paul Léon. He has a thick dossier which he's always consulting." I realize that Henri is totally exhausted so I try to persuade him to get some rest.

The night goes on. An air raid. While the R.A.F. is doing its job, it occurs to me that today is the 21st. We'll offer up this, the first day of our imprisonment, for all the communities of Saxony and Thuringia. Jean and Marcel are dozing. Alone in the dark, Camille is suffering from his colic attacks. As for me, I am anxious about how well I might endure other interrogations: if they succeed in making me talk, how many of our comrades will be arrested? And what is going on now in Sonderhausen? In my present state of mind I imagine the worst possible scenario. Sometime later I would learn the details of what had actually happened there as follows:

Leaving the church, André Yverneau warns the others about my arrest and rushes to the barracks. Rousset had already done what was necessary. The jar that contained all my papers had disappeared and the side of the locker bearing my name, which I shared with André Dupont, now only contained clothing. These precautions greatly facilitated matters. André Yverneau leaves for Kleinfurra where he warns Milo; and until very late in the evening, they both write to all the communities in Saxony-Thuringia to alert them. About 11:00 Milo and André go on foot to Sonderhausen. When they arrive, they sort out and conceal all compromising material. After a short rest Milo leaves on the 5 a.m. train to Kleinfurra, taking along with him my briefcase with everything in it.

They don't know about us at the factory until Thursday morning. Then a conspiracy is uncovered. It seems that the French *lang* (local factory representative) was in fact a spy. As a result, others have been arrested at Nordhausen and Frankenhausen. Herr Saul is on edge every time he hears two French people conversing together; the women gossip and the prisoners, old hands about these matters, say it's really God-awful luck. Lucien agrees to conceal my notebook among his papers. "Pipe" has lost his desire to smoke. It's a tremendous blow to Jean Carton. A very nervous team reels from the shock. Even when anticipated, bad news like this has disastrous over-all effects. The next day, Friday the 21st, André Yverneau goes to the police station to try to get first-hand information. He is told, "*Beschet nicht da*" (Beschet is not here). "He's no doubt already left for Erfurt or Leipzig," André writes to Pierre Sournac, "He was probably arrested because he had in his possession the envelope containing some pages of Henri Perrin's clandestine (prison) journal that he received from Jacques Etevenon on Wednesday morning."

For his part Milo leaves Saturday the 22nd for Nordhausen to take control of the situation. "I'm sending you a hurried note from Pierre Giraud's room in the Montagna camp," he writes to Pierre, who has been detained at Oberfgerbra.

> "Later on you'll learn why I'm here.... This has been a remarkable week for reasons you're well familiar with. I've really been shaken up by it.... I'll always remember the night trip I took on foot be-tween Kleinfurra and Sonderhausen with André. We talked about the events of the day and, in the deep woods under a star-filled sky, we prayed together for Paul. My eyes were brimming with tears. One never forgets such moments. Then we spoke at length about our comrades at Erfurt. You now know the aftermath. I did what I had to do.
>
> "Yesterday evening André was at Kleinfurra to complete the group discussion of the *Acts* started by Paul. I'm going to postpone the all-day conference arranged by him for Nordhausen on the 14th of May—a prudent step. Moreover, the guys at Eisleben, Gottingen and elsewhere must have written you about this matter. On the 7th I'll go to Erfurt with André to see the Directors who are still in a state of shock at the news that Camille was arrested Wednesday morning. Louis Zacher,[5] who had just come to Sondersh, was the one who informed us. The police came and got him out of bed. Let's not get all excited, but we now have to be sure to proceed very cau-tiously. André was supposed to go to Weimar tomorrow. But hav-ing been detained at the factory, he wanted to go see Camille that very evening. He was leaving on foot to take the train at Honebra when Zacher arrived. Jean Carton went after him and dissuaded him from going there. I saw André Yverneau after he had come back and we talked for a long time. Then I decided to return to Nordhausen to warn André Dupont so that he would return to Sonderhausen. I found him with Paul Giraud's associates at the Welcome Center. We spent the evening together—we read from the *Acts of the Apostles*, had a discussion on the Holy Spirit. I slept there and departed with him the next morning. Good night, Pierre, in union with Paul and Camille, very sincerely yours, Milo."

---

5   Jocist Representative from Annonay who would succeed Camille Millet at Erfurt.

DELICATE CONVERSATIONS

Day-time noises are now reaching us within our prison cell. At about eight o'clock Wincklers comes to get Jean Tinturier for an interrogation. He would not be brought down again until 6:00 this evening. Still no sign of food, but the *Schupos*, most of them nice old guys, lead us through our morning rituals. We then settle down for the day in the back of the cell, each to tell his own story, starting with Camille who recounts the details of his arrest. (We all must do something to keep ourselves occupied!)

Camille and Michel were awakened about 6 o'clock on Wednesday the 19th, by noise coming from a suspicious conversation taking place at the entrance to the Rosen Müller building. They recognize their boss's voice among those speaking and hear people coming up the stairs. The door opens and two Germans break into their attic room. One of them, a short, soft-spoken man about fifty, introduces himself. "We're the Gestapo," he says in French. "Are you Camille Millet? Get dressed." During this time, Michel, while still in bed, is asked to identify himself and is also told to get dressed. He complies while the two cronies are ransacking the room. With great self control Camille lays out for them all the mail from his family, thus giving himself enough time to locate his list of the names of the militants, fold the paper and put it in Michel's béret, which he then places on his own head, as the latter prepares to obey the orders just given him by the two Gestapo agents to go down stairs. "I thought it was only a routine search," explains Camille, "but while descending, Michel spots handcuffs in the briefcase of one of the inspectors and warns me. If they get a kick out of arresting me, that's fine, I'm ready," he says to Michel now being led below. When the search is concluded, Camille leans out of the window to warn Michel, now posted in the garden: *Zu zieuteras les couvrantes du paddock*" ("See that everything in the room is covered up"). "I had to be sure to tell him," continues Camille, "where to find the rest of the papers without revealing the meaning of what I was saying to the others, who could understood French." Camille finishes his business and comes down, accompanied by the two police officers who let him give a final handshake to Michel. "Don't be alarmed. I don't think it's serious, a matter of a day or two at the most, then he'll be back. Don't alarm his parents." While the inspector is sharing these observations with Michel, Camille departs forever from #6 Grenzweg. Michel now finds himself all alone in this well-known little greenhouse, living among the Italians there who have, for once, been rendered speechless by Camille's arrest.

The afternoon goes by. About 6 o'clock, again voices, keys. "Jean Tinturier must be coming back," Marcel Callo surmises. I rush to the spy hole and ask him:

"Have you been there a long time?"

"They're not very smart, you know."

"Were you beaten?"

"Not me, but he was. Wincklers wanted to check out my responses to his questions on the spot and offered me a little tour of Schmalkalden this afternoon. Thus I was able to see Kuehn and Donati again. They've attended to everything that needed to be done. The police made a clean sweep of my food supply, but I was able to save a little something for you, some eucalyptus lozenges that I had in my pocket."

"What did you talk about?"

"The Chaplaincy, Communism, but he has less intelligence than a *lycée* drop out. I think he really wants to bring this to a close as soon as possible, now that he has the major players in hand. One thing to worry about, Camille, they don't seem to know much about Erfurt and they grilled me all about it. I pretended not to know anything, but they don't seem to be satisfied."

"Is Henri with you?"

"Yes. He's sleeping, or trying to."

"Have you had anything to eat?"

"Not yet."

"That will have to wait for tomorrow, good night."

Again a terribly long night. About 8 o'clock in the morning, the Alsatian interpreter comes to find Camille and promises us a "stamm" at noontime.[6] Then a long waiting period during which we pray. Marcel Callo tells us about his native Brittany. René, who has completed his apprenticeship as pastry cook, regales us with his delicious recipes. About 11 o'clock there is an air raid. Then many comings and goings. Will we have to wait until Monday to be interrogated? The adjoining cell is opened. Then ours. "Beschet?"

"Yes, here." It's my turn. No luck, I have to leave just as the soup is arriving.

---

6   A meal served every day in restaurants and which did not require a food ration ticket. (trans. note)

I'm not proud of my mental state. I can't pray at all. I simply remember, while climbing three levels of stairway behind Wincklers, that this officer would have over me only as much power as would be granted him by our Father. With this thought in mind, I'm relatively at ease as I sit down in the cushioned chair Wincklers offers me when we enter the office. The room is very well lit, large, with glassed-in bay windows and walls adorned with bright paintings and a huge portrait of Hitler surrounded with panels of SS propaganda. We go through the identification preliminaries; I'm not at all eager to let him know that I'm a Jesuit. "You are a seminarian?"

"Yes, enrolled in the *Faculté* at the Université de Lyon."

"How long have you worn the cassock?"

"Since Nov. 1939."

"And you don't yet say Mass?"

"No, I've had to go through a very long program of studies."

"Why?"

"I want to be a Doctor so I can teach in the Missions."

"So, a missionary? And your parents?"

"My father served as a Colonial Officer from 1914-1918 and in 1929, as a result of wounds suffered during the last war."

"Have you a brother who is a soldier?"

"My brother is in charge of a camp in the Alps."[7]

He pauses, and after a minute or so says, "If you don't answer me as you should ...." He shows me his bludgeon and revolver, both lying in the open on his desk.

"I'll try, Sir, to answer your questions as best I can," I tell him through the Alsatian interpreter. The latter advises me to be precise and to the point so as to avoid more questions if I don't want to prolong the interview—and I certainly don't! Both seem, however, to be quite tired. Wincklers gets up, then both of them go out leaving me alone in the room, no doubt to give me time to think things over.

I cast an inquisitive glance around. On the desk there is a chalice decorated with flowers and another next to it, which bears traces of beer; there are also various ecclesiastical objects on another table. I found out later that Wincklers had made Jean Tinturier drink beer from the chalice, before he himself took a drink, and that he had forced Camille to eat unconsecrated hosts, hence there could be no doubt

---

7   Actually, in the Vercors, site of one of the largest *Maquis* (clandestine camps for young resisters often located in mountainous regions) in France.

about what was driving this particular SS officer. He also made his secretary the gift of a crucifix which she promptly threw into the waste basket, calling it *Schiese* (shit). I also learned that between the two sessions, during which he severely beat Roger Vallée with his bludgeon, Wincklers had made him dress up in priestly vestments, thus provoking loud guffaws from the others in the room. I keep looking around me discreetly and see, scattered over his desk, Marcel Carrier's correspondence, and prominently displayed with it, the letter from Jacques Etevnon in which he had disclosed the identity of the Jocist leader at Weisenfeld. I resist the temptation to make it disappear: they've probably set a trap. On the other tables, rosaries, books, cookies, jam, magazines, cigarettes and various other objects are strewn about in complete disorder.

Wincklers comes over to hand me a plate on which three spoonfuls of spinach keep company with four morsels of potato. *Schmeckt's?* ("Isn't it good?") *Ia, aber nicht viel* ("Yes, but it's not very much"). As I eat, my spirits rise.

"Tell me about your trip from France." I give him a brief description. "Isn't it correct to say that your Chaplaincy has sent you here as emissaries to carry out anti-Nazi projects?" "No, rather we've been sent on a mission to become, by our presence and generosity, companions and means of support for our brother workers conscripted to do forced labor." He gives no sign of believing what I'm saying. I go on further to insist (without unfortunately being able to produce the document in question) that "Just the other day I received a letter from the Chaplaincy congratulating us for not having taken any political stance." He still remains silent; I wonder, is he going to explode? I later found out that by reading André Vallée and Camille's mail, Wincklers had learned about the protests of the Belgian Bishops and of Cardinal Liénart of Lille concerning the imposition of the STO, as well as Cardinal Suhard's letter protesting the imprisonment of Father Guérin. But apparently wanting to lead me on, he continues: "Yes but don't you presently aid and abet the JOC movement and its support groups?" I explain to him how Catholic Action functions through its discussion and support groups in meetings held on Sundays for Jocists and Scouts. "Then you do have an organization and that is absolutely forbidden (*streng verboten*) in Germany!"

"How can you prohibit spiritual activities whose goal is to maintain the morale of young workers whom you have forced to leave from their homes and whom you've deprived of all legitimate charitable care?"

I go on to explain the precise objectives that we are currently trying to realize here and now: to dismantle black marketeering among the French; put a curb on gambling for money; and discourage as much as possible sexual promiscuity among our workers with German women and others as well. The inspector is taking notes. There is a brief pause. Then he brusquely asks, "Have you ever gone to Weimar?"

"Yes."

"Why?"

"Carrier and his friends wanted to have a seminarian give a talk to them about the Bible. This book was all that I took with me for baggage." Knowing that he was informed about our trip of April 2nd, I describe it at length. It seems apparent that I've now gained some of his trust. He offers me a cigarette which I willingly accept, after all he's only giving it back to its legitimate owner.

Then he tries a new approach: "You're fighting against the Communists."

"For us Catholics, atheistic Communism is an error condemned by Pius XI in his Encyclical *Divini Redemptoris*. But we don't use the same procedures as you: instead of destroying, our intention is to love." I had excellent friends who were Communist. At this very moment I remembered Meisner, the metal fitter at the Glockmann workshop, who asked me to help him in his work solely as a personal favor, because he did not want to force me to "collaborate," hence betray my personal convictions. And how many times did he stand guard and warn me of our boss's approach when I was writing letters on the sly in the workplace?

"What opinion do you have of the German worker? He doesn't work like his French counterpart: We're not used to pretending to be working while actually doing nothing, when the boss makes his rounds. I've found some to be excellent friends, and others who are bad characters, just like back home." Showing no reaction to what I've said, he then changes tack.

"You're a good Frenchman. What is the better way for this war to end as far as your own country is concerned? With victory for Germany, or England?"

"Sir," I responded after some reflection, "the Anglo-Saxons have taken from us our colonial empire and a part of our fleet, while Germany is holding as prisoners within its country two and one-half million Frenchmen. France will give credence to the first of the two and will begin to give us something back." He jots down my reply.

"Do you think that France will be able to get back on its feet again all by itself?"

"Yes, its Christian and humanistic traditions and its present-day program of Catholic Action are strong guarantees that this will come about."

"You don't take a side in all of this?"

"How could we since as Catholics we claim responsibility for everyone?"

"So, you have good relations with the German clergy?" The trap was only too obvious. I replied by praising the helpfulness, generosity and discretion of its members. For almost the next five hours we went on discussing the same topics. The interrogation ends with the question: "What do you talk about among yourselves in your groups?"

"About sports, France, and God." Wincklers shakes his head.

"You're still a believer?" When I don't reply, he adds, "That's why you're of such concern to me," and he gives me a long stare. Then getting up, he directs me to an adjoining room where he has his report typed up. It makes mention only of my faith commitment and my religious activities, so I can sign it.

Wincklers takes me down to another cell. I throw myself down on the boards. I'm totally exhausted and have talked a great deal. But have the words that I've spoken fallen in with the seeds of wheat that the master of the harvest has stored in his grange, after it has been separated from the chaff on his threshing floor? I'm amazed that we can bear witness to our faith as Christians in such a banal way. I also feel so miserable because of this hunger that constantly keeps gnawing at me. Even so, it all went very well, perhaps even too well. I wasn't even maltreated, and by desiring this I had perhaps manifesed too much vanity on my part. I had disclosed nothing about the communities of Northern Thuringia and Saxony; I had described our activities and our contacts with our friends at Kleinfurra and Nordhausen as consisting of nothing more than smoking a few cigarettes together in the Welcome Centers. We didn't talk about Neumühle, or Saalfeld, the Jesuits, or Victor Dillard. I've even reached the point of finding it grotesque that I've been imprisoned for so little reason. Wincklers should have had me released since he had no real grounds for keeping me here. To be dealt with so unjustly on such petty grounds really irritates me. But I'm nevertheless enduring this suffering that I so much resent because of the hope that I harbor deep within me that I may be called upon to bear witness. But how difficult it is to find anything positive about being imprisoned for having worked for the good! I seem to be such an unlucky person!

It's getting dark. Sounds reverberate around me. I hear the grating noise caused by someone setting a full pail on the floor at the entrance to my cell, before my door is opened. I spring to my feet; the soup has arrived. Very shortly afterwards I am aware that Marcel and René have just been brought back to their cells; their interrogation was supposed to continue until Monday morning. We'll have to spend Sunday in this filthy hole.

"IN COMMUNION WITH THE ENTIRE CHURCH"

At dawn I'm dragged from half sleep by moans originating in the adjacent cell. They're coming from Russian women who must have been picked up for being out in the city at night without proper authorization. Outside the trams are starting up once again. At this very moment Christians are coming together. Today we were to hold a district conference for all of the leaders of Southern Thuringia, at Arnstadt. But I recall the *First Letter of Peter the Apostle*

> "to all those living as aliens in the Dispersion, Christ suffered for you and left an example for you to follow in his footsteps. He was insulted and did not retaliate with insults; when he was suffering he made no threats; he was bearing our sins in his suffering on the cross. Through his wounds you have been healed. You had gone astray like sheep but now you have returned to the shepherd and guardian of your souls." (2/21-25).

Just the other day I had meditated over this text in the factory, with the study day in mind, because it resumes the liturgy of the Second Sunday after Easter. René, Marcel and I feel a great calm coming over us. Holed up in the lair of the Gestapo, nothing matters anymore for us except God, the ever-constant guardian of our souls.

We sing *the Kyrie*, the *Gloria*, and join in our offertory prayers with all those throughout Germany who are coming to the altar this morning to receive Him. The women have left off singing their lament and now begin the *Kristos voé kressie* ("Christ is risen") from the Easter liturgy. Feeling somewhat more like his own self after having his soup, René Le Tonquèze recalls that on this very day we were supposed to meet with each other at Arnhardt but, "We've been tripped up by these folks. So let me tell you anyway," he continues, "what we've been doing at Suhl."

"In the beginning there were only the three of us: Jean Haméon, Gilbert and myself. Then others began to work with us. It's amazing what friendship can accomplish. We operated together as one, and it was really tremendous to see how our work was branching out: visiting the sick in the infirmary and the hospital, bringing them presents, doing little odds and ends, distributing books, and lifting their spirits. We also had to take care of the men in the barracks who, for the most part, admitted that they didn't know what to do with themselves and lay about lifelessly on their mattresses. The most popular sport in the living quarters where 120 men lead a disgusting lifestyle is boxing. Twelve days after our arrival I had my first real experience. A guy was sleeping above me when about 15 rugged fellows came around to strip him and wax him over with shoe polish. We hadn't yet gone to bed. I get up and tell them, 'I'll bash the first one who comes up.' They exchange a few words among themselves and then sheepishly slink away. On another evening as I'm coming in, I see some guys making chalk drawings on the curtains of naked Adams and Eves in various lewd poses. I ask them if it's their own mothers and fiancées they're making fun of here. What I say shocks them, but they don't want to let up in front of the others. Taking a rag I erase everything. No one makes a move. Let me tell you, this never happened again."

"Were there women in your camp?"

"No, not in mine, but there were some in another camp. What a sad situation that was! Once when some pregnant women went for a medical exam at the factory, they were told by the doctor: 'I'm going to give you an injection to relax you.' In reality the injection caused them to have an abortion. We took up the matter with the head of the factory; he weighed in on our side, and as a result, there were changes in the medical staff. Another time we had a friend who wanted to fool around with a young woman and wrote to his future fiancée the following: 'I'm going out with a German woman so that I can learn the language and have enough to eat.' Another person, a youth club director from Brittany, constantly takes advantage of young women who want to go wild and party. But let me tell you something." And René goes on to tell us how his chaplain in France reacted to his intentions to help these women. The priest raised his arms to heaven, like a good mother, and proceeded to scold him. But René replied very appropriately, "Didn't Christ save prostitutes?" The Chaplain retorted by comparing himself to a mother duck who, after brooding her young, sees them rushing onto the pond. In her view it's still too soon for them to go near the water alone; but these young ducks already know how to swim.

"So," René continues, "I then got to know how bad the situation was for women. I remember a young eighteen-year old Jocist with whom Jean Haméon had come in touch as she was leaving the 11 o'clock Mass one Sunday. She in turn consigns to our care another young woman who had been thrown out of her own home in France. This young person had been placed in an orphanage by her parents who then made her go out with a young man she didn't care for. Out of pride, as she put it, she volunteers to go to Germany. In her camp there are 22 women: things are pretty ugly there. Having come as a virgin, she and four of her friends weren't able to stay that way for very long. I try to get her back on her feet and lend her a copy of *A la découverte de l'Amour*.[8] The book makes the rounds of the camp; one day I meet one of the women who says, 'Hi there, you're the man from JOC. You people have some pretty good stuff to read!' The book had made its mark. Another young woman from the camp wrote me to say: 'You're more fortunate than I am. Just think that a person like me, who shares your same moral values, can never expect to marry a man like you. When I was 12, my father abused me; I've suffered ever since because I've never been able to resolve this loss of a part of myself. Moreover, if you could only know what torture I've had to endure. Do I have to turn bad because of this? I swear that I've never had sex with any man. Thanks for your confidence in me and your friendship that has been so encouraging. But will I be strong enough to hold out? I feel I've nothing more to lose.' This is all so terribly sad. Fortunately for myself I was able to locate a POW chaplain who lived in the French POW *Kommando*. We used to go to confession to him through the barbed wire or hear Mass said outside the wall. From that point on, 'Iron Wire' (as he was dubbed by our own group) had not the slightest problem ministering to all those coming to him. And we also attended sessions of directed meditation led by Jean Tinturier

---

8   ("The Discovery of Love") by the French physician, Doctor Goust. (trans. note)

who had just come from Schmalkden, to raise our spirits. Don't you remember, Marcel?"

René never ran out of things to tell. We all felt as if we were really in a church, and we benefited every bit as much from what we were doing here as we might have in attending Sunday services. René concluded that, as an only child, he had had to learn how to do the washing, sew, and share his bread. "I wrote letters to encourage and counsel others that amazed me when I reread them. Can you imagine, a simple guy like me! Thank goodness that Christ was there with us. Otherwise I would have become a thief like the others."

The night seemed endless. We couldn't sleep and were cold and hungry. Today, Monday the 24th of April. This morning Marcel Callo and René Le Tonquèze have gone for their final interrogation with Wincklers. We aren't given anything to eat at noon. About 3 o'clock, we have to unload a coal truck in the courtyard; every time the main door opens onto the street, I can't help looking at the passersby until a *Los Mensch* ("Get a move on") snaps me back to reality. We talk very little. However, René tells me about how lucky he was, at the moment of his arrest, to have had on him the letter from Cardinal Liénart, in which the latter specified the ways in which the JOC was very different from a political party. "You bet, we've got other things to do. The JOC amounts to a form of devotion, but a party is more often than not concerned with a power struggle."

Meanwhile Marcel Callo is busy destroying all the papers and photos that might incriminate us.

Tuesday evening, we are joined in our cells by three Russians and a Frenchman, and the very next morning, the Russian women are let out. The Frenchman, a POW, transferred as civilian worker, had been badly beaten. I try to bandage his bruised ankle with a rag. He had struck his boss and will be discharged after having spent six weeks in a *Strafeslager* ("disciplinary camp"). He's a good guy who tears up when we explain why we're here. He offers to take messages to our friends outside because he thinks he'll be let out before we will. The little Russians are using newspapers for smoking material. Sleep is out of the question.

Thursday, April 27th, they come to get us about 5 o'clock in the afternoon. —"*Alles mit!*"—("Take everything with you!") We're quite weak from eight days of fasting. Wincklers sends us off after allowing us to rinse our hands and offering us a slice of bread to take along. I take advantage of a moment when no one is looking to pocket a half round of bread. We go out into the city. Obeying all the commands given by the two Gestapo secretaries who follow close on our heels, we take infinite pleasure in once again moving about on the street with others. The offices are emptying out and a crowd of people is reading the latest communication posted by the *Thüringer Zeitung*. But there is a vast difference between them and us in that we can no longer go where we want to. We finally arrive at No. 2 Steinmühlenallee, the address of the Gotha City Prison.

CHAPTER FIVE

PENTECOST, 1944

WE BEGIN OUR LIFE IN PRISON

Number 2 Steinmühlenallee is built like many other prisons with its two-story grey building shaped in the form of a T. One enters through a little door and, after passing through a small garden, you have to climb three stairs, at the top of which a huge guard opens the bars and greets you with a bunch of keys; then the bars close behind. We meet Jean Tinturier leaning against the wall in the corridor, looking feverish, with dark shadows around his eyes. We go through the usual formalities: we are weighed, vital statistics taken, and are given a medical exam. We have to wait in line a long time to deposit our personal effects. The officer in command, about 55 years of age, buttoned up in his green uniform, with graying hair and angular features, his elbows planted squarely on his desk, peers at us through antique spectacles planted on the end of his nose. This worthy functionary is waiting conscientiously, his watch in front of him, for 6:30 p.m. to come around so he can go off duty. The *Oberwachnmeister* ("Chief Inspector") finally comes around to bring us to our respective cells, but not before supplying us with trousers, shirts, underwear, and shoes and socks. The laundry man, a German convict who is serving a term for trafficking in the black market, says to me in a friendly voice: "*Du, Franzose: schön Kammer*" ("A nice room for you, Frenchman"). I am to spend the night in cell no. 68 and will share it with a Russian, but tomorrow I'll be given a cell (no. 72) all for myself. He hands me a small bowl of soup; I hesitate, not being used to such abundance. While closing the door, the *Oberwachmeister*, moving his right hand up and down before his wide-open mouth, says "*Fressen, fressen, ia mein Herr!*" ("Eat up, Mister").

Silence reigns in the prison. My Russian has come back, and sitting resignedly on the edge of his bed, looks me over as I arrange my mattress and blankets. In a hurry to check out my surroundings, I give the scout whistle and the JOC greeting through the door. I hear a resounding echo: Camille, Henri, René, Marcel Callo, and the two Vallée brothers are all here on the same floor. Frightened by this outburst among Frenchmen, the Russian begs me to cut it out. We quiet down only after we've whistled the *Salve Regina*.

I come close to Ivan, a tall blond Ukrainian whose right eye is badly bruised. "*Gestapo, viel Kaput! Du Katholik?*" ("The Gestapo, it's all banged up. Are you Catholic?") The question surprises me. I explain to him that there are many French Catholics in the prison. "Good friends," he said, "but nothing to eat: that's war for you." I wanted to talk some more. "Go to sleep, Frenchman, sleep, it's better. We have to work tomorrow." And I followed his advice.

The following morning, rise at five o'clock, coffee, a slice of bread. Yvan makes me sit on the bench while he arranges the mattress. At 6:00 we assemble in the courtyard to leave for work. Surrounded by his guards, the prison superintendant takes the roll call. We separate into columns, and, by chance, I find that we'll all be in the same group. "We're going to work for Wagner, an important market gardener in the city," says Camille, who has just managed to sidle up next to me in the line. Lecoq, Carrier, Pourtois and Tinturier aren't allowed down. They're being held in secret.

We spend the day planting potatoes. At noon soup is brought to us from prison. The boss awards us with a mess bowl of *Kartoffeln* ("potatoes") taken from the farm's hog rations. Our guard, Herr Rausch, or "the dago" as we decided to name him, has a nasty look about him. He always bullies the Russians and today he drew his revolver on a Pole who had saved a pear to eat with his bread later on in the day after returning to the prison. Sometimes he becomes good humored and, with exaggerated gestures and loud cries, explains to us what we are to do. When he comes up to me, he first looks me over and pointing to Roger Vallée, asks: "*Du Pfarrer wie Roger?*" ("Are you a priest like Roger?") I say yes and he leaves snickering, as he shifts his rifle from one shoulder to the other. When he comes back, he hands over his overcoat and briefcase to the two Vallées, whom he already considers as old hands and worthy of his trust.

At six o'clock in the evening I take possession of my new cell (no. 72) and make an owner's tour of it while waiting for our *Abend-Brot* ("evening bread") and then to bed. During this time, Camille, who had managed to get some paper and a pencil from the Italians working at Wagner's, writes to Michel:

> Let me give you a few details about how we're spending our lives here. Each of us has a small cell measuring two by four meters painted in light gray, which is sparsely furnished with a more-or-less comfortable bed, a folding chair, small table, shelf, wash basin, chamber pot, broom and hygienic bucket. We're wakened at 4:45 a.m.; I say my prayers and tidy up the place. They bring us coffee and we go down for the 5:45 roll call. We then go out to work for produce farmers. At 9 o'clock we take a short break, have our soup at noon, and return to prison at 5:30 when we are put back in our cells for dinner at 6 o'clock, then to bed. The food isn't bad though there's not enough of it. But in certain civilian labor camps, the workers get even less than we! Every week we have a change in linen, every two we take showers, and every Saturday we get together in a friend's room to get a shave. We work in teams of ten, and there are eight Jocists in our group. Up to now we know nothing about what will happen to us, but we expect to learn something before Pentecost. Soon we'll be processed and perhaps released? But have confidence, God is watching over us; we place our trust in Providence and are confident that we will once again be victorious with Christ.

This message wouldn't be sent until a few weeks later. But by writing something, you are already made to feel less alone. You also are able to agonize a little bit less about how to lessen the grieving of those from whom you've been so abruptly separated.

My neighbor on the left, Marcel Callo, has just called out to ask me what day it is, because he wants to make his own calendar. "The 28th," I reply ... I hadn't stopped to think until now that on this very morning of the 28th somewhere a priest has offered up Christ for me and that in all these communities of people exiled from France, there are brothers who have worked and resisted on my behalf; indeed at this very moment, many of them are probably coming to the communion table. When we left France, we had promised to offer up our daily prayers and communion for each other. Today it's my turn to benefit and I deeply feel the power of the Offertory part of the Mass, of which I am presently the focus and beneficiary. The Lord holds His friends in the palm of his hands, and they find their peace in Him.

"I, the prisoner in the Lord, urge you to lead a life worthy of the vocation to which you were called" (*Letter of Paul to the Ephesians*, 4/1)

I now feel properly disposed to make a seven-day retreat as a prelude to this new phase in our witnessing as missionaries. I'm filled with a feeling of happiness, because, living in the depths of this prison, I no longer feel the need to worry any longer about what I have to do to survive. Such things will be granted day-by-day, hour-by-hour, drop-by-drop. My only remaining desire is that I be led according to His will. He has chosen and arranged this present situation for me, and has fixed the length of time it will last so that I might bear better and more lasting fruit. I remember all my companions in captivity in this my most meaningful prayer of the day. I believe that God has heard it and that it has already been sanctified by the conditions we're presently enduring and the sacrifice we have made of our personal freedom.

The following day, as on the one before it and those that were to come after, we worked for one of a number of bosses.

We spent our first Sunday degerming potatoes at Wagner's under a shed protecting us from the rain. Our work group made up almost entirely of French prisoners, a favor granted them by the prison superintendent who is very well aware that they don't like to stay in the courtyard to cut wood. We are taken to the farm by Herr Brunschweig, or "*Bouboule*" as he has been nicknamed. The oldest of the prison guards, he lives in the building with "*Bobonne*," his wife, who is in charge of the women prisoners. A cavalryman and then regimental cook after the battle of Verdun, where he was wounded in 1916, he stayed in the military to serve as prison porter (concierge). Short, stout, chubby-cheeked, red-faced and rheumatic, he always moved about with the help of a cane whose handle served as support for his enormous posterior. Every morning he would take along a sack that would come back every evening filled with food and fresh produce given him by the bosses for whom we worked. Bobonne, pleasant and thrifty housewife that she was, counted a great deal on them as a means of replenishing their food supplies.

Snuggly ensconced in his overcoat, the collar rolled up, his face beet-red, and his gloved hands secured in his belt, Bouboule distractedly watches over our group now working alongside Italians from Wagner's farm. We're sitting in a circle around a huge pile of tubers. "*Heute ist Sonntag. Ich habe kein lust.*" ("Today is Sunday and I'm feeling really depressed"), a Neapolitan woman with the profile of a Madonna sadly laments every ten minutes. From early morning till now we've been working in the tired, half-hearted way common to prisoners everywhere. André Vallée, who can't get used to this calculated way of killing time, proposes that we sing the Mass. This helps us to pass the time for at least another hour or so. Marcel Callo starts us off with a few Jocist songs and Roger intones several psalms from the readings for Vespers. Bouboule doesn't mind because the work is progressing even though we sing. He comes over and asks us where we've learned all these musical pieces. Henri Marannes, who is the best versed in German of all of us, begins a lengthy explanation. Bouboule looks perplexed. Not understanding what is being said, the Italians are nonetheless intrigued. Because he is more or less able to speak their dialect, Camille translates for them. The Neapolitan woman is visibly moved and avenges us by bombarding Bouboule with scraps of potato, at which we all break into laughter. "*Nicht so laut—Allez, moussieu, travaillez, Capisco italiano—Tirho!*" Bouboule brings back to order (in all our languages).

The boss, wearing high boots, a brown coat, the Nazi Cross on his boutonniere, and smoking his Sunday cigar, comes on his inspection tour. We hum *Jeunesse debout, entends l'appel suprême d'un monde qui meurt!* He remains silent. The Italians win out, it's Sunday and this calls for singing. All of us in chorus—French, Italians, Russians, and Germans—intone *la Paloma.*

But there's a small cloud on the horizon: Marcel Callo is suffering from a stomach ailment. After having had to fast for a week while living at the mercy of the Gestapo, he hasn't been able to recover on the meager prison diet. We lay him out, flushed with fever, over the potato sacks. Bouboule gets moving when the Neapolitan brings him hot tea and he asks the boss to have Marcel transported back to prison by car, to which the latter acquiesces. Camille suggests that I thank Wagner in the name of us all. When I do this, he is rather taken aback and seems to be thinking: "A little bit more of this and I'm the one who is going to break down and feel guilty (he was rather prone to weeping), whereas these young people seem quite relaxed, quite indifferent and show very little contrition for other wrongdoings."

"Don't you find that we're a pretty cocky bunch after all?" Camille asks me during our return. "They mustn't be able to understand us at all. But there's nothing to be done about it. If we're happy as larks, it's because God our Father takes care of his flock."

And who can ever take our joy from us? It's more intimately a part of our makeup than even our passion for freedom.

They're amazing, these Frenchmen who always see the best in everything and instinctively view it all from a Christian perspective. They're indeed wonderful optimists! Never can they be divested of their cheerful attitude. "*Franzose immer lustig!*" ("The French are always in good spirits") they used to say at the Brunnquell factory. And so it was that Bouboule had to renounce his whim of having us march in step through the heart of Gotha, because he couldn't keep up with the accelerated pace set by René (walking at the head of lines), in defiance of the commands "*Langsam! Langsam!* ("slower, slower") shouted out by Herr Brunschweig.

Monday, May 1ˢᵗ, the Feast of the Worker. The "dago" takes us to work at Herr Reich's tree nursery. As is my custom, I take up the back of the line where one can talk more easily. Camille recounts how the Feast of Labor was celebrated in Paris in 1941 and describes the Mass for the Worker celebrated at Notre Dame Cathedral. And today is the feast for workers who everywhere give shape and form to matter and in so doing, honor and reflect God's own handiwork in creating the world. We pray for saintly workers just as we do for saintly priests, kings, and all other kinds of people.

We'll offer up this work day at Reich's as our own Labor Day Mass. I'm offering it for those young Christians who have to their honor dedicated themselves entirely to this mission for Christ, and in particular, for those walking ahead of me in line this morning, my companions in prison. Each of them has distinguished himself in his own profession. They are specialists who do top quality work: Camille who is so appreciated by his boss in Erfurt;[1] Henri who repaired all the typewriters in his factory at Gera;[2] René who was a blue ribbon worker at Tours; André Vallée and Marcel Callo, typographers at Montligeon and for the newspaper *Ouest-Éclair*, who constantly discuss their work. They've also distinguished themselves through their profession of faith among their comrades in the factories, and even more recently before the Gestapo. They still bear the marks of the beatings they have

---

1   He grew roses there.

2   Which allowed him to circulate about the entire plant.

received but it remains for them, as well as for me, to win distinction in what is presently a new profession for them. We now have to engage in a battle within ourselves and accept our imprisonment as a kind of sacrament whose visible sign, even more significant than the deprivation of our freedom, is time itself, this sword which penetrates into the most intimate parts of our souls and bodies and brings along with it all those things that are not from Christ. Lord, I sincerely desire and now make it my firmest intention to imitate You by bearing with all harassments, my own weaknesses, and the genuine poverty I feel in body and spirit. And didn't You deliberately choose to appear in this weakened and diminished state before the eyes of men?

No, workers must no longer be treated like work-horses harnessed to every nondescript plow which they drag out of sheer habit until the day they drop. Workers have to learn to promote their own freedom. The worker must not be confounded with the tools he uses. And is it his fault if this happens? He's been exploited so cavalierly, this poor hand laborer. The worker must not be taken advantage of any longer. He must be given proper respect and must be allowed to comport himself as a son of God his Creator, or else the world will force him down and he won't be able to rise up again. We must see in him, and he in himself, that Carpenter of twenty centuries ago, the Son of God, who for twenty years of his life, sawed boards and would today be a fitter or mechanic. Who will make this clear to them all? Perhaps those among us who have become a part of this group at a particular moment in time and have since been willing to dirty their hands and accept the consequences.

The work we were now doing—hoeing parts of the plant nursery—wasn't very taxing and allowed us to discuss matters like the above throughout the entire day. Toward evening we meet up with POWs who are working for the same boss as we, and they promise to provide us with writing paper and pencils when we next meet. André Vallée asks them to run errands for some friends in town while we sample a liter of pea soup with bacon, a pleasant surprise that we didn't expect. As we return to prison, a guard informs us that Jean Tinturier is in the hospital with diphtheria.

Returning from work has gradually become our time to relax, and whether bad or good, the day is finally over. The two Vallée brothers, more often than not at the head of the lines because of their familiarity with the city, arrange our return so as to allow us to pass by various places of interest: French camps, a butcher shop displaying a cuckoo clock on the outside by which we can tell the time, a POW mess hall, movie houses, etc.

One evening, we went by the convent of nuns where Jean Lecoq regularly said his Mass. "A penny for your thoughts," I said to André with whom I was in line at the time. "Christ is there and we can't go in." If only we could bribe our guard with cigarettes, enter, receive communion, pray and then leave!—a wild dream since: none of us can make a move. But He has chosen to be among us. Didn't He assume a human form and say, a long time ago, "Don't be afraid, it is I." Couldn't He break our bonds and take away our sorrow at having to pass so close by without being able to come near Him? The Divine Being is hidden and chooses to be present without appearing in person, because He prefers to be worshipped by the consent of the willing rather than receive the prostrations of those overwhelmed by appearances. André understands, as do I, that He wishes us to serve as an example and do as He has done. The worker is not more clever than his boss, nor the apostle greater than the one who has sent him. Here in prison we share our existence with Christ the Worker, who is silently bestowing his grace on all of us.

Farther along at a turn in the road, the column comes in contact with two Grey Nuns ... a rustling of veils, perhaps something like this must have agitated his own Mother's veil when He met her in the street that led to Golgotha.... They had first become familiar with Jean Le Coq's team. Ever since then, especially in the evenings when we would be coming back that way, there were always some veils to be seen through the branches of their garden hedge. Pretending to be trimming the privet, they would wait until after the guard passed by to beckon to us with smiles. They were there to provide a connection between those who had been imprisoned for a similar cause—intermediaries between Him, the silent one who had let himself be caught in a trap that he had chosen for Himself, and us who had also been rounded up as criminals.

The week has gone by. This morning a teaspoon of imitation fruit jam on our daily slice of bread reminds us that it is Sunday. This tiny extra supplement is also a symbol of the much-appreciated rest that we take on the seventh day. We wait a longer time than usual before going down to the courtyard for roll call. Perhaps we'll be going back to Wagner's where we were last Sunday.

Silence reigns in the cells and the corridors. Right next to me I hear footsteps. Marcel Callo must be killing time by pacing about his cell. Through the open fanlight I hear the rustling of very fine rain. Sitting on my stool, my head in hands and my body cramped in a ragged work outfit, I listen to it fall. By now I am used to all the things common to prison: the police, handcuffs, cell walls, bars, keys, guards, forced rounds in the courtyard, food rations, silences, semi-darkness. We've all had to resign ourselves to these things from the moment we were locked up. But now there's this rain that will bother us all day long, since a prisoner doesn't have the right to find shelter: he must work. You have to accept it as something imposed and over which you have not the slightest control. There's also the bread and liter of soup that you have to accept, saying thank you, from the hands of a robber like Schliesser, who is well-known for fraudulently reducing our bread ration and passing on to us only the smallest portions. How terribly important does the obtaining of one's daily bread loom in the day-to-day existence of every prisoner! We still find kids who point at us in the streets and ask, "What are they?" And their mothers bend down to them, saying, "You see, if you're not good, you'll end up in prison like them." And indeed, we're generally viewed as being extremely imprudent, even stupid, by the others. Gréaux, Bordes, other Frenchmen and many of the Germans in prison don't understand the reasons for our arrest. Then there's always that unknown person abruptly arriving no matter when, or this period of waiting that you know you must pass through, as if you were going into a forest in the dark of night, being almost certain that you'll bump against stones and stumps positioned before you. I keep looking for a companion, like a mountain climber who, during the night, stretches out his hand toward an invisible guide who might go before him, because I've lost all confidence in myself. I'm even horrified by how freely my mind still operates in fabricating a multitude of plans that I could possibly use to regain my freedom, and by the way it encourages me to wander about in memory and conjure up the faces of those whom I would like to see again. I'm tired of the dialogues or the replies that I imagine myself engaged in and which I am determined to use to provoke my guards and inspectors whenever I am next interrogated. We have to consent to this spiritual captivity and find rest and quiet strength by acknowledging our absolute powerlessness to do anything for ourselves and others. Once arrived at this point and forced by all this exterior deprivation to ignore the clamor raging deep within yourself, you have to cut it off and say, "My God, all right, I accept my situation." Since this is so, Lord, take for yourself everything I have including my freedom. We need only receive your breath which sustains us each minute that we live, as we await the small pittance that we get from the hands of those who, at any moment of their choosing, have the power to put us to death. We are in need of nothing more.

The rain lasted all day and we worked in the muddy fields until evening. The Russians in the group shared the best of the potatoes among themselves; we weren't able to sing our Mass as we had on the previous Sunday. Upon returning Camille wrote in his diary: "Today, rooted up leeks at Offhaus's ('Tutur's') place. Bad weather, cold." The following morning we had to put our damp clothes back on again. My retreat was over.

A BUSTLING PRISON YARD

Tuesday, May 9ᵗʰ—"Callo?"

"Here."

"Beschet!"

"Here."

"Hier bleibe" ("Stay here"). Is there something new? An interrogation? Panic. Today we won't be going to leave for work on the outside and will stay to cut wood with Schliesser in charge. This man Schliesser, a convicted thief, enjoys the confidence of Herr Petri, the prison head. He manages the kitchen and operates the electric saw like a mad man. He's responsible for all deliveries and supervises the shipments of wood. An old veteran of the penal system, he forces all the younger guards in the house to put up with his changing moods. Only Bouboule can stand up to him. He uses his contacts with the truck drivers to engage in a bit of black marketing in tobacco and other merchandise. His methods of punishment are very simple: he needs only to pocket the cigarettes (one or two) that he habitually distributes to the prisoners on Sundays. He rewards his friends with additional food. First and foremost among them are the Germans, and then some Russians and Poles who will do anything to get more to eat. The French are his *bêtes noires* because they don't want to do anything, spend all their time talking, and wait for him to bellow an order before they do a drop of work.

We have only one way to defend ourselves: provoke him so that he'll screw up and thus allow us to gain the upper hand over him with Bouboule or the prison head.

In this genre of sport, Gréaux, a former POW become civilian worker from Bordeaux, robust and with dark curly hair, who has escaped, been recaptured and returned to prison four times, is past master. Being a nervous type, Schliesser has often broken the blade of his saw. Gréaux, who assists him, needs only to line up the logs a bit crookedly to cause this accident to reoccur as frequently as possible. Schliesser, who can't see anything after a few minutes of sawing because his glasses become covered with sawdust, lashes out at himself, the saw, and then at Gréaux. The latter plays the innocent. Exasperated, Schliesser accuses him of peeking through the windows of the women's quarters and threatens to thrash him. Gréaux warns him that his fists are more than strong enough to deliver a knock out punch. Enraged, the latter jostles him. Gréaux pretends to be just as angry and goes to complain to the prison head. Schliesser is then called in and Gréaux comes back. We weren't able to hear the dressing down that Schliesser receives at the hands of the prison superintendent, but we're happy to benefit from the results: the saw won't be repaired before day's end, thus we can work at our ease. During this time, Gréaux, playing the good apostle, explains to Bouboule how wood is sawed in France and tells him that Schliesser is an incompetent with whom it is impossible to work. His hands in his pockets, Herr Brunschweig blinks his eyes, half convinced, and seems rather to enjoy seeing Schliesser in such a bad mood. The latter returns to the kitchen where, from time to time, he peers out of the windows without daring, as is his habit, to shout at the prisoners who, for quite some time now, have left their axes lying on the cords of wood.

We still have to keep busy. A vehicle has just entered the court. Without waiting for orders, Gréaux takes us to unload the cardboard material on the truck. Then afterwards we'll have to load it up again with the boxes the women prisoners have finished making. From the bottom of the stairs the superintendent surveys these comings and goings. We climb up to the second floor of the women's quarters to set down what we're carrying. Gréaux carries the largest load in only one trip while it takes two of us to bring up the rest. Looking ridiculous as he fondles the old horse pulling the wagon, Schliesser seems oblivious of what is going on. So we finish the job.

Now we've come back to our place in the courtyard. After a while Gréaux returns, rubbing his hands as he triumphantly informs us that he has put one over on the old woman guard and was able to see his girl friend because the door of her cell was open. She even managed to pass him a note. He goes off with tired step to the large tank surrounded by wooden planks in the corner of the courtyard which serves as a toilet. He settles down in there to do his reading.

The sun is already high: "What time is it?" a Russian asks Marcel Callo. To respond he undertakes a dangerous expedition. He has to stop his work, cross the length of the courtyard to the opposite side where the toilet is located, the only direction to which prisoners are allowed to go, and then position himself on the slant under an office window from which one can consult the time on the clock hanging on the wall inside, provided no one has intentionally covered its face with a cloth to conceal its hands. Marcel is already on his way back. Too late, the fidgety Nazi *Oberwachmeiser* ("Two Stars") has just opened the door which connects the courtyard with the corridor of cells. He yells at Marcel from the stoop. The latter doesn't respond and gets off with merely getting his face slapped. From his vantage point in the toilets, where he is furtively reading the letter from his girl friend, Gréaux remarks: "I told you never to leave your place without taking your axe with you." This comment causes "Two-Stars'" attention to fall on Gréaux. He asks him how long he's been there because he ("Two-Stars") had spotted him going to the toilet area from a window on the third floor. While carefully pulling up his shorts, Gréaux tells him: "*Machine kaput, Schleisser, etc.*" "Two-Stars" approaches the saw and contemplates the damage done to it by Schleisser. Gréaux explains the situation, shaking his head. "Two-Stars" signifies his assent saying, "*jung, jung.*"

Because there is dust coming in from the door that "Two-Stars" had left partially open, someone must be cleaning the corridor. A broom being swept back and forth seems to suggest, by its agitated strokes, the sweeper's desire to cross the threshold once the coast is clear. Marcel throws a piece of wood against the door and a man appears. Marcel moves close to the sweeper. "Are you French?" he asks.

"Yes," the other replies, as he ventures out to do the stairway entry.

"Are you from JOC?

"Yes. I'm Jean Lecoq, the priest at Gotha. Do you work in the courtyard?"

"Not always. The others are outside today."

"I clean your cells and empty the sanitary buckets every morning. Leave some paper under yours." As he talks Jean scoops up the dust and goes to throw it into a hole at the end of the courtyard. Coming back he passes very close to me, but "Two-Stars" then calls to him from the stairway entrance where he had once again positioned himself. We stand looking at each other for what seems a very long time. Jean must have understood what I was wanting to say.

Mittag ("noon"): we stop work. Before locking us up in groups in the basement cells, Schliesser gives us soup, served, of course, in tiny mess bowls. Gréaux notices this just in time and slips out among the Germans. He accomplishes his mission and we are allowed three quarters of an hour to enjoy a liter of soup consisting of dehydrated vegetables, while the women walk about in their clogs as they take their recreation in the courtyard. The Russians in our cell have appropriated the bed and chairs for themselves. There is nothing left to do but wait for the end of the break. In another corner, a Pole holds his mess bowl between his knees, waiting for seconds that won't come. We hear Schliesser's voice resounding from some place near the kitchen. After having brought soup to the people on the second floor, he has taken the kettle with all its remaining contents back with him. If there is an air raid, we'll be able to prolong our noontime siesta; the Russians are already dozing and one of them is snoring. The hot sun beats down on us. It's one o'clock. "*Los aufstehen!*" ("Get up"). Once more there is the jarring sound of axes on wood. At two o'clock the men working in the cells take their walk. About twenty of them turn around in a circle in front of us, like caged wild animals in the zoo. Jean Lecoq is among them. It took him a number of times round to finally place himself behind Marcel Carrier. Many of them are involved in the same little game. This is the only time we have during the day to communicate with others, when we must use single words more meaningful than sentences, words that have been chosen and weighed the night before, in the form of questions or answers, with the responses to them having to be awaited until contacts are resumed the following day. During the exercise several prisoners break away from the line and approach the toilets. This affords them one more chance to communicate, even though Bouboule is watching the area. One of them takes a longer time. Carrier comes near him but they can't talk. Bouboule has already reassembled the group, and the men are taken back up to their cells.

About 5:30 p.m. the work groups return. We can talk more freely now that the woodcutting has ended in the courtyard. Schliesser has collected the axes. André Vallée is suffering from phlegmon on his right hand and goes to the office to ask for a doctor. Camille reports that they had spent all day terracing—during the morning in the court garden behind the prison where they had dug a reservoir, and in the afternoon, at the hospital where they had to reinforce the sides of the bomb shelters. The work wasn't too hard and they were given a supplementary serving of food as a bonus for good performance. They had no news about Jean Tinturier, who must now be in another hospital reserved for those suffering from contagious diseases.

The next day Callo and I go to work in the courtyard with Gréaux and Schliesser. The saw sees more action than usual. At 10:00 a.m. Schliesser takes a little break in the kitchen and returns a short time later very distressed and nervous, repeating several times: "*Ausschiffung. Normandie.* ("Landing. Normandy"). So it seems they have finally landed: Schliesser has seen these headlines in a newspaper belonging to one of the guards. He chokes on the words and becomes almost incoherent. Gréaux grills him a bit to try to get more information. We conclude that it's probably nothing more than a *bouthéon*.[3] But if only this were true! Our imaginations run riot. We feel suddenly connected with all of France in the depths of this prison. And we entertain the mad hope of returning before autumn, far sooner than we had expected. But shouldn't there be some kind of announcement? Maybe there's an armistice. "Soon war over, Mister," remarks Schliesser, while going back to the kitchen. Does he really think that the Americans will set him free, a robber like him?; as a convicted criminal he'll have to serve out his eight years. But all of us "political" prisoners will return before anyone else, as soon as the Allies get here; that's only logical. See how we're now talking as if we have priority status, when in fact we're still officially classified as criminals. I never thought that a prison courtyard could be the scene of so much commotion.

Schliesser has come back with a newspaper: Gréaux put him up to this daring act. Cause for disappointment, it contains only a military communiqué that alludes to the possibility of an Allied landing, in the North of France, possibly in Normandy, with the return of good weather. This won't be such a bad thing, the article goes on

---

3 A slang expression used by prisoners to mean a rumor. (trans. note)

to say, because if the Anglo Saxons finally decide to wage war on the Continent, we'll be in a position to hand them a very decisive defeat.

The day ended with our unloading a coal wagon. We still had a long time to wait for our liter of soup. About 5 o'clock Schliesser offered us a slice of bread (weighing about 75 grams). We all receive our *Stuck* ("piece") except for a Russian, who has arrived around noon and is not authorized to have a ration card. Schliesser pockets this man's share. But this Russian has been working with us for the past hour. During this time, all of us, Gréaux included, have depended on the strength of his powerful *mujik* ("peasant") arms to do a large part of our work. Gréaux sits down to nibble at his slice of bread; mine, which is smaller, is burning my fingers. I share it with the Russian; Schliesser and Gréaux have both seen me do this but say nothing. "*Spassibé*" ("thanks"), says the Russian, and signaling me to back away, he unloads my pile of coal immediately after finishing his own. I protest. "*Egal. Karachov.*" ("That's O.K., good friend").

While working at the hospital, Camille managed to talk with French patients. He learned that André Vallée had been transported there to have his phlegmon treated. After having to put up all morning with Schliesser's shoutings in the courtyard, I have the good luck to be sent at noontime to work at the hospital with Henri, Camille and the others. We are guarded by a good old gramps *Schupo*. A farmer, he only wore the green uniform because he was obliged to. Having just come to see his brother André, who is recuperating from his operation, Roger Vallée is accompanied by Herr Rausch—the "dago." Apparently in rather good humor at the moment, he informs us that this is the visiting day for the hospital. Our work team is divided up into two groups: after the first one loads a tipcart with dirt, the second unloads it and shovels in the dirt to bolster the foundations of the air raid shelter adjacent to the hospital buildings. A decrepit wagon driver goes back and forth dragging both wagons drawn with a single animal. We've all agreed beforehand to slow down departures of the wagon to be unloaded in order to allow for fewer trips back and forth. Our *Schupo* doesn't mind at all. The only thing that matters for him is that the five of us are there with him when he has to hand us over to the "dago" at 5:30. The hospital visitors have already gone; evening is beginning and still no sign of Bédouelle.

Bédouelle is André's right hand man: he promoted Catholic Action with him at Gotha and works in the *Kommando* located there, where he is in charge of food supplies and the mail service. He belongs to the Welcome Center staff and has taken on the task of visiting the sick at the hospital. About 4 o'clock a fellow comes by on a bicycle; ten minutes later he returns and slows down in front of us. As soon as he catches a glimpse of him, Roger rushes towards him calling out "Bédouelle, Bédouelle?" The other hands him a package containing rations for three meals and some chocolate. Roger shows all of this to the *Schupo* before the latter has been able to react. The policeman enjoys the chocolate and lets us share the rest. Meanwhile I manage to have a quick exchange of words with Bédouelle: as he slowly moves away I follow him, shovel in hand and pretending to be distracted. He'll come back tomorrow—we'll be able to write—he'll address everything and see that it is put in the mail. If he can't come, we should try to find contacts among the French patients who take their turns around the park in the afternoon. I agree to all of this and pick up a pencil and some paper that Bédouelle has let drop from his pocket while getting on his bicycle.

That evening I write as follows to all my brothers—Pierre, André, Jacques, Jean, André Dupont, and Emile Lebrun—who have been with me at Sonderhausen:

> I take this opportunity to send my very best regards and want to reassure you about how things are standing with us here. We're still awaiting a decision from Weimar. Our day-to-day existence is both calm and boring, though time passes terribly slowly. But Christ has instilled in our hearts so many things during these days that seem to go on forever! I gain nourishment from your friendship, an authentic kind of sacrament which, for the time being, serves as a sort of substitute for the Eucharist, if you can ever even imagine this as possible. Since Monday, I've spent my days thinking about each one of those friends of mine who have remained in France, as well as all the rest of you over here in Germany. I'd like to be able to list the many acts that I've performed specifically for each one of you! I've been able to discover more about Christian friendship here than in any other place that I've ever been; I've also gotten to understand how every apostle is goaded by the conviction of how absolutely necessary it is to abandon oneself completely to the Father. By doing this, we can gain strength, wisdom, and discipline in the ways we react to the things and events that we have to endure, from the most extraordinary to the least significant, because in our situation, we have to depend entirely on Him, hour by hour, day by day. I

couldn't be more happy—we're united as one on this path that we've taken.

In signing my name "Paul," I felt very humble to be thinking that I was committing myself and writing in the same way as he, who when he was traveling the length and breadth of Asia, constantly gave encouragement and support to the Churches and experienced trials and imprisonment before spilling his own blood while working at Peter's side to found Rome for a second time. How heavily our surnames can sometimes weigh on us! I took another piece of paper which was to be sent to France.

It's impossible to describe what deep feelings I have while writing you, my dearest Father and little Mother.[4] From this time on, my love is intimately joined with you, the ones who have done the most for me and who are now suffering the most with me for His sake. Will whoever first receives this letter see to it that it gets to the other? I'm living among friends and together we offer up the tasks we have to perform every day—often very hard but usually healthy kinds of work—with all our other minor heartaches as well. God is good and Christ is a real and tangible presence amongst us, tending to our needs. I couldn't be more happy even when things don't go so well. I get enough sleep, the food is adequate. My body is holding up and my soul is thriving. Don't worry. Rejoice because there is need for suffering if the mission seed is to grow. Christ has chosen us for this honorable task. There's nothing to fear. From a distance, we tend to make mountains out of molehills; and if there be mountains, have faith sufficient to uproot them and cast them into the sea. May what I am writing fill you with true joy. Deprived of the Eucharist, we are nourished by fraternal charity and the Holy Spirit will accomplish the rest. What a wonderful Pentecost we're going to have! Yours, in the immense peace of our Father.—P.S. Father C., I feel very linked closely with you each morning when you say your Mass.

Darkness had fallen over these few written lines which, for the moment, were helping me to overcome deep feelings of anxiety that I'd now been experiencing for a long time.

"With one heart, all these joined in prayer." (Acts 1/14)

---

4   Letter written by Beschet to Father Charmot at Mongré and his mother at Lyons. (trans. note)

The Feast of the Ascension, 18th of May. Yesterday evening coming back from the hospital, Camille confided in me his feelings that he was wasting his time here. Of course he sees that being in prison for the sake of Christ is certainly something worthwhile, but he misses not being with his team at Erfurt and not being able to pursue the projects that he had wanted to put into effect. Cut off from those of like mind with whom he has been living, he admits to having seemingly lost his spirit of commitment, and he accuses his friends here of being of similar mind. We're in the same prison for the same reasons, subjected to the same persecutions; but we view all that we suffer from our own personal perspective. We've all withdrawn into our innermost shells and are living as recluses, remembering only what we've lost and using this as the reason for putting up with our present situation. We view each other, he says, as if we were earthenware dogs, as we wait for our release so that we can once more resume our work. We're like the apostles looking fixedly at something far away in the distance but uncertain of just what it is or where it may be. We've been "arrested" but is this any reason for us to have to "stop" doing our work?

Today Bédouelle was able to bring us some mail at the hospital. Lying on the floor of my cell, under the cover of my blanket, I read the following letter, written in a handwriting so familiar to me.

> Mongré, April 29th 1944—I'm a bit late in sending you my usual monthly letter of the 28th but I have some things to tell you that I would not have been able to convey if I had written sooner. I've learned from some of those recently repatriated[5] that you've been the victim of an accident, and I'm wondering if my letter will get to you. This news, which of course pains me very much, was accompanied by a divine voice which filled me with peace and confidence. For the rest of your life you'll remember the part you are now playing in the Passion of Jesus Christ. And your having drunk this drop from the chalice will have left you with a special thirst, the thirst to start up again, or rather to continue onward. Take courage! By pushing yourself to the very end of your endurance, you'll ultimately see the beauty of God's plan. A building that has only been begun makes no impression in the eyes of those who pass by. It has

---

5   The Jesuit students and seminarians from Neumühle who had been expelled and repatriated at Wittenberg, April 28, 1944. Two of these five came back a bit sooner.

first to be finished before it can be admired. My paternal blessings, Franciscus.[6]

So our duty is to go forward as one toward a common goal. This letter, received along with a note from Jacques and André provided me with details about what had transpired since we were arrested, but even more importantly, it reconnected me with the spirit of the community. Hence, once again God has provided a family for those who were abandoned and has delivered those in captivity by bringing them happiness. No longer would prison for us be that barren place where one feels the terrible solitude caused by the absence of everything we so sorely missed. Only rebels live by themselves in arid places. Because we have acted as "resisters," we must not allow ourselves to become rebels. Yet the boundary between the two is so easily crossed.

"Lord," the Church sings out today, "You have ascended on high, You have freed those in captivity, You have graced men with many gifts, You are, Lord, the God of salvation …." To receive these gifts we have had to empty ourselves, and we found our exit door on the very day of our arrival in this country whose intention it was to confine us as prisoners within its borders, but which instead made us become open to the entire world.

This next week proved to be one of prayer, unexpected events and waiting. Upon our return from the hospital on Saturday, we are searched. "Two-Stars" finds the mail we've been hiding on our person. Because it was his day to have been in charge of us, the "dago" is compromised. He immediately has our letters translated by Jean Lecoq, in whom he has complete trust. The latter informs him that there is nothing to all of this and no need to involve the Gestapo. The "dago" believes him and gives everything back to us, saying that we have to be careful and, above all, must in the future never bring anything back with us on our nightly returns to prison. On Monday the 22nd, we are given a rapid but thorough medical examination. The following day we have to go to have our pictures taken at the *Kriminal-Polizei*. On Thursday, they ask us about our personal history and profession. The prison regulars are mystified by these procedures. Gréaux predicts that we'll be sent to a concentration camp; and indeed others will leave from here a week from now to go to Buchenwald or to a *Strafeslager*. Wincklers, the inspector who was in charge on the day when we were

---

6 Father Charmot.

photographed, tells us nothing. Pourtois and Callo have to go for a follow-up medical exam. On Friday evening an exasperated Camille writes in his diary: "An *Arbeitslager* ('work camp'), yes or no?" This all helps us to develop a deep feeling of solidarity among ourselves, as we wait to find out the further kinds of sacrifice we'll have to make.

Sunday, May 28th, the prisoners bask in a warm sun during the morning roll call. "Oh, Camille, just take a whiff, it smells like summer!" says René as he goes down the stairway. The prisoners are drawn up and stand in their columns. Silence. A branch of cherry blossoms spills over the wall in front of us. It stands out in full bloom against the large patch of blue sky visible above these huge grey buildings. A clear and brilliant day. It's Pentecost, the summer feast to which have been invited the 175 men and women of this prison, who will spend the whole day cutting wood. The logs have been in place since yesterday, like altars which have been made ready in the churches the day before great feasts. Will the others understand any of this? Now ten of us are scattered throughout the various work groups, like yeast in dough. Our ten logs will be ten altars and our bruised and bloodied hands will be joined in one common action bringing together the sounds of wood being chopped simultaneously with the elevation of the host and the chalice in the churches all over the world. Everyone must be included in this sacrifice—especially this poor Jew, with his shorn head who labors next to us. He's just come out after having been in prison for a month, chained and subsisting only on bread and water. In bludgeoning him, an inspector took out two of his gold teeth and immediately pocketed them. His only crime: to be a member of his race. His fiancée, also a Jew, wasn't sent down to work in the courtyard with the other women. We can hear her calling down to him from time to time. Over there is this huge fifty-year old German who abused a fifteen-year old maid servant and who has been serving his sentence for the past two years. Then there's this enormously fat man Hermann, an opera singer who took it upon himself to satirize the regime in a musical review that he directed in the provinces. He is counting on the director of the Gotha Opera to have him released because he has made an engagement to sing for him there during the summer season. In the meantime, he brings us his basket of wood to be cut while whistling some airs from Strauss or Rossini. There are these two silent Russians who escaped from Düsseldorf as a result of the bombings and who were recaptured after they had wandered for two months from farm to farm.

They've been sentenced to six weeks at the Römhild disciplinary camp. There is Gréaux who continues his games with Schliesser and whose "little woman in yellow" has positioned herself beside him. There is "Perpignon," a huge *Méridional* ("Southerner") just arrived yesterday evening. His only offense was to have struck his *Lagerführer* who had insisted on making him work in the camp after his factory had given him an exemption because of his injured legs. Sweating and weeping at the same, Perpignon continually rails against German "Kultur." "Ah *péchaire!* If my little woman could see me here!" Camille is thinking about his first meeting with his fiancée Marcelle. Marcel Callo keeps talking about places in Brittany, his newspaper *Ouest-Éclair*, and his Welcome Center at Zella-Mehlis. Jean Tinturier and André Tinturier are both sick in the hospital. Near me Roger Vallée murmurs a psalm from the Pentecost liturgy. He is thinking about his seminary in Sées. Our prayers rise like those of that prisoner some twenty centuries ago and help us to remain united in heart and soul. So here we are gathered together with all the Christian communities of Germany, in the *Stalags*, the *Kommandos*, the STO camps, and the prisons. Everyone in all of these places must feel their hearts bursting this morning! We are reunited with all the churches of France, with these silent but prayer-filled cloisters, these half empty but patiently-waiting households, these barely productive workplaces, these fields where old men have once again taken up the plough as they wait.

It's thanks to all these channels of love that Christianity is taking on a new form this morning. God's spirit fills the Universe, and He by whom everything exists is speaking and expressing himself through us in this Catholic form of prayer ascending silently but persistently this morning to the very heart of God.

Monday was much like Sunday. Two heavy air raids during the afternoon give us the opportunity to remain for quite a while in our cells. We later learned that several French cities had been reduced to rubble during terrible bombings that had taken place around this same time at the end of May, a week before the Normandy landings. Gréaux took advantage of the air raid to tell us about some of his adventures.

Having escaped and then been recaptured three times, he spent some time at Rawa-Ruska. After this he became a civilian worker at Stettin, where he engaged in the black market behind the back of the *Wehrmacht* ("German Army"). He escapes once again one day in April. He had gotten to know a woman back there. He is an appraiser by profession and operates in the same way in his love affairs, never letting himself be tied down to any bad deal. He winds up his business, disposes of everything, and goes away on his bike. He is arrested by a *Schupo* on the road from Gotha to Eisenbach. He doesn't believe in Christian chastity, but our situation is of interest to him. He's a good guy but the only thing he's ever been taught is how to turn everything in which he is involved to his own pleasure. He treats women just as he would any of the objects that he appraises. He confesses that we ourselves wouldn't be very successful in his profession. "It's not your style!"

"Yet," responds René, "we have the same desires as you, but we control ourselves."

"You're lucky, you don't live all alone."

"But there's this also: For us a man isn't the same as a dog who takes his pleasures on every street corner."

Such were the things happening around us as we went about our work in the Gotha prison on Pentecost Sunday, 1944.

CHAPTER SIX

THE MISSION CONTINUES

AFTER THE APRIL ARRESTS

L et's return to Sonderhausen.

Several days after the 19th of April, André Yverneau made a number of visits to the police lieutenant's office to obtain any kind of information that he could. The latter finally made him understand that he would have to go to the Gestapo headquarters at Weimar.[1] André seizes the opportunity and asks his boss Brunnquell for the authorization to do so. Visibly unnerved by such audacity, the latter consented to his request with unaccustomed dispatch. Rare indeed are people who want to visit the Gestapo, and they therefore have to be humored.

Once in Weimar, André hoped to learn news. Received by the doorman at the Gestapo headquarters, who politely asked him to write out his request for information—to which there would be no response—he returned without having found out anything. Any signs of life would have to come from the prisoners themselves.

Mail received from Leipzig confirms through another source that Clément Cotte was definitely arrested on April 4th. They also learn that Henri Perrin had been liberated on the 22nd and was given twenty-four hours to leave for France. Many other priests and seminarians have also been harassed or forcibly repatriated.[2]

The storm rages on, carrying off most of the shepherds of the flock.

In his camp in neighboring Bitterfeld, from which he is coordinating all apostolic activities in the central region of Germany, Paul Léon

---

1   Weimar is the administrative capital of Thuringia.

2   Abbé Louis Rolland, of the Lille Diocese, would be the last volunteer chaplain in the Leipzig area to be repatriated by force in July of 1944. From this point on, the Saxony-Thruingia region would be without the services of its three most important missionaries.

sends out new directives: "After all these 'hard blows,'" he wrote to Milo, "I invite you to take to heart these words of Abbé Guérin":

> I went to prison as the national chaplain for JOC and will still hold that position when I get out. We were militant Christians when we came to Germany and we won't have changed when we leave. To be sure of it, let's keep our activities functioning, including regular visits to all our communities to the extent that it is possible, so as to help them keep up their fervor and maintain their ties with each other.

Working in the Sonderhausen-Kleinfurra area, Milo brings about a revival of Christian life which, after a certain time, will be even more on the increase thanks to clandestine contacts that have been forged with those in the prisons.

Very near by at Nordhausen, René Tournemire's team continues to promote its own activities. André Dupont, together with Albert Dupasquier,[3] frequently comes from Sonderhausen to make the rounds with them—despite increasing police surveillance and the much heavier, back-breaking work load that has recently been put in effect for the night shifts at the Montagna and Nieder-Sachswerfer camps.[4]

At Orbergebra, Pierre, who has just been transferred from Kleinfurra, has personally been involved in activities that are especially very well suited for this locale with its large numbers of Russians, Ukrainian women, and workers of other nationalities.

From Sonderhausen, André, Jacques and Jean still go off to visit communities in the vicinity of Sommera, Mülhausen and Artern, where they have established very vital contacts among the various groups. André Yverneau is profiting from a transfer from his factory that has allowed him to establish a group at Langensalza.

At Weimar, a scout named Robert has taken Marcel Carrier's place. After a period of somnolence, this community has also come back to life. "I'm happy to have received your message," Robert writes to Milo, who has just sent him a clandestine circular letter from Paul Léon,

---

3   A Seminarian POW, transferred as "civilian worker" who had been operating since March 1944, at Stolberg, near Nordhausen.

4   Near Dora where there was a concentration camp affiliated with Buchenwald.

and I've shared it with all our friends here and in the immediate vicinity. Let's hold our activities to this limit and everything should go well. Soon we'll take a trip.[5] We're keeping close watch over the hospitals, the library (both the main one and the other for the militants) and are always careful to act appropriately. Causing very little commotion, we are holding on, while being as prudent as serpents. Best to you, Robert.[6]

In Marcel Carrier's camp, where they too had to be very much on their guard, Félicien, his friend from the very first moment, has regrouped the comrades with the help of a seminarian from Sommerda who comes to visit him from time to time[7] and who is in charge of providing support for the hospital.

At Gera to the South East, Yves continues Henri Marrannes's activities with his "monastery,"[8] and he will continue to organize meetings up to the very day when he will be forced to return to Stalag IX C, his former prison camp. Because he is a priest, he will no longer be able to benefit from the limited mobility to move about allowed to the other POWs. The same will be the case for Father Dubois-Matra at Eisenach, where Louis Pourtois's friends have also resumed "the enterprise,"[9] despite the fact that their factories are now under constant bombardments.

THE REVIVAL AT ERFURT, CAMILLE'S LETTERS

Life resumes its course everywhere, and particularly at Erfurt, where, once Camille was arrested, everything had pointed to the weakening or even ultimate demise of the mission, much like what happens to a young plant that has suddenly been deprived of its nourishment.

---

5   To hold a retreat.

6   Robert Aubugeau, Troop Leader from Poitiers, who organized the Scout STO conscripts in Thuringia.

7   Paul Galli, who worked at Sommerda with Abbé Louis Maga, from Lyons.

8   The team of the Directors from Gera consisted of Henri Gauthier, seminarian from Maximize (Ain), Louis Bacle, Jocist Director from Nantes, both of them STO members; and Joseph Pommeret, a Benedictine novice and POW transferred as civilian worker.

9   In particular, Albert Perussel from Nantes, Robert Lartigue from Bordeaux, and Maurice Bruyère from Saint-Etienne, all of whom were Jocists.

During the month of March, Camille had discovered Loulou—Louis Zacher—from the Ardennes—an employee at the Postal Service (PTT) and a militant Jocist. Assigned to the parcel post department at the railroad station, Loulou had no fixed schedule for time off and found it difficult to participate with Camille's team. Yet despite the problems of arranging his time and having to submit to the daily inspections and searches which he had to undergo whenever he finished work, Loulou managed to maintain his activities with his friends in STO and among the POWs working at the Erfurt Post Office.

When he was transferred from his former job on April 11th, a week before Camille's arrest, Loulou could finally lead a normal work-day schedule. To be granted this transfer that he had been requesting for such a very long period, he had listed his qualifications and filled out his application for the position of apprentice blacksmith. It thus became easy for him, thanks to help given by the French POWs who connived ways to free him up so that he could spend the larger part of his time (up to the very end) in the various WC facilities of the train wagons parked on the tracks in the railroad garage, where he would take care of his mail and prepare for meetings. One of the very first letters that he wrote was to inform the Chaplain's Office in Paris that he would assume the position left vacant by Camille's arrest.

Loulou will thus take over from Camille with his own particular dynamism, providing the others with the benefit of his background and valuable experience gradually acquired through hands-on involvements in so many areas. He is able to organize a community of the DAF in the Erfurt camp, whose members regularly attend Mass on Sundays. Given the difficult condition under which they now have to live, such an habitual observance might even be viewed from the outside as bordering on the heroic. But they would have to be persuaded to go beyond this and learn to do more than simply remain "good boys." René Guédon invites them into a room which his boss, an auto mechanic, has placed at his disposal; this place, like Camille's green house of the past, will soon become the headquarters for the regroupment of all the militants in Erfurt.

Because they have to be constantly on the move, they have to be able to be in close contact with the leaders of each of the camp barracks. Loulou provides services for everyone and thus gains free entry into just about all the living areas. His great success is due in part by his being able to provide hot plates and fuse boxes, acquired from the

Brunnquell Co. that André and their friends from Sonderhausen regularly arrange to send him.

After a three-week-layoff agreed upon for caution's sake, the other teams gradually resume their normal life. Loulou and Michel Vacherot cover the city, the suburbs, and penetrate into the camps, thus helping to raise everyone's morale. Some of the others, however, retire from the field—the game is not worth the candle, they say in explaining their motives, and they decide to continue to live as Christians, though practicing a non-committed kind of observance!

Yet what has happened to Camille continues to be a matter of agonizing concern for all his friends. Michel goes around to knock at every prison door in the city without finding anything out. Then a month later, everyone at Sonderhausen is very happy and relieved when a letter arrives from Gotha. The details and reasons for his arrest contained therein spread quickly throughout the entire French communities of Erfurt. The men pass around to each other the few brief sentences written on a post card received through the regular mail in which Camille exhorts Michel to "support Rosalie."[10] "Better days will soon be here," he adds. In other letters smuggled out secretly, Camille is able to express himself more freely: "I am with you every moment; be prudent, do away with all compromising papers, but we have to have leaders everywhere who think and act as Christians. Explain clearly to everyone around you why we are in prison, and try to make the other militants understand that whatever we have to endure for the Faith is infinitely worth while." He gives further advice to Michel and promises to pray for everyone:

> Come on, have guts and try to brace yourself now for whatever difficulties you may have to endure, and take every effort to become more active. Accept the kind of person you are while striving to gradually strengthen your inner self. I am praying for you, Michel, you whom I hope to see again before three months are out, and our entire team as well. Every day I say at least a decade of my rosary for you and often offer up for your intentions the hardships which I'm presently finding the most difficult to bear. While vividly remembering all those nightly excursions we made to the camps throughout the city and all of the long evenings spent in the green house or

---

10   That's to say, the JOC in Erfurt. The address of the national office of the JOC in Paris was: 12 Avenue Soeur Rosalie.

in my room, I ask God that you may continue and bring to harvest what we have sowed together. My best regards to everyone.

No sign of being afraid and, not a single complaint. His letters that they pass around to each other make the blood course through their veins. Michel, who was briefly at a loss as to know how to act, pulls himself together to become Loulou's right-hand man, and he constantly declares to whomever will listen: "They can't do any more harm to me than what they're doing to Camille, and I couldn't be happier if I were to join him!"

And what about Camille's neophyte, Joseph? One might have feared what would happen to him once the Gestapo had taken away his best friend, "the one who had shown him the truth," as he liked to say over and over. Joseph continues to visit the hospitals, talks about his Camille with the sick and relates the circumstances of the latter's arrest with the passion of someone evoking the memory of a best friend. Refusing to observe the visiting hours posted in the various hospitals, if a nurse chases him out of one room, he quietly goes to the next ward. The men at Gotha are never absent from his mind. He "swipes" white rolls and bread ration tickets from the bakery where he works and gives them to the sick or to those among his friends who haven't enough to eat.

Since the Normandy invasion, packages have stopped arriving from France and food supplies have progressively dwindled. One has to be satisfied just to get soup at noon and survive the rest of the day on three hundred grams of bread, while the work load continues to increase, now counting for more than 72 hours a week. Loulou and Michel have decided to take on the job of bringing food to those in prison and make this known openly. Starting with the first collection, they have to send out several consignments because there is always too much to be contained in only one parcel. This will continue to be the case to the very end, even during those darkest days of December and January.

One person, without any reserves on hand, stops smoking and gives away his last cigarettes. You run into him yawning in the streets and without any tobacco to alleviate his hunger, yet nevertheless very happy to have done this for Camille and his companions. Another has received his last box of noodles from France: One day he brings it in to an astonished Loulou who doesn't know what to make of it. "I'm taking this to you before your next appeal for donations," he explains, " because I'm too hungry and will certainly eat it all if I keep it!"

And Camille's letters stimulate even greater apostolic generosity. Within the DAF itself, the team launched by Loulou becomes very active. Their members meet one evening a week behind the camp buildings to read letters from the POWs and to pray and reflect together on such topics as love, the family, and the Church. This has become all the more necessary now that they have come out and identified themselves as Christians in their attempts to revitalize the camp; hence they are constantly being questioned on matters such as the above and have been required to take stands on these issues in the responses they give.

One night Loulou comes back from having made the rounds in the city. All his friends are asleep in the room. Since the electrical current is off, he lights a candle and settles in to take care of his mail. About one o'clock in the morning, he hears footsteps in the hallway: Bernard is coming back and seems somewhat annoyed to see that Loulou is still awake. After hesitating momentarily, he asks him if he would stop writing his letter for a few minutes and lend him the use of his candle. He then goes out. Outside there are footsteps, then a woman's voice. Loulou listens attentively and hears German being spoken. Immediately he knows what's going on. A few days ago a comrade had proposed that women be allowed into the living quarters. The occupants found themselves divided into two camps on the question and a stormy discussion had ensued. This evening Bernard was bringing in a German woman to sleep with. Now Loulou understood why Bernard had been more or less disturbed to see him still up and about at one o'clock in the morning, and he also suddenly remembered that Bernard was the one who, during the debate, had argued most strenuously in favor of allowing women into the barracks.

Then Loulou awakens two or three of his friends and briefly tells them what's going on. "Don't worry," says a huge fellow who goes to stand near the door. "If she comes in, I'll hit her with my suitcase and take her out through the window feet first." Without waiting for the woman to enter, Loulou goes out and tells her: *Geh weg!* ("Get going"). She doesn't hesitate for a moment. Bernard isn't able to keep her from leaving as she quickly runs off.

Now everyone in the barracks room is awake. They ask what's going on. Bernard very angrily explains the situation to all his friends. "God damn you, Loulou! Why did you do that? We're free to do what we want here!"

"If you want to sleep with women, go and do it in town; but never here. You don't have the right to bother your comrades."

"But we're not bothering them; they're not the ones who are sleeping with anyone!"

"That may be, but just tell me what would happen to the spirit of friendship we have for each other if everyone starts to bring in women! You'll all look at each other out of the corner of your eyes and become jealous of one another. Also, maybe you want to catch something, but not me. I want to go back to France in the same shape as when I left!"

The discussion continued until 4 o'clock in the morning. Calm is finally restored and everyone goes back to sleep. At 6 a.m. the police break in, make a search, and find nothing. After they depart, Bernard, now teary-eyed, finally understands, thanks to Loulou. If the police had found him sleeping with a German, he would be sentenced to go to the *Strafeslager* at Röhmild for a period of eight or ten weeks.

Faced with such problems as these relating to love and religious matters, Loulou asks André Yverneau to provide background material for use in discussion groups. Despite having to work during the night shift and being constantly under police surveillance, the latter often goes out from Sonderhausen to visit the Christian community at Erfurt. He recommends books and articles that they might consult, brings along printed material, and urges them to read the *Acts of the Apostles*, pointing out to them that at Kleinfurra, Nordhausen and many other communities, the militants are already carrying along with them pages from this apostolic text, which they read, meditate upon in bits and starts during work, or use for the evening discussions in the cafés or the barracks. Thus they taste of the spirit which animated the first Christians and feel they are living in their company. Peter, Paul, Andrew, James, John, Philip, and Stephen become their everyday companions. They speak the same words and perform similar deeds; and the prayer they say each evening eerily resembles that said by the first Christian community of Jerusalem, when its members were imploring the Lord to have the Apostle Peter set free (Acts 12/5).

They too have someone to whom they have given their support and for whose return they are also anxiously praying: Camille. He now writes them rather regularly owing to the assistance he receives from Bédouelle and Henri Choteau on the outside. At Erfurt they wait for his letters with great impatience and quickly pass them about when they arrive. Some of the men copy out passages of the letters and then use them later on as matter for meditation. Thus Camille still lives among them, tells them how life is going, and asks for news about themselves; he recommends that they act prudently but expresses his conviction that Catholic Action should not be suspended out of fear, which though certainly understandable under the present circumstances, is nevertheless unworthy of Christians. He also describes the workings of grace that he discerns operating within himself. In his diary entry for March 28th, he writes: "Pentecost eve, feeling down." But in another letter he says, "What tremendous fruits we'll all be able to draw from a life like this which, though sometimes not very happy, we always joyfully accept as being given us by Christ. My inner spiritual life has evolved and taken on another form, and I shall leave here more sure of myself than I was when I entered. Pray for us during Mass and when you receive Christ, think especially about our own situation, which is not to be able to receive the Eucharist, for the present at least, in its real species. But I've now discovered a new way of acting—through prayer and sacrifice: this is more difficult, you have to remain patient in doing nothing and not seeing anyone; but we'll come through it all because we're constantly in prayer."

Supportive of each other and united in this way, the Erfurt militants feel at one with Camille and are committed to living the same kind of Christian life, even though they know that their situation is quite different. The leaders swap their tobacco for potatoes which they give to their teammates for food in the evening. After having offered up prayers for their brothers, they return to their barracks and spend their nights together in friendship. Many share all their possessions in common, and when someone needs to go out, he puts on "the community's clean pair of trousers and jacket" taken from a single wardrobe.

At the reception of the Eucharist on Thursday evenings—a program inaugurated by Camille—at least three or four new French people are in attendance every week. Loulou, Michel, Joseph Prin and René Guédon understand what's happening and insist on talking about this to others. As a result, they snag Henri, a Catholic grammar-school teacher—someone with rather lukewarm beliefs when they first meet him, but who eventually will take charge of the community in the North Erfurt region. The Ursuline sisters had put their chapel at Camille's disposal, with their chaplain's consent. Using a great deal of caution, the members now go there regularly. When the convent was later destroyed in a bombing, the hospital then became the Welcome Center for the Jocists. They come and leave here in small groups. Normally twenty-five or thirty people arrive after their twelve hours of work; they have had to wash up, shave, change clothes and ask a comrade from the barracks (who is not always very willing) to get their soup for them in the canteen. But the guys would come back buoyed up and reenergized because, through their prayers and the reception of the Eucharist, they had been able to step away for a moment from their exhausting lives as slave laborers.

Remarking on the growing number of communicants, the hospital chaplain proposes to Loulou that there be a special Sunday Mass for the French. Each time it is said, the *Kyrie*, the *Gloria*, the *Credo* of the Mass, and the Lourdes hymns are enthusiastically sung by all. On every Sunday more than 150 French people hear the word of God preached to them by a priest who talks to them just as if they were at home. When Louis Maga, the STO priest from Sommerda, can come, he has his work cut out for him. They rush from all sections of the city to go to confession to him. Louis is locked up until noon in the little chapel's confessional box and, for the rest of the day, he listens to men—young and old—who express the need to talk about their innermost feelings. While walking up and down the streets and alleys of the camps, Louis offers them the peace of Christ which they always gratefully receive.

Loulou, who is feeling an increasing burden of responsibilities with the growth of the mission, would have liked this priest Louis to take up residence in Erfurt. But the Gestapo was closely watching the situation and blocked all requests for his transfer. Loulou asks André Yverneau to augment the number of his meetings with the leaders and insists that Milo propose a whole day retreat for all the militants in Erfurt. The latter, who is spending his Sundays travelling about the province, arrives with André, whom he had met while passing through Sonderhause one Sunday in June, after both of them had been working the night shift. They are just on their way to Loulou's place to prepare the afternoon meeting when a Frenchman runs into the barracks. "Quick, get out of here!" he says. "The *Lagerfürher* has just phoned to inform the police that there are some strangers in camp." Without any further ado, Milo and André jump out the window and go through an opening in the grating. Several minutes later the police arrive and check everyone's papers. The only arrest they make is that of a Frenchman, recently arrived at camp the evening before from Nordhausen, whom the others had forgotten to alert.

Loulou arranges to have his friends notified about the meeting as they exit from the various Sunday masses. Many of them are exhausted and others are not able to attend. About twenty arrive in little groups from all sectors during the afternoon and come together in the woods. They sing with hearty voices and find the site very much to their liking. André, text in hand, explains to them how through their Catholic Action in Germany they are living in the same way as the first Christians. And each one offers examples to illustrate how this Biblical text aptly relates to their own lives: "The great number of the faithful lived together with one heart and mind. No one considered as their own what belonged to him but everything was shared in common among them.... No one was wanting among them." More or less consciously they had chosen the same means in bringing themselves together. "Everyday they took care to be in attendance at temple, but it was in their homes that they broke bread: they took their meals with joyous and simple heart. The Lord increased each day the numbers of those on the road to salvation." Weren't they praying and acting in similar ways? "While Peter was locked up in prison, the Church never ceased praying for him ...." Peter and John underwent interrogations, received the 39 prescribed lashes, but they joyfully set out again and did not let this prevent them from going forward. Hunted by the police, persecuted, stoned, left for dead, cared for by his brothers who then arranged for his escape the following day, Paul sets out once again to bring the good news to another city. And before them, before their very eyes they see Milo and Henri, these indefatigable travelers, still at liberty and speaking to them about all these things: The analogy is striking and they all feel grafted to the same root as these saints of twenty centuries ago. Loulou and those around him can no longer sit quietly by. Milo has taken all these things to heart. In a calm manner and using words with which they are familiar, he suggests methods that they might use to evangelize the others:

First, they should introduce a team initiative to create an atmosphere conducive to instilling in the men a taste and desire to live actively as committed Christians. A camp in which such an environment already exists (he mentions his camp Kleinfurra as an example) could then slowly and progressively educate the mass of workers. As far as the work of evangelization is concerned, this will be realized through personal contacts and by people who have been adequately trained. Milo goes on to say that everything he is explaining here revolves about theories or techniques for doing things, but that the surest way to accomplish the mission is through authentic witnessing on their part as Christians committed to the needs of the masses of workers.

It begins to rain and the group reassembles around Milo and André under a tree. The discussion goes on for a long time still. They all are in agreement, and Joseph has the final say, reminding everyone of Canon Cardjin's expression: "When everyone begins to push the cart, it will move forward and will then be able to keep going all by itself, even through the ruts. Our faith is too great for us to give up!" They prayed for those in prison. Then Milo and André returned that very evening without a mishap, leaving the men at Erfurt united in their resolve to carry forth the mission.

THE COMMUNITY AT ILEMENAU

Let's now leave Erfurt. About sixty kilometers farther South, between Suhl, Arnstadt and Saalfeld, perched at a height of six hundred meters on the foothills of the Thuringerwald, is Ilemenau, a small city of fifteen thousand inhabitants. Among the inhabitants are some 600 German Catholics and about 350 French men and women who work in the various factories located in the city. It is at this quiet and wooded area that a team of seminarians, coming directly from Angoulême, arrived in July of 1943.[11]

During autumn of that year, the Vallée brothers had come from Gotha to put this new community in touch with the ones in Southern Thuringia. Thus in February of 1944, when the Messerschmidt *Waggonfabrik* factory of Gotha was bombed, Ilemenenu took up a collection and sent packages to the victims of this disaster. But the difficulties caused by lack of rail connections prevented the team members in this city, who had already become very active, from participating in the clandestine meetings at Erfurt and Weimar. But this also allowed

---

11   Henri Tesseron, a priest ordained immediately before his departure, with Lucien Boilard, Léopold Crémaud, Gilbert Herand, René Valtand and Albert Marie. There they joined Jean Pervis, from Laval, POW in *Kommando* 840 of Stalag IX C, and Abbé de Marescot, the *Kommando* chaplain.

them to avoid being caught up in the dragnet set in motion during the month of April.

For work fit for slaves or mad men, the few Germans assigned to it seemed more or less mentally disadvantaged.[12] Despite the harsh physical endurance that it demanded from these committed Christians[13] and the moral inertia to which quite a few laboring in this locale had succumbed, the team continued to expand its work.

This small isolated region was not totally spared from the turbulence affecting the surrounding areas and also had to contend with troubles of its own. And the Gestapo was keeping a close watch over those to whom it had knowingly given considerable free rein. Henri Tesseron had already been quietly warned on several occasions to stop delivering homelies to the French during their Sunday Masses. He could also no longer celebrate Mass for the Germans in their own church, and the comings and the goings of the *"Pastoren"* were currently under very strict scrutiny.

Every two weeks Father Tesseron, accompanied by Léopold or Albert, goes to celebrate Mass at Grossbreitenbach, a small industrial town of 5,000 inhabitants located 17 kilometers from Ilemenau. Thirty or so young French people have been vegetating in this backwater since their arrival in November. Mass is said in a room of a restaurant that has been rented with the greatest secrecy. But unbeknownst to them, the Nazi Party also is in the habit of holding its meetings in the same building. One day two *Schupos* pay them a visit.

The more conciliatory of the two checks the identity of the suspects while his colleague searches the house from cellar to attic. Not having their passports with them, the men overwhelm the policeman by showing all the identity cards and photos contained in their wallets, which touches the old man very much. A former POW imprisoned in France during the last war, he waxes nostalgically about the country.

---

12   They worked in a glassworks factory which manufactured glass beakers for thermoses. They labored twelve hours a day in a tropical and fetid environment with virtually nothing to eat, carrying incandescent bottles on shovels from the blowers to be annealed in the ovens, without any break. Here a worker would have to walk an average of 16 kilometers a day.

13   They had to make constant trips on empty stomachs at all times during night and day to get communion, without mentioning the very many hours spent tending to the mail, engaging in conversations, giving instruction or ministering to their comrades.

Then suddenly becoming greedy when he spots the portable Mass valise, he asks whether it might not contain chocolate or coffee. While this is going on, his colleague returns sputtering. Shortly after, they both depart reassured and seemingly no longer suspicious.

Somewhat later in July, after Mass, Albert Marie, who had accompanied Henri, offered to take back to their camp several militants who had come from a considerable distance. This small group had proceeded only about 500 meters through the woods when a *Schupo* on motorcycle, accompanied by a *Hitlerjugend*, approached them from the rear. It was some kind of ambush. Once identified, Albert is brought to the local police station where the *Schupo*, who has now taken his revolver out of its holster, treats him correctly.

After being searched several times, Albert has to undergo the classic forms of interrogation and is forced to provide a full explanation for every one of the papers he has on him. There is a question about the contents of one of them in particular, regarding the meaning of the words "big hunt" (*grande chasse*).[14] "This was a hunt for bed bugs that was held in the barracks," he explained. Several similar replies to other questions of this sort threw the police off the track. Albert had quickly realized that the interrogation was being conducted because of a report no doubt prepared by the Gotha Gestapo after the April arrests: predictably, the interrogation dealt largely with questions suggesting the JOC's anti-Nazi stance and the clandestine activities of the various groups. During all of this, Albert played the role of the innocent seminarian.

Finally, at the end of the afternoon, after seeming to hesitate several times, the police announce that they are going to transfer him to their barracks at Arnstadt. Albert gets his back up: "What! You're arresting me for no reason! You have no proof! There's no evidence against me." The others, now more or less embarrassed and believing themselves victims of some kind of misunderstanding, still feel they have to execute to the letter the orders that they've apparently been given. After several telephone calls, they prepare a report in four copies. Making them rectify a few details, Albert signs it. About 8 o'clock in the evening—another phone call—and, his papers are then given back and he is allowed to leave. The interpreter calmly explains to him that he must never again step foot in this part of the country if he doesn't want to

14   This is still another equivocal term used to mean a meeting of a Catholic Action group.

be sent to a concentration camp. Because there are no more trains that evening, the now obsequious police officer invites Albert to spend the night at his own home while waiting for the one that which will depart on Monday morning.

Albert declined the invitation and proceeded by foot and on an empty stomach to travel the twenty kilometers separating him from Ilemenau. The Ilemenau community will thus be able to cautiously continue its activities of Christian witness up to the very end. "The results of their efforts didn't seem to produce much of an effect on the outside," Léopold Crémaud acknowledged, "But Christ was present in their midst and they were able to tear down many longstanding prejudices."

"In fact I had the pleasure of meeting a 40 year-old POW in that fiendish glass works factory to which I had been sent. Six Frenchmen were working there, three of them prisoners. In the final analysis we got to know perfectly well the kind of person that each of us really was (and which we had been concealing up to now under the standard blue worker's outfits that all of us wore). I was struck in particular by the oldest one among them because of the great interest that he seemed to have in religious and philosophical matters. A few days before Easter, as I was passing through his work area, he calls to me from around the stack of crates where he is stationed to come over to help him. I go but find that this is only a pretext on his part. He confides in me his ardent desire to make his First Communion and starts to tell me about his life. After he was baptized, he received no religious education. Then the vicar of his parish had caused a public scandal. "Don't you see, that from that day on," he explained, "it was all over for me."

"They're all alike, all equally disgusting," I had said to myself at the time. As I see things now, I judged him perhaps wrongly but certainly too quickly. But you know how it is, people expect so much from a priest and can never overlook anything that he may have done or pardon him for anything! But during the time I've been living with you and have seen for a whole year how you deal with our comrades, with Germans, and women, I know it is possible to remain faithful to one's vows. And you're not the only one! I've met other priests just like you during my imprisonment. We don't know enough about you priests. This would be easier done if more of you lived like us! I'm grasping for something to help me remain faithful to my wife; that's why I want to make my First Communion."

He was able to do this a few days later, about 6 o'clock on his way home from the factory to his barracks.

Here again the grain had grown and sprung forth like the blade of green wheat which each day surprises the farmer as he returns to his fields.

WITH THE SAALFELD COMMUNITY

At Saalfeld, situated forty kilometers to the East, where the two Vallée brothers had gone to make contacts, Maurice Lefebvre and his companions also experienced very difficult and very distressing days following the April arrests. There as well they had to engage in a battle of wits with the Nazis, but they managed this without too much difficulty. They were aware of being under surveillance but Father Link—a German priest there—who was very well informed about everything, provided a watchful eye and constantly reminded them to use caution. The head of the Welcome Center is summoned by the police and undergoes a lengthy interrogation concerning the activities of the seminarians. But this POW transferred as the civilian worker knows very well how to maneuver. Sensing oncoming danger he pretends not to know anything and reassures the Gestapo commander. But the police chief of the Werkschutz factories has become very stirred up and has now put into effect very heightened security measures.

So at Saalfeld, as in all the other cities of Thuringia, apostolic activities are forced to adapt to the situation and go more or less underground. General meetings are no longer held in the *Gasthaus* or in the church, but a growing network of personal contacts comes into being. Friendship becomes the means by which the more committed are able to respond to God's grace. Activities are no longer pursued in the open, unless they involve personal acts of witnessing by individuals or those performed within the confines of the group. Christians are very conscious of having much less support upon which to rely from the outside, but they are spurred on to bear witness as best they can in union with their brothers in prison. Despite their fatigue, many read from an oil-stained Bible that they place on the motor of their machine. Guy discusses the readings with two Protestant POWs; Marcel provides Louis with a theme for meditation every morning, and Maurice is eager to discuss such matters with anyone who cares to listen to him, whether or not they are believers.

The word of God continues nonetheless to spread about more and more. Henri Noyelle and Jean Reynaud pursue their work as official leaders of the Welcome Centers and provide countless services in this capacity, even though their activities are now directed mostly to organizing recreational programs.

This kind of devotion to duties requiring risks taken in common becomes the best defense against egotism and a shield against the slow, crushing burden of time passing, which demoralizes and wears down even the most optimistic. So it is not unusual for a guy going back after work to the "Russian Kommando" (the seminarians's barracks) to find at table an unexpected guest or a new occupant on his mattress.

These people could be French POWs, fugitives, escapees from the *Strafeslager* at Röhmild or from one of the Buchenwald *Kommandos*, and even Canadian parachutists. The "Russian Kommando" puts them up for a few days, and to facilitate this, has to dip into its reserves of the remains of the latest packages received from France. It also provides them with civilian clothing, railroad tickets and money. The "Russian Kommando" has thus become a launching pad for escape and a secure relay station for all those on the run, and this is common knowledge to everyone, with the exception of the police, the nurse, and the *Lagerführer*, despite the frequent visits they make there at all hours of the day or night.

This kind of charity, provided at such peril to the lives of everyone concerned, wins over the sympathies of a large number of the men and makes the entire camp aware of the many kinds of activities Christians are performing in their midst.

Hence despite the growing fatigue everyone feels at the sharply increased number of air raids and their anxiety in confronting Nazi ragings, now at an hysterical pitch, Christian witnessing is once again on the rise. New groups are being formed in the environs: at Unterloquitz, Eischsict. Though people everywhere are sick to death of the war, individuals acting with tact and patience achieve miracles in operating on their own turf. Recreational activities succeed in providing a more healthy environment and conversions begin to materialize. In one barracks Jean Ducruet manages to create on a number of occasions a family-like and virtually Christian community within a group of labor conscripts who had at first shown especially strong resistance to having to participate in the STO. He begins by moving all the women out of the barracks; then a statue of the Blessed Virgin

that he displays in a prominent place is witness to the gradual disap-
pearance of the pornographic pictures that up to now had decorated
the surrounding walls.

To the very end, wherever a militant was actively engaged, the goals
of purity of conduct and inner happiness were offered for all to emu-
late. Looking back now, all of those who had been personally involved
in this experience can attest to the tremendously solid bonds of charity
and friendship that they were able to forge with the mass of workers.

CHAPTER SEVEN

A NEW CENACLE

THE JULY 2ND EXCURSION

For a long time the Sonderhausen community had been contemplating a special project to which the *Kommando* chaplain had given his assent and his blessing: this concerned bringing consecrated hosts to the prisoners at Gotha. So on Saturday, the first of July, after having informed Henri Choteau,[1] André Yverneau leaves the factory earlier than usual and goes back to the barracks to get the sacred species that Maurice Devise, a seminarian working the night shift, had gone to obtain that very morning from the *Kommando* at Schutzenhaus.[2] André knew very well, saying goodbye to his brothers, that they would be praying for him even more intensely than ever before while he was taking this trip.

The train rolls on to Erfurt. André wants to see how the hosts have been placed in the box. Ever aware that he might be arrested, he thinks it would perhaps be a good idea if he took communion now. He proceeds to an unoccupied area, removes the small precious package from his pocket, and carefully opens it: Christ is present in these tiny bits of hosts. For his communion, he removes a few crumbs and then carefully wraps up the rest.

Having to wait three hours at Erfurt, André benefits from the layover to carry Christ to a Trappist at the hospital, who had not received for a very long time. Two *Schupos* stationed at opposite ends of the long line of passengers who are proceeding to the exit closely scrutinize everyone passing by. André feels his heart beating rapidly. This isn't the first time he has encountered *Schupos*, but today he's not alone and he trembles in fear out of concern for Christ, whom he is carrying on his person. Fortunately, he is once again saved by his German cap

---

1   A Jocist and member of the Vallée brothers's group at Gotha.

2   The "the hunters' house" where the POWs and Father Danset lived.

and briefcase. In the meantime, the Trappist, who had been informed of his coming, had arranged to go out into the hospital park at a designated time. André comes up to him, and behind a nearby bush; the priest kneels and receives holy communion. Now after so many years, Christ is once again passing through the streets of Erfurt!

André next goes to find his friends who are holding their meeting in René Guédon's barracks. He places the small box on the table, they pray and the meeting continues with the Master now in attendance. The topic under discussion was how to extend Christ's dominion over the hearts of everyone, beginning with those present. The Nazis, apparent rulers of the moment, might control the streets; but He, passing by in silence, was quietly making his way into all their hearts.

Once he arrives in the Gotha station, André will have to recognize the Jocist who is waiting for him somewhere in the crowd. Going out he notices a hatless young man who looks like a Frenchman. He passes in front of him without either one saying anything to the other. André then proceeds ahead and sits down on a bench a little farther on. The travelers are streaming out of the station and heading toward the center of the city. The young man remains alone at the top of the stairs in the station, casting one last glance. No one! André then gets up and approaches him, saying in German: "Do you know how I can find *General Weverstrasse?*"

"Yes, I live there. What number?" Our friend is having difficulty replying in German.

"Perhaps you prefer to speak French?" replies André.

"Yes, I'm French."

"I would like to go to 142 General Weaverstrsasse to the French camp."

"That's exactly where I live. Whom do you want to see?"

"René Gauthier."

"Very good, I'm René Gauthier, or to be exact, there is no René Gauthier. It's a name I borrowed. I've received your letter." (So the young man knows who I am.) "I've come to wait for you, only I didn't recognize you with your hat. I was just leaving because I thought that you hadn't been able to make it. Let's go somewhere where we'll be in less danger." Thereupon Andrè delivers Christ to Henri. They conversed for a short time and André received first hand the most recent news about the prisoners.

When he returned to Sonderhausen, André was reminded that he had gone to bring Christ to his brothers on the day of the Feast of the Visitation.[3] How could he not have succeeded?

ONE EVENING WHILE RETURNING FROM WORK

The Gotha prisoners are now working every weekday at the Courthouse and the Hospital. Their Sundays are normally spent at Offhaus's (nicknamed "Tutur's") farm. The owner takes a perverse pleasure in making us weed his cabbage fields only for show. While doing this trivial job we immediately became soaked from feet to waist and remained wet throughout the entire day, because of the abundant amount of dew that normally collects on this plant's special kind of of leaves.

At present our team is just about complete. Jean Lecoq is no longer confined secretly in his cell but is working with us on the outside. Thus we've been able to go to confession. The POWs who are now civilian workers come in contact with us during the course of the day and, out of friendship with Jean, bring us newspapers and bits of food. With his phlegmon now cured, André Vallée once again has resumed his position of leadership as the group's senior member. Jean Tinturier has also come back to prison after spending eight weeks in the hospital, where he was well cared for. While there, he was able to receive visits from Kuehn and Donati, coming from Schmaklalden, where Christian activities quietly continue to function. But like Louis Pourtois, Jean was classified upon his return as unfit to work on the outside and now remains alone in his cell during the entire day. We send notes to them during the week through the intermediary of the prisoners who cut wood each day in the courtyard of the prison. We also share news with them every evening, before returning to our cells, by talking loudly with the others right under their windows in the courtyard. However, our contacts with the people we meet on the outside have become more and more chancy: now we rarely go to the Hospital where packages and letters from Sonderhausen and Erfurt remain undelivered. Since the end of June we haven't once run into Bédouelle or one of his friends during the course of the day. On Sunday, July 7th, a small, evil yelper of a man (we call him "Pug Dog") whom we'll eventually tame, makes us come back from Offenhaus's farm by a round-about way.

---

3   The Feast of the visit by Elizabeth to her cousin Mary.

He must have suspected something, and since we had neither cans of sardines nor a supply of chocolate ready to offer him, he refused to let us pass through the center of city on our return that evening.

Because of the monotony of prison work, the lack of news, and the daily flow of petty, insipid events, we feel our energies dissipating more and more from day to day. We've now been in prison for one hundred days. Suppose they've forgotten us! Bureaucracy moves forward so slowly, secretaries are so indifferent and documents so easily mislaid! It is to our friends throughout Thuringia, who pray for us and continue to witness in our places, that on this Saturday evening, July 15th, I once more appeal for sustenance:

> I'm asking you, dear Milo, and all our "Brothers" in Kleinfurra to remain in union with us. Here we're forced to play "the patience game," and we derive a great source of strength from knowing that by being in prison we are gaining grace for all the young people of France and the rest of the world. Let's pray and suffer for the intention that our generation may become a holy one. We need saints, great saints to find solutions to resolve the conflicts the world is going through in our own times. And why shouldn't they be us? Let's pray especially for Marcel Carrier who, since the beginning of May, has been without news from his wife and kids back in Orne. Here we're waiting every day for God's will to be accomplished in us. We can't give up hope. Pray for me that I may not prove to be too weak in the company of my Jocist brothers. For days now I've been in a pretty miserable state. Put Jacques Etevenon back in touch with me by letter. Send me some news about Paul Léon and don't forget to take care of Nordhausen. Send my warmest and friendliest regards to Pierre Giraud: I pray very often for him and his fiancée, and for all of you as well. Goodbye, send the note that you'll find attached here to Sonderhausen after reading it yourselves. Remain constant in your faith and united in Christ.

> My dear friend Jacques, It's been impossible for a long time now for any of us here to receive any mail or packages. Still no White Bread.[4] We're famished. I feel united with you through the prayers that I offer up for each one of every evening, remembering everyone of you to the extent that I can (as you were when we were living together during our nine months of exile). It is a wonderful thing to gain merit for those whom we love in Christ. I think that I'll be better able to say Mass after this adventure. Despite feeling wea-

---

4 The Eucharist.

ry, I ask the Lord to keep me here as long as is necessary. I don't want to be lacking in generosity nor fall short of the sanctity of our group. For we must become saints; only by suffering in Christ's name can we be elevated to the stature of those great apostles that the Gospel demands and which the Society of Jesus has already given to the Church. We must become like them. Make a novena to Saint Ignatius that we all may be set free soon, if it is for the greater glory of God. In solidarity with all of you in Christ.

The next day, Sunday, our group is returning to "Tutur's." Weida comes along as our guard: this big nineteen-year-old kid has fought on the Russian front. Wounded and discharged, he has reentered the military as a prison guard. He is bored with this work and, as a compensation, what he likes to do best is to try his luck with all the blonds or brunettes he encounters in whatever areas we are sent to work. Most of the time he dozes off or loafs on the side, after having put either Jean Lecoq or Henri Marannes in charge of alerting him when the owner or the policeman in charge make their rounds.... "The big guy" thus leaves us completely free, provided we do the minimum of work required. Every morning he never fails to ask the question: "*Kamaraden?*" ("Will you see your friends today?") "*Vielleicht!* ("maybe"), we reply, so as to prepare for any future eventuality. He was just as happy as we last month each time Bédouelle or Marceau—our new contact from the outside—would bring us something, and he had good reason to be! And here is what happened on this particular Sunday.

After the ten o'clock Mass, Marceau had come to find us in "Tutur's" fields; and at the stroke of noon, he brought us bread, sausages, some newspapers, but no mail and very little news. The English radio, "the little one" as we called it, has been silent during this period. It appears that things are at a standstill around Caen and Falaise. *The Thüringer Zeitung* is preoccupied with vivid details about the destruction caused by the V1 rockets in areas of London. While Marceau is talking with us, Camille slips the letters we have written just last night into his pocket. When he leaves us he goes to seek "absolution" from Weida by offering him a cigar. "*Alles gut, Franzose, Auf Wiedersehen!*" ("That's fine, Frenchman, so long").

The weather is wonderful and we are feeling happy. Maurice Chevalier and Charles Trenet's songs will keep us going this coming afternoon. About five o'clock the group gets into formation; as we return, we nibble discreetly on our provisions. Weida walks at the head

of the line. At a short distance before the farm comes into sight, André
Vallée, who heads up the column, turns around and signals to Jean
Lecoq who is at the back of the line with Roger. He has just recognized two Jocists from the *Wagenfabrik*, Henri Choteau and Henri
Bonvot, and points them out to Jean. Knowing well how to proceed,
the two come up from behind and shake Jean's hand, quietly uttering
only the words "Sonderhausen, communion." They engage his hand
again and Jean feels the little box that Henri Choteau is slipping into
the hollow of his hand.

Weida hasn't seen a thing. The column files into the courtyard of the
farm and disbands. The "big shot" goes to get his tip and enjoy a *café
au lait* with the proprietor's wife. The Russians come to life and go off
to steal tomatoes and cucumbers that they see in Tutur's greenhouse.
Letting us know where he's going, Jean then disappears inside the living quarters of the ex-POWs currently working on the farm. Once
inside there he gives us communion one after the other.

Remaining outside to serve as cover, I see two of my friends near
the door to the entrance who seem to be waiting for something. I approach them. "I've a package for you," says one of them. "Where shall
I put it?"

"Wait …" A door opens. I throw a glance at the person who is coming through: it's the daughter of the owner's wife. Scandalmongers
claim she's a gift given to the Offhaus family by a French POW of the
last war. My friends disappear. I have to pretend to be doing something here, and I do this by simply advancing directly toward this
young woman; I then take from her hands the large pot containing the
soup sent for us from the prison every noon, which she was returning
to us after just having washed it out. I put the container down near the
entryway and uncover it. Then I rejoin Jean in his room where we both
consume the remaining morsels of the host.

We come outside. The Russians are back and have also returned
with their own booty. Weida calls us back in line and asks several of
us to take care of the dahlias that Offhaus's daughter has just cut for
him. He looks for the soup pot but glancing at it before he does and
noticing that its cover is back on, I call out to Camille and René: "Take
it but be careful, it's full and we have to bring it with us." Forced to
shove out of the way two Russians who are descending on it, Camille
and René grab the whole thing and then take up places at the end of
the column which is just moving off.

Choteau and Bonvot reappear and follow us in order to be reassured that everything has gone well. We exchange a few rapid-fire sentences with them as we march: "You've received Him, have you?"

"Yes, everyone has."

"I've been carrying the hosts for two weeks."

"Who brought Him?"

"André Yverneau, from Sonderhausen."

"Come back here every Sunday."

That evening I sent on my thanksgiving in a brief note addressed to André:

> This July 16th, Feast of Our Lady of Mount Carmel—written immediately after the return from work after 88 days of waiting. "He" has traversed the entire city of Gotha with us on our return to prison. André, I recognize your fraternal faith through all of this. You are indeed Peter's brother, possessing a less exuberant but fiercely constant, almost "stubborn" charity. This time you really accomplished your goal, and we are all sharing our thanksgiving prayers with you. I can't express all the things I am feeling in my heart. Silence is the best form of praise. In receiving Him, I have really been able to reach out to embrace all of you. Thanks again. Continue to take care. We all are united in our prayers of thanksgiving and in the peace of Christ.

Upon our return we have been able to pass on food and newspapers to Louis Pourtois and Jean Tinturier, who had spent their Sunday cutting wood in the courtyard. But we hadn't been able to bring them Christ. However, we're all presently sharing the same kind of life and observing the same form of the Mass, if one can judge from the contents of a letter that Jean Tinturier wrote to his family on the following day, which did get to them and which they managed to save:

> I am one of the ones who stay inside ... I'm all alone in my cell, face to face with a drilling machine. We work sitting down and it isn't too tiring. Sundays we're taken down into the courtyard, which has given me the opportunity to meet the only other comrade working inside like me. He comes from Besançon.[5] Though he doesn't seem very impressive on the surface, I quickly came to realize when talking with him that he was a very mature and strong person. To be alone all day long is something new for me, and it reminds me in many ways of the seminary. But more than the seminary, it's like a

---

5   Louis Pourtois.

novitiate. We own nothing: and here we most certainly observe the three vows (chastity, poverty, and obedience). We have few pressing needs and hence have only to be preoccupied with ourselves, I mean to say, with our personal salvation quite in ways suggested in the "Exercises" of Saint Ignatius. I had never before made my novitiate and am profiting greatly from this. It's in essence very simple: a few commonly-said prayers—I've forgotten all the others—offered throughout the day to allow me to remain constantly in God's presence; and in my present state of poverty and deprivation, I find that I'm at peace with myself. I'm now spending my thirteenth Sunday without having heard Mass, but I've discovered, however, that our Christian faith possesses an incomparable abundance of riches. I say my rosary morning and night: wasn't it originally used by lay brothers as their breviary? A lay brother, yes, that's exactly what I am at present. I also spend time thinking about my past life, reviewing each of its events—what there has been of good, and more particularly, what of bad through it all. I also think about the future, about my vocation, and I ask God to lead me solely according to His will; in this way everything will come out well. Jean.

Being in prison affects each of us in similar ways. Marcel Callo admits to his mother that what he misses most are her cherished letters:

I have absolutely no news from you. At times I find my solitude almost impossible to bear, and it's all I can do not to be overwhelmed by the sadness I feel. But in the long run, I have a Friend who won't abandon me for a second and who knows how to console me during some terribly oppressive moments. With Him we can stand anything. How thankful I am to Christ for having sketched out for me the path that I'm now following! I offer up my present difficulties and sufferings for all of you: you my dear parents, you my dear little fiancée, for Jean,[6] that his ministry may be fruitful, and all my friends and comrades. How sweet it is to suffer for those whom you love! Every night before falling asleep, I think about the future and review my good qualities and my faults; I resolve to become better by following God more and more closely. Little by little I'm preparing to build that charming little home where Marguerite and I will live together when I return. Every night my thoughts also turn toward France: I'd love so much to see her resplendent and prospering once again. All of us who have suffered will rebuild her and will know how to restore her real face.

---

6   His brother, Jean Callo, priest of the Diocese of Rennes.

To remake France or rather to assure her going forward: how many of us have not thought, throughout these long days in prison, about the historic vocation that our country has been given?

During these days, as we prepare for the feast of Saint Ignatius, I see again and again in my mind's eye this immense and nondescript multitude of French people, a mass diverted from its path, a grey ocean extending up to and churning over into these camps and prisons. From a distance I indistinctly hear the splashing sounds of huge numbers of people. They are the ones who have passed along this way with me, yet how many others will there be who will still have to suffer like this? We've shared in the sufferings of all those people who Péguy has written about,[7] the neither Christian nor pagan, the living dead. Proceeding through this mass of people has given us a great thirst, and now that we're alone, we ask for something to slake it. The only response to our request is in the apparition of a well dug on the very site where we are living, and whose water has sprung up inside us as a living stream; and others in their turn will be obliged to experience the same. We have needed the solitude and deprivation of this long period of imprisonment to develop a deeper faith within ourselves. My Jocist companions claim to be revolutionaries, and they've certainly thrown themselves into battle. But Christ has not wished them to remain se-

---

7   Charles Péguy (1873-1914), an encyclopedic essayist, publicist and poet who was killed on the battlefield at the very beginning of World War I. From the moment of his death he would become a legendary hero, writer and thinker in France. During his brief lifetime, Péguy had developed a political theory, more exactly termed a mystique, advancing a Christian form of socialism along with a campaign for political and moral renewal aimed at purifying the roots of the Republican tradition and values. He grafted on to these the mystical vision that he saw as France's unique vocation that it had been called upon to fill from its earliest Christian origins (the conversion of Clovis) throughout the centuries, advanced by such luminaries as Joan of Arc and other French Christian saints, heroes and thinkers up to the modern age. Péguy's vibrant civic patriotism and deep religious faith made him an enormously influential figure in French resistance to the Nazi Occupation in general, and among members of the Resistance in particular, especially among French Catholics. His works were often cited and used as inspirational texts serving to legitimize and encourage opposition to the Nazi presence and hope for final victory. His life, works, and involvement in developing a Christian form of socialism would be further reasons to endear him to members of the JOC and all its affiliate movements. (trans. note)

cluded in their nascent Christian communities; rather, He led them
out, so they may receive the grace that comes only to those who truly
suffered in His name, and to show them that He, who is first among
all who have served, desired to be more intimately united with them.
They now know—as Péguy explains it—that a revolution ultimately
comes to depend upon the inexhaustible resources to be drawn from
one's inner life, and that men do not ultimately make revolutions because of motivations from without, but rather from what they are inspired to do by forces rising from deep within themselves.

But there are nights when we can't stand it any longer, when our
nerves are frayed to the breaking point. We would like to rouse all the
earthly powers, since God seems to have wearied of using his own.

On the evening of the 29th I paced for a long time up and down the
length of my cell. We can't go on like this. They have to do something
about us.

> It's inconceivable that twelve Frenchmen, one of them a priest and
> three seminarians, can be interned here solely for their religious ac-
> tivities. (This evening marks our 102nd day in prison.) Someone has
> to inform the Nuncio's residence in Berlin and send them a copy
> of Rodhain's circular letter.[8] Still not having been judged guilty or
> innocent, we're in limbo. Will we have to remain in the "shadows"
> until the very end? I've received all the official letters, dear Jacques.
> But everything possible must be done to bring our case to the at-
> tention of the Welcome Center at Weimar. Do everything that you
> can. The Nuncio has to be informed. Let me repeat again that it's
> impossible to believe that twelve Catholics are being held in prison
> solely because of their religious activities.

Writing these few lines calmed me down and made me think of the
people at Sonderhausen:

> I would like to see you again because it would do me a great deal
> of good to be with all of you: Everyone of us here will have been
> greatly marked by suffering and we should all profit enormously
> from living together in our newly formed community. All this will
> be resolved when He sees fit. At present, I no longer want to worry
> about when I'll be freed. If I'm feeling down, it's more because of
> the silent battle in which we're engaged here rather than because
> of the situation in which God has placed us. And we offer Him
> everything, even this weariness that we feel when saying our prayers

8   Written on May 19th, 1944. We had gotten wind of it by secret mail.

of thanksgiving. Soon we'll be at a new turning point.[9] The political events that loom threateningly on the horizon will lead to the
greater glory of God. Once liberty is restored and people's minds
and bodies are comforted and again made whole, the Church with
all its members will be able to resume its missionary role. While still
having to suffer for some time, we'll eventually be able to harvest the
fruits of our trials. We must be thankful for having been the recip-
ients of such wonderful graces. We have been specially chosen—
despite our insignificance—to participate in the passion of Christ.
How wonderful it will be to have played some part in His glory!

God, who alone sustains all of us here in a community of prayer,
conversion, and sanctification, will send us out again when it suits
him, in the same way that he has brought us together. Pray often
for me so I won't have disappointed you when I return. Don't worry
at all about me. I'm depending absolutely on Christ for everything
that I do. You're the ones whose labors have been responsible for
having initiated my beloved comrades here into a life of prayer and
self-sacrifice. I often speak to them about you. They're carrying on
as a team and learning, as they ingenuously inform me, the driving
motive of our Jesuit Society: which is to love. We'll still have to
suffer and gain merit by living in such obscurity so as to be in the
vanguard for the renewal that is to come—a role we must assume
if we are not to sin against the light.... Let's all live in unison and
remain attuned to the rhythm of the heartbeats of our Lord, as our
Father,[10] whose feast we'll celebrate in two days time, has desired
that we do.

The 31st of July. "We're in very good spirits," declares Camille.

We're finishing a novena to Saint Ignatius for the intention of gaining our freedom. We'll stand fast despite everything, especially since
it's for the sake of Christ. We have no news about our situation
and hear nothing being said about it. No one seems to understand
what's going on. But we're being led through it all by God's love.
I should have lots to tell you, dear Michel, when I see you once
again.... We're beginning our 15th week. It's been a long but splendid period of time.

---

9   The Allied offensive in Normandy was now imminent.

10   Ignatius of Loyola, founder of the Society of Jesus.

REUNITED IN THE "KIRCHE" (CHURCH)

One evening, "Two Stars"—the head prison warden—greets the column in the courtyard as it returns from work. Still another inspection? Now what has he come up with to bully us again?

He had not at all appreciated Jean Lecoq's reply the other day to his question "Where is Cherbourg?" Jean had answered, "Now it's back in France." Upon hearing this, "Two Stars" had turned pale: And in fact, the Allies had just recently driven to the South of Auvranches.

We wait silently until he finishes roll call because he is holding a sheaf of paper in his hands. Are we just beginning the ceremonials that routinely take place on the evenings before departures for Buchenwald the following morning? We're in a state of fright. We had somehow managed to put this eventuality out of our minds since that time when our attention had become side tracked by military events occurring on the outside. Henri Marannes is ashen, André Vallée remains impassive as his brother Roger moves over to his side, Camille tries to keep smiling. Jean Lecoq's name has not been read out. Was he going to be separated from us? They're probably going to send him back to the POW Stalag. Taking delight in our prolonged silence, "Two Stars" then brusquely gives the order: "*Alles mit dem Pfarrer Lecoq in Kirche!*" What does he mean, "Everyone is to proceed to the church with Father Lecoq!?" We don't appreciate the joke. While "Two Stars" bursts out laughing, the "dago" explains to Jean that because the prison is full— they've just arrested a large number of recently captured Communist militants—all of our team will now be housed in the same room— "the *Kirche*." This is a large cell on the uppermost level of the prison, with one big window looking out, where a minister used to come every Sunday in the past to perform religious services for prisoners—hence the reason why "Two" Stars referred to it as "the church."

A few moments later, we find ourselves all together—Jean, Henri, André, the two Marcels, René, Fernand Morin,[11] Camille and I—in this "upper room," as Roger would later baptize it upon his arrival there.[12] Jean Tinturier will come to join us a little while later, at the insistence of a police officer who had always been well-disposed toward us; but we will not be able to obtain the same favor for Louis Pourtois.

---

11   He arrived in prison after his arrest on the 27th of July.

12   The upstairs room (Mark 14/15), (Luke 22/12): ("The Cenacle").

We put down our mattresses along the length of the wall, around a large table. Camille fashions a cross out of everlastings that we hang on the wall for all to see. To "Two Stars'" constant remarks, we invariably reply: "Well, we're in the "Kirche."

Then we spend our finest days of living as a community. We are also working on the outside during what is now the harvest and threshing season and thus can make contacts with the POWs. Through them we receive news, packages, and other supplies. The guards turn a blind eye, but we have to be careful because "Two Eyes" remains unbending. We often come back with puffed-out jackets and shirts or well-lined caps. We are also provided with bread, crackers, jams, and cigarettes thrown to us by a comrade who is often on the lookout for us at the edge of the sidewalk or at a bend in a road when we are filing past in the evening. In the room everything is considered common property: razors, paper, bits of string and other minor odds and ends useful to prisoners everywhere. Each of us has his designated place around the table at which Jean Lecoq presides. From the very outset, André Vallée has insisted that we take our meals together in a leisurely fashion: and it is not an easy matter to have to wait to eat after a long and frustrating day of work. Camille and René have the permanent task of chopping parsley. Marcel Callo cuts up and scrupulously divides in equal and fraternal portions the supplies on hand for each day. Jean and Fernand Morin tire themselves out translating clippings from German newspapers. Marcel Carrier offers his habitual rumor or prognostic of the day. Henry, who is our tobacconist, has all he can do to divide up and apportion tobacco and matches.

These evening hours provide a real break from the very demanding work we have to do every day. Even Camille, who is the most resilient among us, has to admit:

> Tonight, dear Michel, I don't have enough strength to write. I'm really all done in. This week we've threshed four days without stopping, and believe me, that's a lot. It's true that it's not all bad because our bosses usually feed us quite well: bread, potatoes, sausage or eggs, beer, coffee, cake. All this makes for contented stomachs and raises our morale. We're currently divided into two work groups, but we come together at ten every evening. We conduct our lives as members of a Christian community, praying together and reading

the Mass for each Sunday.[13] We are now hoping we'll be able to get to a church, perhaps less than a month from now.

A little later on he writes:

It's been some time since you've received any signs from me, but once I tell you that I've been working as part of a threshing team, I hope you'll understand and excuse me. We thresh every day except Sunday for various bosses, at one farm or another. The best food isn't always allotted to those who do the hardest work, and André Vallée and I are now the only members of our team who can keep going all day long without a break. All the others have to be sent back to work for the truck farmers. But in the evening we are eventually reunited and share with one another the day's ups and downs, all of which we offer up to Christ in our prayers. On Sundays Father Lecoq gives a homily for the Mass, and on Thursdays Paul Beschet or Jean Tinturier prepares and delivers a commentary on the Gospel. This evening, at the request of René Le Tonquèze, we are beginning a novena to little Theresa, asking her to help us find sufficient patience to endure our remaining days in prison, because, let me tell you, Michel, the way things are going for us, we're really going to need it!

Christ had taken possession of the hearts of each and every one of them.

One evening in August, Camille received a letter from Marcelle, his fiancée in France. I can still see him, tears in his eyes, showing me what she had written: "You are too generous, my dear Camille. I'm afraid that the priests are getting to you. And I don't think you'll come back to me!" For several days Camille struggled with himself, alone and in silence. Christ's stern words: "He who does not hate his father, his mother, or his own life, cannot be my disciple..." kept repeating themselves to him again and again. It was only sometime later, one evening after we had been discussing all the things that could possibly happen to us, that he vehemently exclaimed: "After all, if the JOC needs martyrs, we can certainly do that!"

---

13   The Jocists of Gotha had procured for us a missal from Abbé Godin and two copies of the *New Testament* from the Ségond Press, printed in a convenient size and format that always seemed to pass through inspection and escape the attention of the guards.

FOR THE CAUSE OF CHRIST AND
CATHOLIC ACTION

During September a new circular letter, sent from the Sonderhausen-Kleinfurra region, alerted all the Christian communities about the preparation for a pilgrimage to Lourdes that the Chaplaincy was in the process of organizing for those returning, and provided information and directives as well on how to organize the preparation of a *Livre d'or* ("Golden Book").[14] Replies flow in from every area. Those in prison are elated to hear about this and also begin to prepare for their own return, which they want to make in the company of their brothers on the outside, whose works they've been supporting through their sufferings in prison. Their fellow workers on the outside won't allow themselves to be outdone in generosity and organize evenings of prayer at Nordhausen, Erfurt, Weimar, Gera, and Saalfeld. Things have calmed down considerably, and events on the battlefields increasingly give rise to the hope that freedom is near at hand.

At Gotha the prisoners are already planning for the future. As for me, I take the opportunity provided by several days of rest in my cell, granted to allow for the healing of an abscess on my arm, to write a long letter to Jacques, sent the 25th of September:

> Prison will have been a revelation for everyone, and even more than this for some. None of us is familiar enough with the Bible: I'm constantly made aware of this during every one of the "cenacles" that we hold here on Thursday evenings. But I am still hoping very much (now more than ever) to see you again soon (how we'll celebrate!), because I don't believe that, given the events of the moment, we're going to have to remain here for more than six months. For obvious reasons, I know nothing whatsoever concerning how or when we'll be freed. My first goal will be to get together with you immediately afterwards to embrace you before we leave for France. At present everything's in God's hands. We'll find living quarters for this winter wherever He sees fit. Together with Jean Lecoq, we've requested the Welcome Center to appeal our case, in the name of the French people, to the Procurator General at Gotha, as soon as the cessation of hostilities or any operation of this kind will allow.
>
> Our contacts with Henri Choteau are few and far between and very difficult to arrange. We haven't received any White Bread since

---

14 The "Golden Book" would be a compendium listing those who had been deported and given their lives for the Christian cause. (trans. note)

July 17th. This we miss very much. What news do you have about
everyone? Give our regards to people at Saalfeld, to Etevenon,
Dillard, etc. Best wishes to you all.

But once again another storm was rising which would eventually
strike the members of the flock and scatter them far and wide to other
sites that God had chosen for them, where Christians could still bear
witness for their faith. All of us, in the prisons as well as the camps, felt
more or less confusedly that Jesus Christ had not finished disclosing
to his own all that they would have to suffer in his name.

On September 27th I had my last opportunity to write the following
message to the Thuringian communities that were about to undergo a
second persecution:

"Dear André, The everlasting peace of Christ be with you! My cell
door has just been closed. It is one o'clock in the afternoon and I
have just finished a liter of cabbage soup in which a few beaten
scraps of potato were lying at the bottom of the mess bowl. I'm still
not working because of my abscess which is on the mend. There
has been another air raid over Gotha this morning. The Germans
fired back only after the Americans had taken the opportunity to
discharge several machine-gun rounds. This war will pass away and
be followed by the renewal. May little Saint Theresa of Lisieux, to
whom we have prayed for so many days, grant us the grace to become new men for this renewal. If only I could describe to you all
the dreams about the apostolate that I've been having here. Deep
within me I feel a great strength compelling me to conjure up and
imagine everything that I think should be brought forth and accomplished in order to inaugurate the kingdom of Christ; and often
afterwards, when alone again with myself, in this shrunken body, I
then feel wretched and break into a sweat! Fortunately there dwells
within me Someone who can provide us with more than we can
even imagine to ask. Aren't you experiencing similar things in your
own soul? He is teaching us André, about Himself. What a wonderful cause for joy!

We've also had a new alert regarding our own situation. Our
papers have come down from the Gestapo at Berlin, and we were
shown them very late Monday evening. They've examined our case
and it seems that a decision has been recently taken which threatens
to put us in a new situation, effective as soon as these papers are
sent back from Weimar. What awaits us? I don't even want to guess.
But what I know for certain is that, if the Master wishes, I shall
return to take my place at your side, expecting to encounter once

again along my way everyone whom, in my prayers at Mongré, I had asked Him to allow me to meet, no matter when and wherever he had planned for me to go. At any rate, André, do rejoice with all of us—our whole family—because of the reason for our imprisonment. This is for Christ—everyone understands that it is for the sake of Christ that we've been working. Their major error is to have set themselves up in opposition to our cause: for no one can serve two masters. That is why they have understood: *"that we were guilty of having threatened the security of the Community of the German State by our Catholic Action in the service of our French comrades during the time we have served in the STO in Germany."* What will they soon decide? Here in prison, where we seem to have gained the affection of quite a number, people have mixed reactions depending upon their own personal inner convictions. A number of guards and the prison head have shown themselves to be more than considerate toward us. The "boss," Herr Petri, will alert us as soon as he knows anything. We may very well be sent to a concentration camp. In the meantime, we live inspired completely by the *New Testament*: We read and reread the *Acts* and the *Letters* written by Saint Paul from prison. If I am to be leaving for a work camp, chances are that I might be repatriated before you; but if I can, I'll try to rejoin you so that we'll all come back together.

Courage to you all: we're proceeding along a beautiful road and are making other people envious. May we prove ourselves worthy to the very end of this cause that we refuse ever to give up. But if we could only again have some White Bread. We're so famished!

Upon receiving this letter, André once again boarded a train after Henri Choteau had managed to inform him from Gotha that there were chances for them to get to see our group on Sundays.

Overcome by fatigue, André had fallen asleep on the train and had to be awakened by a fellow traveler who politely told him: "This is Erfurt!" André goes to the place where Loulou's Jocist cormrades live and takes part in a meeting before getting back on the train for Gotha.

Henri was waiting for him as he arrived. Throwing all caution to the wind, he rushes toward him saying, "André, they all left yesterday morning!"

"Who? Where to?"

"Yesterday at 7:15 a.m. they were put on a prison train en route to a concentration camp. André Vallée had us pass the word on to Fernand Morin who is still in prison." André cannot bear to listen another moment, so crushed is he by this sudden and brutal blow, and he seems oblivious of the crowd now pushing the two of them toward the exit. For a few seconds he reviews in his mind everything that he has heard about the death camps and sees passing before him the faces of his brothers, those prisoners who have just now become infinitely more dear. After a moment's hesitation, he reenters the station to check the directory for train departures: "There's nothing left for me here, Henri. I can't stand being in the place from which they've been shipped to a concentration camp." But there was no train departing from Gotha that evening.

"You can come sleep in camp if you want," suggests Henri. "One third of the guys work nights and you'll easily find a place."

"O.K., let's go. Do you have André Vallée's letter?"

"Yes, here it is." André slowly read and reread it, without caring in the least if he too was now running the risk of having himself arrested. The letter ended with these lines of hope in human justice that his good brother Roger still believed they might possibly find at Buchenwald or Flossenbürg: "We'll only be deprived of our freedom. Perhaps we won't be badly treated. Let's remain hopeful!"

Where are they now? André recalled some lines from a recently-received letter: "Rejoice with everyone, with the whole family, because we've been convicted for the sake of Christ.... "

"Come on, let's go to the camp." Without uttering a word, André follows Henri. At the entrance, Henri gives him an identity card. "It belongs to someone in the military, but everyone here needs an Ausweis.[15] Just put your finger over the photo and they'll let you in." The guard turns on his flashlight and allows them entry. Henri wants to introduce his companion to Bédouelle, but they find him asleep and don't wish to waken him. They knock on the door of another room. Someone opens it: "So it's you, come in," and the other closed and locked the door behind them. The people in the room were gambling for money, despite this being strictly forbidden.

André settles in on the third level of a bedstead as Henri leaves him. Since the prisoners for whom he has been carrying the hosts can no longer receive them, André consumes them in the darkness, then

---

15   Without the "Ausweis," the workers could claim no formal identity and were subject to immediate arrest. Without it they also were not able to procure ration cards entitling them to have meals or obtain food in the factory cafeterias or worker kitchens in the Kommandos. (trans. note)

communes at length with Christ about those whom he already fears he may never see again. And he prayed throughout the night while the other guys continued to gamble.

At dawn Henri returns to bring him to meet Bédouelle. As they're talking about the horrors of the concentration camps, a young woman comes into the room, smiling and looking very cheerful. "Hello, Henri, hello Bédouelle, hello, Mister! I don't seem to know you. You can't be from around here?" André was about to reply, but Bédouelle doesn't give him the opportunity:

"Yes he is, he works in town and has come to see me about a soccer match that we are going to play this afternoon. Henri is going to take care of the details with him." Then he says to Henri: "Now that you've got all the information, go along with André to René's place, and hurry up or you might may miss him." Without a moment's hesitation Henri leads André outside; "Quick, let's go," and he explains: "She's probably the woman who denounced Lecoq and the Vallée brothers to the Gestapo; she might try to telephone the guard to have us arrested." But the soldier only glanced casually at our cards and let us pass.

When they arrive at the station, both go their own separate ways but promise to remain in contact by mail.

At Erfurt, the communities are in a state of panic. Some members have become completely demoralized and can only think about what Camille and the others will have to suffer. Others, outraged, cannot hold back the insults that they hurl at the Nazis and the SS. But all are very proud of their comrades now bearing witness for their faith. Michel and Loulou take André to the hospital to visit some of the sick. Among these is a young *Bordelais* (man from Bordeaux), who had just spent eight weeks in the *Strafeslager* at Röhmild for having struck a German woman. When he had completed his sentence, the comrades took him to the hospital because he could no longer stand up on his feet. After being treated for three weeks, he could sit up in bed only with great pain and wasn't disposed to divulge his life secrets to anyone around him. When André had told him the story of how Camille and his friends had been arrested and explained the reasons for their conviction, the *Bordelais* threw his head back on his pillow and shouted out in pain and anger: "O what swine, what bastards!" Then calming down, and looking up at André, Michel and Loulou, he added, his voice filled with concern: "And to think that this is the way that they treat people like you."

Christ had gone down this road as well, doing good to all, and had also been convicted and scorned as a jailbird. And he was still calling upon others to follow him along this same path!

When André returned to Sonderhausen during the night, he learned that Milo had just yesterday undergone his first interrogation by the police at the factory. The Gestapo was seeking information.

The latter had patiently pursued its investigative work and Weimar had sent along Inspector Winckler's reports. With the arrest and interrogations of Henri Perrin and Clément Cotte, the Leipzig police now knew full well how to proceed.

As a result, during the early part of September, a new wave of arrests unfurls in Saxony, specifically in areas around Halle and Wittenberg.

Inspector Schade makes good use of the excellent information he has obtained about Halle: August Eveno, the Director of the group at this city, is arrested on September 6th in the factory and will remain in a jail cell until November 20th. On the 12th, in Schkopau, Pascal Vergez, clandestine chaplain of Mersesberg, and on the following day, Colbert Lebeau, Jocist Director at Merseberg, both join Auguste in the same prison.

Paul Léon is arrested in his turn. The following Tuesday, the 19th, Roger Martins, Director at Bitterfeld, is taken by the police to the *Lagerführer's* office in the Antoine camp. Transported to the prison at Bitterfeld, he joins the STO priest, Louis Doumain who has been incarcerated there.[16]

Finally, Wittenberg sees its two Directors snatched away: Julien van de Wiele from the Neumühle camp and Eugene Lemoine from Schleicher. André Parsy, from Eisleben, is also arrested and will join them in the prison at Halle on October 4th.

As for the Halle-Wittenberg region, about thirty young men are arrested and taken to the "Mill"—the *Präsidium Polizei* (Gestapo Headquarters)—in Halle. About half of them will be quickly set free. After a second interrogation, some others will then be let go—among them Marcel Regnault, Director at Halle. The remaining nine will be detained—after several interrogations—to await their sentencing.[17]

---

16   Louis Doumain had already been interrogated by the police on the 10th of February, 1944.

17   They would be sent on November 20th, 1944 to the *Arbeitslager* for disciplinary action at Zöschen.

At Leipzig, only Jacques Etevenon seems invulnerable and continues to pass on information to one and all.

At Nordhausen, René Tournemire is under surveillance. But because he takes precautions and is actively aided by his boss, Madame Roegner, he will be able to avoid prison.

Milo will remain on the alert for several weeks. At the end of the month, the police come to arrest him, and Julot as well. After being locked up in a police railroad car while being transported from Halle to Leipzig, the two finally arrive at in Erfurt, where they join "Brother Félicien" who had been arrested at Weimar.[18] At the end of the final interrogation, after being severely warned, they are told: "We know that you are the leaders of Catholic Action in Thuringia, but we don't have sufficient evidence of your meetings. You're free to go, but don't let us hear anything more about you again." Somewhat disappointed, Milo and Julot will go back to Kleinfurra alone. They'll recommence and continue their activities up to the very end. Himmler's police would have many other matters with which to occupy during the winter months to come.

---

18 On September 19th. This friend of Marcel Carrier would be set free on December 8, 1944, subject to the same warnings as Milo and Julot. The prison at Erfurt had just been partially destroyed in a bombing raid which also demolished a section of the walls in the cell in which Brother Félicien and his comrades had been confined.

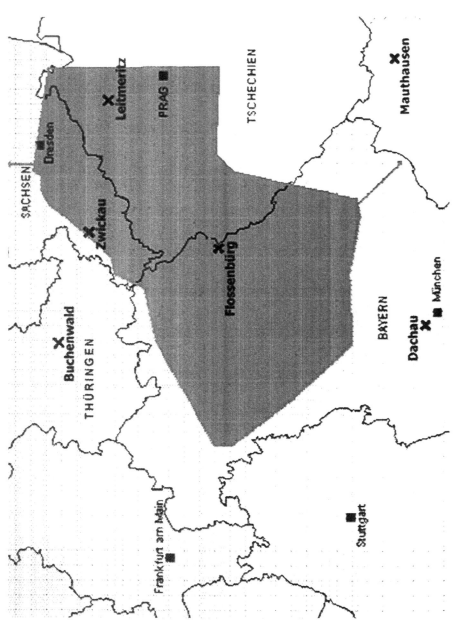

Location of the concentration camps Flossenbürg, Buchenwald, Dachau, Mauthausen, and the external camps of Flossenbürg, Leitmetitz, and Zwickau. The dark area designates where the external camps of Flossenbürg were located.

PART III: HELL

CHAPTER EIGHT

FLOSSENBÜRG

OUR DEPARTURE AND ARRIVAL AT THE CAMP[1]

On the evening of October 6th, 1944, "Two Stars" assembles us in his office. "Tomorrow, (you) leaving!" We are given back our civilian possessions—watches, wallets, pens. Henri retrieves a package that they had kept from him and we spend our last evening sharing its contents. Some delicious "Gauloises" and sweets from home. The "Pug Dog" grants us the favor of keeping lights on and Fernand Morin, who isn't going with us, will take charge of writing goodbye notes to our friends. Then night prayers. "This is going to turn out all right, guys, since we've got little Theresa in our corner," René keeps repeating. Marcel Carrier reminds me of the prison *Kommando* which bordered his camp in Weimar. Having shown it to me from his window when I was visiting him there last April, he had said: "Several times I shouted out the Jocist call from here and one day a fellow responded. So certainly we'll find some of our men where we're going." I have trouble falling asleep, plagued by my recurring memories of the entrance to the camp at Dora and convicts leaving to work in the tunnel—scenes that I had witnessed more than once while at the Niedersachswerfend camp at Nordhausen, when I was still prey to the persistent illusion that freedom was very close at hand.

---

1 At Flossenbürg in the Oberfalz in Eastern Bavaria, near the German Czech border, Himmler's SS established in 1938 a concentration camp for criminals and the like. Some political prisoners were sent there in 1939. Then during the War, other political prisoners numbering 30 nationalities filled the facilities of the camp and its 95 work camps (*Kommandos*) in Bavaria, Saxony, and Bohemia.

At dawn, our constant guard "Pug Dog" takes Fernand away and gives us something to eat. He had selected eleven portions of bread, one for each of us. "It's the last you're going to get so save some," he counsels. At 7:15 the *Schupos* take charge of our group. No handcuffs, orders the prison head, Herr Petri. After our group had taken a few steps away from the building, he waves a discreet but prolonged goodbye through the half-opened door. He knew, as did the others in the prison as well, why we had been sent there.... My friends and I weren't ordinary prisoners.

It's cold: autumn comes early in Thuringia. We wait for a long time on the platform at the railroad station. Finally they lock us into a prison wagon and for the next week we're dragged from one site to another as we pass through Weimar, Gera, Plauen, and Hof.

At Hof, Jean Lecoq is the first of our group to leave: he is going to Dachau near Munich to join the hundreds of priests interned in that camp.

We join up with a convoy of Czechs and Austrians, political prisoners evacuated from prisons in Prague and Vienna. Soviet troops are advancing rapidly in Hungary and Himmler has to maintain control of his livestock.

"*Los alles zu vier!*" ("Form lines of four"). Quickly obeying, we are given something to eat and have to extend our hands to be handcuffed and tied up. So in the morning mist, seven hundred fettered prisoners make their way to the train station through the streets of the city. It was October 13th. We pile as best we can into an absurdly inadequate number of decrepit third class wagons. I am surrounded on all sides by my chained companions, sitting silently with anguished expressions on their faces. "Where are we going?"

"I don't know. I can see the panel on the side of the wagon that says Weiden-Regensburg."[2]

"Where is that?"

"I don't know exactly..." Their fear weighs heavily on me. We've already given our consent to something unknown that will soon materialize. But having to wait to find out what this might be is so awful. Each one of us has so much time during which to discover his weaknesses, and this endless flow of time itself into which we've sunk is so cruel. Though we say nothing, we feel as one, and praying, we occasionally break our silence, to ask each other, "Are you OK?

2   Regensburg-Ratisbonne.

"Yes, we're OK."

After changing wagons at Weiden, our group gets off at Floss, at the foot of a small mountain range. The *Schupos* tell us that we've arrived. All of us are still nursing illusions fed by vague remarks or comments given us by the police. But these will be quickly dispelled. A rugged SS guard, leaning against the exit door of the station, appraises us with the look a butcher gives to livestock before the kill. We pass before him still chained in rows of four. Then begins our ascent to Flossenbürg.

We hardly utter a word, but with the nodding of our heads, the distressed looks on our faces and the signs of despair that we display, all of us—total strangers to one another barely an hour ago—now seem unusually close. In the midst of a valley bordered by dark mountains, we glimpse a ruined medieval castle, perched on a mountain peak, that will serve as a landmark to measure the progress of this captive mass of humanity proceeding with bowed heads, as if it had become accustomed to this manner of walking for a very long time. After a slow ascent of three hours, we finally arrive at the village that clings to the side of this old chateau. A bell tower arises from among the farmhouses. We brush past a church, once again finding ourselves close to Christ: we're in Catholic Bavaria, and above us, here and there on the outsides of the buildings, we see displayed statues of the Sacred Heart of Paray-le-Monial and Our Lady of Lourdes.

The inhabitants watch us passing by under the sway of the SS, just as they've watched so many who have come before and will follow after. From time to time our column turns to the right to let an SS truck pass.

After making a detour in leaving the area, we come up to a fence rising across the road and know for certain that we have finally arrived. We have to accept this and each one of us recites a whispered Our Father. The third sentence of the prayer stuck in my throat. I couldn't complete it properly and this seemed so strange! So I had to begin it a second time.

The column stops before an immense building of magnificent fieldstone which overhangs a sinister rock quarry. To the left, we can see the entrance hall of the Messerschmidt factory and the SS barracks, and on the right, the villas of the officers and their families. The building's surface conceals a vast amphitheatre in rock on which green barracks are aligned in orderly rows extending up to the immense assembly field that occupies the center place. This is the Flossenbürg Concentration

Camp. Enclosing it on all sides is a three-layered, electrified barbed-wire fence interspaced with granite watchtowers, on which are perched SS sentinels with machine guns, visible against the backdrop of huge reflecting lights. The column comes to a halt before the entrance. The *Schupos* count us once again before handing us over to the Waffen SS. Then well-dressed and healthy looking prisoners, the "Kapos," pass among our ranks, alerting us to an imminent inspection while trying to make off with a number of watches and rings before we're stripped of everything.

Finally we pass through the portals of the entrance gate whose pillars bear the inscription "*Schutzhaftlager*"[3] and "*Arbeit macht frei.*"[4] The *Kapos* place us along the length of wall outside the shower room, to the right of the *Appel-Platz* ("assembly place"). Then begins the classic rite of initiation into the K.L.[5]

After waiting about an hour, we are crammed into a room that is impossibly small and narrow to house the thousand or so that we number. Here we are given the warning: "*Eine Laus, dein Tod!*"[6] Then comes the process of disinfection: after a hasty departure from the entrance area, under an unremitting hail of blows of rubber blackjacks, we enter the immense and immaculate shower room. There, stripped naked and shaved from head to foot, we have to wait, standing in line, to present ourselves to the *Kapo*. The latter, a convicted criminal, administers random blows of his bludgeon to anyone whispering, or to any of the sick or wounded who lag behind. An SS officer, in full regimental dress, presides over the scene.

I wanted to keep my rosary and the signet ring given to me by a French POW that had Christ's initials (X.P.) engraved on it. I conceal the ring under a radiator and keep the rosary under my left armpit. But the *Kapo* in charge makes everyone raise their arms. André Vallée, who wants to try the same thing as I, has already been forewarned: A Czech prisoner has just gotten himself nearly killed for having hidden a medal under his soap. When we come before the *Kapo*, we make the first move, showing him our rosaries. He gazes at us: "You're Catholic?" He hesitates, our bodies are right there facing him, waiting to receive

---

3   Internment camp.

4   ("Work makes you free.")

5   Initials of "*Konzentrationslager.*"

6   ("One louse and you're dead!")

a beating, but he doesn't strike. Assuming a few affected grimaces, he throws them into a trash can. A Czech priest in our convoy trembles at seeing this. He too won't be allowed to keep his small cross. There remains the matter of the signet ring. After the shower we have another *Kapo*. An elderly Austrian manufacturer gets kicked because he tried to hold on to his marriage ring. The *Kapo* looks around the radiators and finds my ring. "Whose is this?" Silence. He repeats the question. Close by Camille is watching me. More silence. Walking slowly while trying to decipher the initials that he obviously doesn't understand, the *Kapo* goes to the back of the bathroom and, vigorously tugging the water chain, evacuates my last souvenir from the toilet bowl.

Several hours later, already very late into the night, our bare feet in clogs and dressed in ridiculous old rags, we are regrouped in an adjoining room where we are to stay until morning on a damp tile floor, without still having had anything to eat. During this time, the louse-ridden camp prisoners pass before us. They'll spend their night in the shower room. This is our first sight of these emaciated bodies which no longer have anything human about them except their skeletons. They're beaten uninterruptedly: little Polish and Russian *Kapos* go wild as they play with these deathly pale bodies. This is a killing field where men are murdered.

I manage to retrieve my rosary from a pile of garbage in the far corner of the room, and I detach its cross and put it under my shirt.

The next day when we are registered, I receive the number 28,907 that I have to sew on the left-hand side of my shirt, above a red triangle and the letter F (*Franzose*-French). We are now officially *déportés* in concentration camps.[7]

While waiting to be assigned to various *Kommandos*, our group is sent to a quarantine block where we begin our apprenticeship in our new life as convicts. Our stay here will be a short one, however, because of the never-ending flow of convoys from which are disgorged other *déportés*, bringing the camp's prison population to over 8,000 men, more than twice the size of the 4,000 for which it was intended.

---

7 The nine of us were all registered at the same time and received the numbers 28901 to 28910.

OUR STAY IN QUARANTINE

Between two endless roll calls which are held between about 4:00 in the morning and 9:00 in the evening, we have to stay outside, penned up in front of the buildings, between the barbed wires, in sun, rain, or wind. In the morning, the only food that we get is a cup of black liquid; at noon, a stingily measured liter of a disgusting and tasteless soup; and in the evening, 200 grams of dark bread and a slice of sausage or cheese. We are hungry in body, mind, and soul. The heavy, feted air is filled with the pungent smell of burning corpses wafting from the nearby crematorium.

Chilled to the bone, our bodies seek out the sun as we lean against the walls of the building. When it rains, there is a mad rush to the stinking, filthy *Abort* ("toilet"). In the jostling that ensues in getting there, the weakest are always crushed. We also have to fight against the cold which is already lashing our bodies through the insufficient cover of our clothing. So we have to form what is called *la boule* ("the ball"). Groups of men press against each other, those on the outside seeking to infiltrate to the interior so as to gain a bit of warmth. From time to time the block leaders yell out orders in bad German, telling us to stop this infernal ballet. Another roll call: they ask for volunteers for special work or announce duty rosters; then the march to work; distribution of soup and new "bull runs," provoked and prolonged for the enjoyment of the Russian, Polish, or German *Kapos*. Men assault each other, some fall. So what! We have to line up again. Have the ones who manage to scramble up to the front ranks assented, despite themselves, to have caused the death of their companions struggling to regroup in the rear? Often one single unguarded second, one simple mistake can bring it on. For here at every moment death is as close to us as life.

Ever in such desperate straits, this fiercely struggling mass of humanity remains in a constant state of turmoil which increases every day, because we are never at rest. Not even during the night when we have to pile together on the same mattress, if one is to be found. While lying there, you have to intrigue endlessly to prevent a bit of bread you have saved for tomorrow from being stolen, as well as the few rags and other meager possessions acquired through long, patient efforts that have to be renewed again from scratch every single day.

The ground is littered with the exhausted bodies of the dying. After having endured the terrible working conditions at the quarry or in the mines, the men return literally decimated. Then warehoused in the *Schonung* ("rest blocks!"), these shockingly emaciated men won't even be allowed to enter the *Revier* ("infirmary") which in any case is permanently overcrowded. In short, they're programmed to die, it doesn't matter where. To facilitate this, they've been placed on a special regimen consisting of half rations and endless roll calls, during which the healthiest must hold up the weakest who are collapsing under the blows administered by the *Kapos* supervising the line ups. How ironic it is! The doctors are ordered to give them phony kinds of aid: a bit of ointment, strips of paper, and a few pills for this mob of ulcerated, gangrenous and diarrhoeic men, including the *Tubars* ("the tubercular"), who tomorrow will be nothing more than ashes. Some of them still crawl about offering an old sweater for bread: what a pitiful black market! A circle forms around those dying in the mud and dust, and the strongest share the spoils of what little remains. From time to time a Russian, tough as any stevedore, passes by dragging by the feet a half naked and still living body which he proceeds to finish off with jets of ice-cold water near the toilets. And all this has to be cleaned up afterwards—a ludicrous task since the cadaver will be stacked in a corner to await the daily morning collection which fuels the crematory ovens. About a hundred are consumed in this manner every day.

Even so, some still manage to cling to life! Isn't there a concert every Sunday on the assembly field! Selections from Wagner and Weber's "Invitation to the Dance" were on the program the other day. Word has it that there is also a library for the Germans; and very near the roll call field there is a block housing boys under seventeen. Assigned to do the housekeeping of the various blocks, more often than not they are also forced to satisfy the sadistic pleasures of the *Kapos*.

Everything is rationed. And who are the ones who can stay healthy in mind and body? Simply said, those who manage to eat. And he who eats has to bully, beat up, and sometimes even kill his companions in wretchedness. Here might makes right.

Only those who have been there can verify all of this. But can any words be found to describe adequately such inhuman conditions, especially since those who endured them invariably felt as if they were living alone and cut off from the others during their suffering?

Our group was soon going to be broken up to go into different blocks, before being assigned to other camps. But each of us has already experienced temptations that we keep deep within us, silent inner struggles and disgusting resentments that we feel we can no longer share with one another. Evil which is so palpable and omnipresent threatens to divide us. Will the love which we have be strong enough to hold out against death?

We feel buffeted by this evil, and as if swept away on an immense ocean; Unable to see anything ahead or behind and living in dreadful isolation, we each ask ourselves why we no longer feel as one with our brothers. But we're alone in facing this all-pervasive evil, and this disgusts us. We're alone as well in confronting a refusal that we don't quite dare put into words but which whimpers within us like the cry of a feverish child. From this point on, we must fight a battle that will only be over at the arrival of a new day. Yet who at this point can afford to despair and accept ending up like those fallen, emaciated and grotesque husks of human beings who are dying all around us! Will we consent to live according to this law of the jungle, or die a slow death, uttering not a word, like pathetic little sheep?

We spend these first days sharing the solitude of this agonizing and debased world. However, a poor man's salvation often comes from one poorer than he. When a communion of saints no longer exists, this communion of poor wretches becomes the order of the day and will remain in place until the first is once more possible.

When Camille—less reflective in nature hence a more feeling person—notices a Frenchman dying in the corner of the *Schonung,* he comes to tell me, "Paul, we've got to do something!"—The action we took of coming together around the body of this dying man restored our group's faith in itself. While Henri Marannes goes to find the Czech priest from our convoy to give final absolution, I bend over the man and gently try to disengage his bleeding head from the barbed wire in which he is entangled. Sighing deeply, he kisses my small rosary cross with blue swollen lips. It's all over; his body might be ready for the crematorium *but he has not refused the call.* Oh the miracle of empty apostolic hands like ours which gain new strength in giving what they believed they no longer possessed.

The very talkative Marcel Carrier has met a lawyer to whom he wanted to introduce to me. A radical socialist and Free Mason, Philippe, from the Charente area, was in the Resistance. We converse for a long time trying to forget how hungry we are. He tells me about his clandestine existence as a resister, then his imprisonment at Fresne, Compiègne and Dachau, places where he has been imprisoned in the

past. He's just coming back from having been interned in a very brutal
Kommando located in a factory[8], where he suffered months of very
hard labor. But he never lost his humanity and with some friends, now
scattered here and there, he formed a group that met to mutually sustain one another by sharing whatever matter they could draw from
their respective humanistic and professional backgrounds. With him
I discuss literature: Gide, Giono, Maurras, and he takes great pleasure
in telling me all about one of La Varende's novels.[9] He injects into his
conversation many allusions to the marvelous cuisine of Normandy.
The following day he confessed that all these kinds of things that he
had talked about served merely to provide him with pure mental di-
versions or means of escape from his present situation. At Compiègne,
a priest prisoner, about whose whereabouts he was no longer aware,
had arranged to say Mass every Sunday.

> I went out of purely human motives. Just to have something to do,
> rather than pace up and down in my cell like a trapped animal. This
> experience left me with a strong thirst. But I know nothing about
> religion, my past weighs heavily on me, and at my age, I don't believe
> that one can start all over again.

This 45-year-old family man, a brilliant conversationalist and very cul-
tured person, confesses that he is more ignorant of than opposed to
religion and humbly asks me to give him catechism lessons. I begin
rather too abruptly with an explication of the *Credo*. He interrupted me several times and I had to respond to a few of these classical
objections that I had thought to be no longer in vogue and possess-
ing no other validity at present than to serve as historical examples
of anti-religious shibboleths commonly in vogue in earlier times: for
example, Joan of Arc had been burned alive by priests; the existence of
hell is incompatible with the concept of charity; and clerical celibacy
is a mere sham or an abnormal state. All of sudden he blurted out: "I
want to pray. Excuse me, but I don't know how to speak to God." Here
a brilliant and very articulate lawyer was now talking like a boy starting to learn his catechism. Philippe obediently repeated the words of
the "Our Father" and learned the "Hail Mary" by heart. Other lessons
followed, including one on the life of Jesus. This neophyte had never
heard anything like it. He found it was all marvelous but very hard to

---

8   A *Kommando* attached to the Sachsenhausen Concentration Camp.

9   *Nez de cuir* ("Leather Nose"). (trans. note)

understand. I said, "Listen Philippe, you're not the first. There was a man among the Pharisees whose name was Nicodemus, a very prominent Jew. He came one night to find Jesus." (John, 3) Philippe was pleased with this story which seemed very much to resemble his own.

While we stayed there, we were saved by the hunger of all these famished people and we ourselves accepted to become poor wretched creatures just like them, because in order to love men you must be willing to share the way they live. One could call this "the game of defeat:"[10]

> You have placed me, Lord, among the vanquished.
> I know that it is not in my power to win or to leave the battle.
> I shall plunge into the abyss, free to fall to its very bottom.
> I shall play out to the end the game of my defeat.
> I shall play it against all that I possess, and when I shall have
> Lost everything, I shall play it out against my entire being, and perhaps
> I shall once again be able to regain everything by having given everything up.
> Those who tread the prideful paths and trample life's humble underfoot,
> Who leave on the tender grass the marks of their blood-stained feet,
> Let them rejoice and give praise to the Lord, for this day is theirs.
> But as for me, I thank you that my lot has been cast with the wretched and forgotten
> Who suffer and bear the burden of the powerful, and hide their faces,
> While stifling their weeping in the darkness:
> For each throb of their pain has quivered in the secret depths of your night,
> And each insult has been gathered up in your magnificent Silence.
> For tomorrow will be theirs.

On Sundays it is easier to go from one block into another. Jean Tinturier located two seminarians, friends of his whom he had known beforehand in France, who were *réfractaires* ("draft dodgers") from

---

10   This passage from the poem "Lyric Offering" by the Indian-Bengali poet Tagore, (1861-1914) which was translated into French by André Gide, was often in my mind during this period.

STO.[11] Roger Vallée hadn't wasted his time either. He found a young
Franciscan STO conscript, "Brother Christopher," along with several
other brother Franciscans. They too had worked together up to the
day that they had been arrested, imprisoned, and sent to the camps.
Separated from them, Brother Christopher ended up at Flossenbürg. I
now no longer remember all the "Fioretti," the little stories about Saint
Francis, that he managed to tell us, as well as the many liturgical po-
ems that he could calmly recite for us from his post behind the barbed
wires, sometimes interrupting himself to go to the aid of one or another of the moribund lying all around him, because he had chosen to
live among them in the *Schonung* block. He presented a clear and living
example of that perfect kind of joy whose image Camille and I would
keep in our hearts during the days to come. I still can remember his
dialogued recitation of compline, which he would deliver at five o'clock
in the evenings before roll call. And didn't we even dare to sing with
him "Nearer My God to Thee" right out in the open at high noon!

Others hadn't resisted evil to the point of being willing to shed their
own blood, but Brother Christopher already felt deep within himself
the joy of living with God in the depths of this charnel house! He and
others like him made this mystery of faith a living reality for the rest
of us through the testimony of their own lives.

OUR TEAM IS BROKEN UP

October was nearing its end. The mass of prisoners was working itself
to exhaustion on the much-trampled Flossenbürg grounds, and their
hopes for an early liberation, so prematurely and even somewhat fool-
ishly anticipated since September, had fallen down over their heads
like the heavy mantle of an early and unexpected snow fall. We were
on the threshold of what gave every sign of being a terrible winter.
Silently each one of us calculated how many more days we would still
have to endure and wondered who among us would still be alive to see
the beginning of April.

Prisoners continue to be shipped off to far away camps: Henri
Marannes and René Le Tonquèze have already departed for the camp
of the Auto-Union at Zwickau. André Vallée, now separated from
his brother, has been sent to Leitmeritz in Bohemia. Marcel Callo,

---

11   Claude Harweg and Marc Hervé.

Louis Pourtois, Jean Tinturier and Roger Vallée have been assigned to Mauthausen.

One morning it was our turn. Marcel Carrier, Camille and I would be part of a convoy destined for Zwickau. An SS medical doctor inscribed a sign on our chests with mercurochrome, and we were pronounced fit to work in factories by the officer in charge of transportation. Anyway we'll be warmer, or at least not as cold as we are here, we say to each other. And since we'll be fewer in number where we're going, perhaps our daily routine might be less lethal, and we'll be able to be together once again with Henri, René and Philippe the lawyer. We might even be able to get in touch with Ligori Doumayrou, the head Jocist in the city of Zwickau, who is probably still acting in that capacity there.

After 48 hours of excruciating formalities that seemed to go on forever, 500 prisoners, in their striped outfits, paraded one last time for the pleasure of the camp commandant before passing under the portals bearing the inscription *Arbeit macht frei*. Would our work set us free?

A bright All Saints Day sun shone over on us as we took the road from the camp to the railroad station, where a number of cattle cars, lined with damp straw, awaited us. We were sixty per wagon and could even reckon ourselves fortunate in this respect. The SS soldiers in charge of the trip, for the most part, old men who had been forced into service, left us in peace during the thirty-six hour trip. Our main concern was to organize the French into one unit to prevent the Russians from pillaging our meager supply of food. We were leaving a hell[12] much concerned about those who are no longer with us, and somehow feeling less threatened by what a still unknown future might bring. How amazing was our hope!

---

12   The Flossenbürg concentration camp was less known in France than Dachau, Buchenwald, or Mauthausen because fewer French prisoners were sent there. Yet it has its own ignominious and tragic history; and only about 5% of the French who had been incarcerated there survived.

CHAPTER NINE

LESS THAN ANIMALS!

AT THE ZWICKAU KOMMANDO

Zwickau, a rather important industrial center in the confines of Saxony and the Sudetanland,[1] is the home of large factories, among which the Horch Company—a subsidiary of the Auto-Union of Chemnitz. More than a thousand Europeans are employed there in the construction of motors for light armored vehicles. Most of the French STO workers here come from Citroen and, along with a few German specialists in this field who have not been drafted into the *Wehrmacht*, comprise an elite group including the most qualified and experienced workers in the factory.

In June of 1944, the camp for the French STOs, located very nearby, was closed down, scaled back in size, and refurbished to accommodate the *rayés* ("striped ones") from Flossenbürg. Its barbed wire and observation towers make it look similar to any of the other SS *Arbeitskommandos* ("disciplinary camps"). For a thousand convicts divided into three blocks who are presently cooped up there, death or the narrow caged corridor leading to the factory are the only ways out. We arrived on the evening of All Saints Day and, for several long months, led the desperately monotonous life of the slave worker condemned to a slow but inevitable death sentence.

Shuffling between the factory and the *Kommando*, convicts who have already been worn out by months in prison, followed by a stay at the Flossenbürg camp, eke out their last ounce of strength.

The interminable roll call ends at about 5:30 in the morning or evening. Before passing by the *Hauptwacht*,[2] the column departing for work pounds the pavement keeping in step with the guttural shouts

---

1   Located due South of Leipzig and to the West of Chemnitz.

2   The guard post.

of "*links, zwei, drei, vie links.*"[3] As the commander is crying this out, the lines jolt from one side to the other and pass under the piercing beams of light from the miradors on the watchtowers. "*Mutzen ab!*"[4] Bareheaded, chests out for a few seconds, and squeezed together side by side, the men parade before the Kommandoführer, a small pudgy fellow surrounded by his *Feldwebel* ("officers").

It's not a long trek to the factory. Our column proceeds in the dark through the muddy terrain and the debris resulting from recent bombings. Sometimes when a man falls, we have to walk right over him because the SS, positioned on either side, keep us from breaking rank by dealing generous blows with the butts of their rifles. At 5:45, this huge man-devouring factory opens its doors, and the column enters and proceeds to its assigned area—the central section of this three-story building is where the prisoners work. Here master and slave enter their common world and begin their labor. If not always demanding, the work is in the long run very taxing for under-nourished people like us. We are always exhausted and find expending any effort at all— even of taking an occasional break—virtually beyond our power.

Our twelve-hour shift is interrupted only with a half-hour pause at noon or midnight, when we swallow the disgusting soup that we have handed to us, usually accompanied more often than not with blows of the blackjack. The SS officer on duty makes the rounds and the *Kapos*, the ones primarily responsible for stimulating the work output of the convicts, hover about. For nothing more than a too lengthy trip to the toilets, a too hurried cleaning of the machine at the end of work, or a conversation with a friend—especially if this person is a civilian worker—a prisoner can have his number taken down and will afterwards become the beneficiary of the "rewards" administered every Sunday in the presence of the *Kommandoführer*.

Sometimes the SS don't wait to punish you before the weekend. I remember having been brought in, about 3 a.m. by a Polish SS guard who had been spying on me for the better part of a night during which I had been suffering from a terrific fever. He had caught me loafing away from my work and conversing with a brother convict. Since the latter was suffering from whitlow and so was also not up to doing his tasks, the *Meister* ("foreman") had agreed to allow us to work together

---

3   ("Left, two, three, four…left!")

4   ("Hats down!")

for the rest of the night. A good deed never goes unrewarded. While this Polish SS was sufficiently moved not to beat the hell out of my comrade, he made me report immediately to the guardhouse to receive 15 blows of the blackjack on my back. Hence the last two hours of work were extremely painful.

In the factory the "striped pyjama" is mostly left alone if he stays close to his machine. Often the German civilian workers, who are basically humane for the most part, only pretend to speak harshly to us when they repair glitches in the operation of the machines, sometimes even muttering threats because they feel that they are being watched. For there is always the possibility that a stool pigeon is lurking about. Some of the German workers even bring newspapers and vitamin pastilles or occasionally leave a cigarette butt or a slice of bread and butter in the mess bowl of some poor wretch who is wearing himself out next to them. I've seen one of these Germans, a tough looking guy—despite the fact that they tried to make them believe that we were all bandits and terrorists—break into tears when one of my comrades persuaded him to feel his scrawny arms. These people had retained their humanity. My *Meister*, a very tough but fair person, was also quite considerate. He had realized that I was incapable of maneuvering the huge drills in the assembly line of which he was in charge, and for a whole winter he assigned me to work with a trolley on which I would transport *"Gehäuse"* motor blocks in cast metal weighing 80 kilometers that often had to be brought back to the drills after being inspected. This work allowed me much freedom of movement and the opportunity to have frequent conversations with the workers of our group.

Very often we engage in rapid exchanges of news items gleaned during the night from the remarks of some French or Belgian STO workers and passed on in a jargon mixed with German, Italian, Russian, and French expressions.

I remember an elderly music master from Warsaw Conservatory, "Mr. Thaddeus," as he called himself. He had been deported September of 1944 at the time of the ill-fated uprisings in the capital, when Russian troops were advancing toward it. Hiding behind a pillar and speaking a very labored French, he would often convey to me how much he was suffering: "Mr. Paul, I can't take it any more. While listening to the sound of these machines, I'm haunted by Beethoven and everyone of his symphonies. But I'm gradually forgetting them. I don't think I could conduct them anymore. Mr. Paul, this so awful, I

simply can't take it, it's so unfair." While saying this, he manipulated
his screwdriver as if he were still holding a wand that was rhythmically
keeping time with the fantastic movements of these monsters of steel.

How many suffered in this way, fighting with themselves! This peasant torn from his Russian steppes, or this professor of history from
Warsaw University, this middle class patriot from Prague, or this elderly diplomat of noble Rhenish descent from Wilhelmstrasse, and
this little Italian Capuchin Friar, Padre Antonio, a preacher from
Milan already in his sixties, whose crime was to have shown charity
toward the Jews,[5] and not even counting all the other anonymous voices who gave vent to their distress with the simple words: "When the
war be over, Frenchman?"

How many, unable to finish their work week, keeled over on their
machines, abandoning their places to others who would end up the
same way. Some who were virtually falling down still refused to be
brought to the dreaded *Revier*, which everyone considered the gateway
to death.

I remember one morning leaning against the wall and struggling for
a whole hour to keep from falling over. Luckily a young French STO
came by my corner, saw me, and before alerting the foreman, gave me a
few mouthfuls of viandox to keep me going—thereby putting his own
life in jeopardy. When the SS guard on duty came by, I simply asked
for a little ether to buck me up, and he complied. How many would
not have died if there had been someone there who could have handed
them a glass of tepid water!

From time to time there is a lull during air raids when we crowd
into the underground shelters. Often the work continues far into the
night. When the luminous globes of the immense central hall are extinguished, it becomes possible for anyone without a regular place in
the assembly line to hide out in unlit areas. The machines keep whir-
ring under the light of the lamps focused on the drills which are grating in the castings. The work area looks like a gigantic submarine that,
submerged and fleeing the enemy, still produces its infernal materials.
Shadowy figures pass by and shout out commands which rise from
time to time above the hallucinating symphony in metal—the frantic
visual drama of a master race exhausting those whom it has conquered

---

5   Padre Antonio left the *Kommando* for Dachau one day in December. He
had heard our confessions several times during the night shift, while resting behind his machine during a break.

and who toil under its yoke, despite the death sentence which is progressively weighing down more and more heavily upon its own head.

I have often huddled in a corner during these moments trying to compose my prayers, while, riveted in their places nearby, Marcel, Camille and the others continue pulling the hand levers or the chains of their machines. But what can a tired body do when it can only finger the beads of a rosary held deep in its pockets? How can the mind continue to operate when the stomach demands this daily bread, stolen from it during the previous night before or which will be denied it tomorrow as a form of punishment? There is nothing more to be said or done. Prayer has now become only the distant memory of an act that a priest on the outside is still performing, even at this present moment, as he raises the chalice above the altar. At present, we no longer so much resemble men but are more like animals in God's presence, but animals who still cling to this elevation even in the lowest depths into which they have fallen.

On the Mount of Olives, an anguished and exhausted man sweated drops of His own blood.

Camille and Marcel came to see me one night during work, emaciated and their faces marked by the long hours of the night shift. Something simply had to be done.

Camille, audacious as always, says to me: "Paul, you have to write. René and Henri have already sent word to Gera by way of the Jocists whom they work together with on certain days in clearing away the debris from the air raids. Write to Sonderhausen and ask them for food. We can't starve here after all." The following night I sent a scribbled message with a young STO from Paris, who worked on machine maintenance in our assembly line. This was a dangerous move, if ever found out, because any attempt on the part of STO workers to communicate with prisoners was strictly forbidden. And anyone found guilty of such an offence could expect to be severely punished, sometimes even sent away to a concentration camp. Terrasson took the matter in his own hands and saw to a number of things. A few days later, packages that we were officially entitled to receive came to us in the *Kommando*. These miraculous acts of charity would continue until the very end, despite the growing shortages of food supplies and illicit trading on the black market. This is an ancient tradition in the Church: A very long time ago the Philippians had provided sustenance for the Apostle Paul who, after going hungry in prison, acknowledged the receipt of similar kinds of provisions with the simple words: "Everything has come to me and I am now in abundance."

Through our work in the factory we could still maintain human contacts with others; but the same was no longer possible in our *Kommando.* There the *Kapos* were in charge of discipline and the management of the block. These were, for the most part, convicted criminals, murderers, or sex offenders with long jail records, usually of German or Polish origin, who by engaging in low and contemptible acts, had succeeded in winning the approval of the SS. Each *Kapo* handled his group anyway that he wanted—with the right to beat up (or more exactly, to kill) whomever he so desired. In payment for these functions, he got double food rations and enjoyed certain advantages: a private room and often a *Stubendienste* ("servant boy") to satisfy his lustful pleasures.

For a long time Block I suffered under a reign of terror exacted by a 25- year-old Pole named Joseph. A former officer cadet of the Polish air force and imprisoned since 1940, he had been transformed by the SS into a first-class murderer. I've seen him break a "miski" ("mess bowl") on the skulls of these poor wretches when they were holding them out to be served soup during this ever violent procedure, and force dazed and exhausted victims, who didn't have the strength to drag themselves wherever he wanted, to drink their own urine. He was in the habit of making the 300 men of the block wait for at least an hour, crowded together in the corridor, under the pretext of waiting for orders, while their soup was growing cold outside. Once a week he made us endure the notorious louse inspection, an obscene and degrading exercise that he would prolong for his own pleasure. Stripped naked and carrying their clothes, the men had to file by him, where, seated on a stool, he inspected their bodies and clothes with a huge lamp. If he found a bug, he would violently kick the guilty one in the stomach. The man would fall to the floor and if he didn't get up, he was relentlessly stamped on until Joseph had his fill. During all of this, the *Stubendienstes* soaked our shirts and underpants in what was supposed to be a disinfectant. We then had to undress and go to bed without being allowed to dry ourselves around the only stove in the room; after spending the night in this state, it was back to the factory, but not before having to endure the interminable roll call outside in the cold. Showers had to be taken by everyone at appointed times, even for those burning up with fever; and these sessions often ended with beatings for everyone.

Joseph had a certain preference for a few Germans and Czechs who used to get packages. The latter had to deliver them to him to be put under lock and key in his living quarters, to prevent their being stolen. Joseph could thus engage in a lucrative trade by forcing the owners of the packages to pay tribute money. I had already made an arrangement with a somewhat less brutal Blockmann to keep my own packages safe. Made jealous by this, Joseph constantly gave me threatening glances. He also took special pleasure in beating up the "French swine."

Christmas Day, with a half package of tobacco in my pocket, I decided to go with Camille to wish Joseph a Merry Christmas. He wasn't expecting such a daring act of politeness. Without mincing words and in his limited French he asked me "Why are you here, Frenchman? Are you a terrorist?" Briefly I respond, "No, a priest." "O, you're a priest! Not good for you. But if you give tobacco, that's good for you." I hesitate to acquiesce, but Camille persuades me saying, "Go on, buy him off." "Yes," I said, handing him the half package, "but on one condition, promise not to beat anymore Frenchmen." The deal turned out well worth the making, though I now personally risked becoming the butt of gossip and envy if Joseph were to be seen giving me any special treatment afterwards. He made a move a week later on New Year's Day, when he assembled all the French in the block to give them an additional liter of soup. From that day on, he treated our French colony with less brutality but took it out on the Italians, Hungarians, and the Jews. He even committed the abominable treachery of betraying his own countrymen, and several Russians, after having confided in him about their plans for an escape, were summarily executed that very night when he had denounced them to the *Kommandoführer*.

A dozen or so people like him are involved in the day-to-day running of the camp. This group is headed by Albert, the *Lagerältester* ("head *Kapo*"), a handsome 28 year-old German, who is said to have killed an engineer for reasons of jealousy. Because he knows so well how to manipulate the "*gummi*" ("blackjack"), it falls on him more often than not to administer "corrections." These take place on Sunday afternoons after the roll call over which the *Kommandoführer* presides in person. The prisoners line up in columns on the assembly field and the "patient," bent over a chair, is beaten according to the discretion of the *Kommandoführer*, who assigns the number of blows merited by the offense. Sometimes the men laugh in spite of themselves: when a person is being beaten, he almost always makes bizarre movements.

In the heart of winter, exercises like these are performed on a smaller scale in the *Schreibestube* ("secretariat").

Only rarely do the SS (the *Kommandoführer* and his *Fedwebels* excepted) go inside the camp. These incursions are always to be feared because they occasion general searches that prove to be very painful for the "pajamas," who find themselves stripped bare of all of the bits of paper or rags used for socks or to insulate their shirts from the cold; and they are severely thrashed if they are found to have in their possession even the most minimal provisions, or a far more serious matter, knife blades fabricated secretly in the factory.

Some searches come as complete surprises. Block 2, where I had just arranged to be transferred with Camille so as to be back again with René, Henri, and our lawyer friend Philippe, was run by Willy, a convicted criminal, sometimes brutal, sometimes a nice fellow, depending on the amount of ether he ingested every day. Seeing me at a loss for what to do with my first package on the day that it arrived, he offered to keep it in his place. Because he was known to have a soft spot for the French, I accepted. One evening after getting our soup, we were preparing to go to bed in our block when suddenly the *Kommandoführer*, his *Feldwebel*, the SS person on night duty, and Alfred and the *Kapos* suddenly burst into the outer room. After the 150 pajamas are pushed into a corner with generous blows of the blackjack, Alfred delivers a speech: he says that they're here because of a possible sabotage attempt they've just discovered this afternoon: it concerns some large hammers found in the flooring of the room. Though many people are grilled, no one gives any information. Then the *Kapos* approach a table and grab the men one after the other to give them a severe beating. Alfred and Joseph take turns with the blackjack, while a bony *Feldwebel* counts the number of blows. My turn is coming—Camille, René, and Philippe have already passed through without uttering a sound, while some of the others howl with pain and humiliation.

Willy, who remains seated during the process, playfully makes a face as he pushes his foot down on those who don't get up quickly enough after their beating. When I arrive at the table, Willy recognizes me, nudges Joseph and calls out to Alfred: "He can't be the one, he's just arrived in the block ..." During the silence that ensues I'm thinking about how much I would like to be beaten like the others. "Move, Frenchman!" Alfred says as he exempts me. The *Feldwebel* stands in my way and gives me a dirty look. I straighten up on my shaky legs and salute. A shade taller than he, I return his stare. "*Franozose,*" he asks, reading my number. "*Ia Wohl!*" ("yes indeed"), I reply in a loud voice. My audacious response (of which he was certainly aware) would ordinarily have won me a good slap in the face. But he does nothing, apparently because he can find no reason. I take advantage of this to remain standing a little in back of him in order to help my comrades get up once they've left the table and are still staggering from the kicks and blows Willy has given them, trying to make them fall down. I felt I had to do something provocative like this to appease my guilty conscience.

Once this sinister comedy had ended, I went to see Willy in his room to thank him. This was my opportunity to exploit the situation. With a sneering grin he replied: "Idiot, I don't want you to end up in the crematorium." I consented to this shoddy little act of diplomacy in order to be able to intervene for the benefit of my comrades, whenever future circumstances would warrant. Willy, who certainly cared more about packages than he did about me, remained a dangerous and fickle partner, but he was at least somewhat less abominable than his peers. And I even found that, from time to time, he still was capable of displaying some vestiges of humanity.

A LIGHTED CHRISTMAS TREE

We were not fully aware of the extent to which our hearts were being gradually hardened by these inhuman conditions and the ever-present instinct for self preservation—or the fact that even compassion becomes exhausted when the body succumbs to its own decay. It may be heroic to share one's bit of bread when every mouthful is the equivalent of a certain number of hours of life; and one can endure obeying a criminal or being beaten by a brute. But to give in to oneself, to make a pact with evil—such things cannot be tolerated. When we went into exile, we had accepted this very painful giving up of our freedom for reasons of charity and in order to undertake a special mission, but we had never imagined how far this road would take us. There is also the experience of a falling down from the self which, like falling into evil, causes one to feel responsible, despite their best intentions, for the sins being committed by others. As a result we feel sullied and embittered and then fall into a permanent state of guilt.

Harassed at all levels of our lives (even the most base and menial), we were descending into a state even lower than that of the animal because we were men.

I was surprised one day at the feeling of disgust I felt rising in me at the sight of a cadaver stretched out in the toilet area. This frightened me very much. I stopped short, and removing my hat and looking squarely down at this person, I repeated three times "I believe in the resurrection of the body."

We definitely had to resist this spiritual degradation, so about ten of us (including Camille, Marcel, René, and Henri) formed a new Christian community.[6] In this spirit we made preparations to celebrate Christmas, meeting at various times on Sundays between the two roll calls, at the back of a block room on the third level of a bedstead. Here we commented on passages from Saint Paul, prayed from a little missal which had miraculously survived all previous searches, and planned how to better share packages which up to now had been too quickly emptied out by so many hands interested only in using the contents for themselves.

On the evening of December 21st, as I was going up to work, René Le Tonquèze who was just returning, took me aside to say, "Thank goodness, I've just received the item we've been waiting for from Eugène Jean, one of Ligori's friends[7] who works in our area. He passed this to me in the toilets." This time the container was a blue celluloid box of Gibbs toothpaste. I put the box of hosts in my pocket and kept it with me for three nights, giving it to René to carry about during the days: in this way we could avoid being searched or having it stolen by people in the *Kommando*.

On the evening of the 24th, we alert our group, along with Mr. Thaddeus and his Polish comrades; about twenty people receive Christ in the shower room alongside a pile of corpses. Returning to the block about midnight, Camille, Marcel and our other neighbors squeeze in around the little box placed on my knees. I slowly read the midnight mass. A Protestant, who is aware of what is going on, offers to block the passageway to our row of beds. Shortly before communion a fellow who has not been alerted to what we are doing there says, "Paul,

---

6   Among these were : René Lacan, a POW transferred as a civilian worker, arrested in Nuremberg for "religious and patriotic activities; Jean Chapellier, Jean Duthu, seminarian, and Pierre Chabert, leaders of "*Chantiers de Jeunesse*" who had accompanied STO conscripts to Germany. They were arrested at Brunschwig for patriotic motives and anti-Nazi activities.

7   Ligori Doumayrou, head of the Action Catholique of Zwickau, whom I met at Leipzig on January 30th, 1944.

We need Him to be here with us now." "Just a second, man, and you'll have Him." Overwhelmed and teary-eyed he receives a host. Camille and Marcel also receive. At the other end of the room the drugged *Kapos* shout and scream with Joseph, while our other comrades doze in a feverish and fitful sleep.

At dawn, thanks to Willy, I managed to slip into the infirmary, despite this being strictly forbidden. Philippe, who had been there been there for quite a while, was making his second First Communion (René and Henri had won him over); and my lawyer friend now asked me to get his "case" in order before he was to receive God, the real one, or as he used to say, Henri's and René's.

Outside in the snow-covered court, a lighted pine tree glistened— the heart-wrenching symbol of a joy that many would no longer have, and a tree which would soon revert once again to becoming an object in front of which we would have to endure countless roll calls during the many days and nights that would follow. I wept only once during my entire stay in the camp, and it was on this particular day, shedding tears of joy.

TERRIBLE THINGS HAPPEN

The first days of January prove to be every bit as deadly as the whole month of December. Henri and René are no longer assigned to digging fortifications but will henceforth be working in the factory. Some of our friends are already dying in the *Revier*, which is virtually off limits to us. At least ten deaths occur every day in the *Kommando*, and other convoys come back from Flossenbürg to fill these vacancies: the latest arrivals are tattooed with numerals starting at 42,000.

I receive a few items of news from Thruringia. People there can write to us in German, and Jacques and André are the same faithful but prudent correspondents as ever. For many long weeks now we've had no news from France. How much longer must we wait to hear, and how many things must have occurred there about which we know nothing?

I'm filled with a desire that won't go away and becomes more and more insistent as the days go by—calling to mind these verses by Péguy:

> "When may I sleep after having prayed
> In the calm and faithful house of prayer?
> When shall we see each other again?

And will we see each other again?
O house of my father! O house that I love!..."

Things happening here have caused unspeakable anguish to those living West of the Rhine. Yet if they had only the slightest notion of
what we were really going through here—fortunately such things are
beyond their imagination—they would be in a far worse state.

"... O my Father, O Mama, when they will have told you
That I am in a country of war and turmoil,
Forgive me, both of you, for having left you,
And for your tears and your lingering sufferings....
Forgive me, both of you, and you my brothers...
Take up my place beside our Father
And console our Mama for my unjust departure.
Console our Mama for my unending absence."

Mama, is she still living? What *déporté* has not felt his mother's presence quivering around him, even during his more nightmarish moments? She alone could tell us the secret of how we might free ourselves from thinking so egotistically about our sufferings, because she
was always more familiar with sorrow. I've seen some men weep because they hadn't loved their mothers enough and have just now come
to some understanding of how much they had made them suffer. Be
assured, all you mamas of the men who won't return, that while they
were here, they loved you to the bitter end.

"Oh, how strangely I love the home where I lived
And how strangely love those whom I loved while being there,
Because I know that when we really love, we remain faithful;
My soul knows how to love those who are not here,
My soul knows how to love those who are far away."

They've expressed these same sentiments to us in far more clumsy
words, these poor buggers who at the end of their rope agree to share
with their companions in misery this their last confession, as if it were
some kind of priceless treasure; and for all of us, no matter whether it

be *he who believed in Heaven, and he who did not*—,[8] this would be our final absolution.

Though still holding out, our group has been shaken to the core by a series of horrendous events. Henri Marannes is suffering from a bad case of bronchitis and Jean Duthu is in terrible pain from badly infected wounds in his legs. When he spit up blood he was sent to the *Revier* and is now with Philippe the lawyer, who is still suffering there.

At the end of January our entire *Kommando* had to undergo the disinfection process and be x-rayed. Three weeks later, a list of three hundred *Tubars* was drawn up with Camille's name on it. The *Kommandoführer* then harangued the group, telling them that from this point on, they represented only worthless mouths to be fed and could thus no longer be cared for, given the increasing difficulties in obtaining food supplies; henceforth they would therefore have to follow a regimen that was appropriate to their new situation: no more employment in the factory, half rations of food, housing in a special block whose entrance was forbidden to the other prisoners, a place without heat, with windows always open, and work assignments of useless but deliberately exhausting tasks to be completed every day. And they were to endure all these things while knowing for certain that they would eventually be shipped back to the concentration camp at Flossenbürg.

All of this was too much for me and as a result, my body simply gave out. One evening towards the end of February, I couldn't go to work and dragged myself to the *Revier*. I had already suffered a moral relapse by even showing up there, since it was considered to be the last step before the crematorium. An Italian doctor diagnosed my condition as a form of pneumonia bordering on pleurisy. Seated on a bench I waited for several hours to receive my room assignment. Fortunately for me, I was placed in room 3 where I was able to get treatment. This room was crowded to the rafters with human castoffs sharing several stinking and infected mattresses. Two days later, Camille, who ventured to come by and look through the windows, saw to it that I got a bit of tobacco. Using this for payment, I was able to get my lungs tapped and receive some injections. Then I spent a period of three

8   A reference to a title of Louis Aragon's poem, *La rose et le réséda* ("the Rose and the Reseda") which the poet wrote to honor both believers and non-believers who had fought and worked side by side in the Resistance and in the prison camps.

weeks of living hell fighting for my life, all of which I prefer to pass over without comment.

During this period of deadly trials, the voice of the Apostle was our only refuge; and we shared with one another these words of Paul, contained in the little missal that we miraculously continued to pass around to each other:

> Well now is the real time of favor, know the day of salvation is here. We avoid putting obstacles in anyone's way, so that no blame may attach to our work of service; but in everything we prove ourselves authentic servants of God, by resolute perseverance in times of hardship, difficulties and distress; when we are flogged or sent to prison or mobbed; laboring, sleepless, starving in purity, in knowledge, in patience, in kindness; in the Holy Spirit, in a love free of affectation; in the word of truth and in the power of God; by using the weapons of uprightness for attack and for defense: in times of honor or disgrace, blame or praise, taken for imposters and yet we are genuine; unknown and yet we are acknowledged; dying, and yet we are alive; scourged but not executed; in pain but always full of joy; poor and yet making many people rich; having nothing and yet owning everything. (2 Corinthians 6/1-10)

Philippe was the first to go, with his death occurring shortly after he had received his second First Communion: Christ had come even to our mattresses in the *Revier*. And René and Henri had managed to be "fed" once again by Ligori's Jocists. Those communities for whom we were suffering were now sustaining us in their turn with these crumbs of Divine life. On March 10th, the Sonderhausen community received these few lines, the last words that I wrote while on my mattress and still suffering in the *Revier*: "Been in bed for a week, I'm a little better now but feeling weak and done in. Life is hard, but I'm experiencing the best moments of my life here." It would serve no purpose to give them any more cause for alarm. For once the censors prevented me from telling the whole truth; and from this point on, those of us in the "death camps" would remain completely alone up to the very end.

CAMILLE'S DEPARTURE—HENRI'S DEATH

During the last days of March I left the *Revier* (my place there was taken by Marcel Carrier, who was suffering from whitlow and early signs of scurvy) to return to the factory. René still remained healthy, but it was heartbreaking to hear Henri's fits of coughing. On one of those evenings, after they had been disinfected, taken showers and been given a few pieces of filthy clothing, the *Tubars* were summoned for roll call. Camille would thus have to leave us to go back to Flossenbürg. But none of us wanted to believe this to be true, because we could already guess what would eventually happen.

Camille was able to perform one final act of charity by sharing the last small package which Schreiber had just sent him from Erfurt and from which he kept only very little for his journey. During a final search given them before his column departed, Camille was stripped bare by some greedy *Kapo*; he tried to defend himself, but was then pummeled by the other—and so it ended. The column lurched off raising a wave of dust and cinders in its wake. Camille passed in front of me, and I saw him for the very last time receding among these hideous human wrecks, stoop-shouldered, emaciated, and consumed by suffering. After having professed his faith, he had been sent out to gain his salvation among this mass of humanity. With him were Jean Duthu and Lucien Marié, who knew that everything was consummated.

Easter, coming after a Holy Week spent in grueling work during the night shift, afforded us the shortest possible break. We passed the day spending long periods of time hunched over a tiny map of Germany, trying to locate the areas of battle we had heard about in the factory from various sources such as the *Meisters*, French and Belgian workers, *Kapos* and even SS people. The French medical doctor, who was the camp's most important source for information of this kind, prognosticated that Allied troops would be arriving in two weeks, at the very latest.[9] What remained to be seen was what would happen to us when this would occur. Rumors abounded, each one more horrible and unbelievable than the last.

As I have said, Easter provided only very little time off. Henri Marannes had not been able to finish his observances for Holy Week—his bronchitis had worsened and was now accompanied by a case of dysentery. René took him to the *Revier* and the Italian doctor sent him to Room 3, where he found Marcel, who was now in a less critical state.

---

9   Doctor Berjonneau from Châtelleraut. He subsequently fell out of favor for having too much care for his patients in the *Revier* and was replaced by an Italian who was well known for his under-handed dealings and total lack of concern for the sick.

Wednesday of Easter week, after the morning roll call and during our departure for work, René called to me from a distance saying, "Riton is dead." He phrased this more precisely a second time: "They killed Henri." This turned out to be a terribly long day. When I came back in the evening I heard, through the window of the *Revier*, Marcel's brief account: "Walodia, the Russian *Kapo* in charge of the room, was the one who finished him off last night by beating him with a wooden plank." Henri, who was in a semi-conscious state and totally worn out, had soiled his mattress in a fit of dysentery. This was an unpardonable act, and when attracted by the odor, the enraged Russian performed like the professional killer that his SS masters had trained him to be, in front of all the other exhausted and powerless comrades, who had become accustomed to such unspeakable acts of brutality.

Oh the wretched, the so terribly wretched spectacle of those, who in the days to come, will be called saints! It almost boggles the mind: that the martyr is himself unaware of what he is when he is living out his role. He seems so ignoble. When they see him, the people are deceived by his miserable state, and unaware of his true identity, shake their heads in disdain without understanding the irony of it all. What a great distance lies between the spectacle of a saint's bruised body and his statue, which eventually will be venerated by the masses. In Henri's case, he wasn't even granted the peace and quiet of a tomb, and no one will ever be able to reclaim his body.

CHAPTER TEN

A JOURNEY OF SUFFERING

"My strength is trickling away,
my bones are all disjointed,
my heart has turned to wax,
melting inside me.
My mouth is dry as earthenware,
my tongue sticks to my jaw.
You lay me down in the dust of death.
A pack of dogs surrounds me,
a gang of villains closing in on me
as if to hack off my hands and my feet.
I can count everyone of my bones…"
(Psalm 22/15-18)

A PARAPHRASE FOR OUR TIMES

We've not been working in the factory since Easter: the Reich is in death throes.[1] The SS are clearly intent on keeping us busy. Starting on April 8th, the day and night shifts have been cancelled and are now replaced by two eight-hour work periods. Air raid alerts and bombings, break downs of machinery and erratic modifications of our food rations are occurring every day. We now get only one slice of dark bread in the evenings and a half liter of disgusting soup at noon. Everything seems to be pointing to the end.

The other evening, leaning against the walls of the *Revier* and facing toward the West, I heard a great deal of canon fire. According to the latest rumors, the Americans are now at Gera, Plauen, and perhaps even as far as Werdau. On Friday the 13th, after soup, the men of the second group are waiting for the summons to go to work. The sun

---

1 The American troops had arrived in Thuringia and were now to the East of Mülhausen. Sonderhausen had probably been liberated.

The Death March ... Onset in Zwickau, April 13, 1945. Break-up of the columns on 23 April 1945 in the vicinity of Schönwald, approx. 6 km east of Flossenbürg. Whoever was not able to flee was shot to death.

beats down on the hot cinders. At one o'clock the first group returns earlier than usual. No roll call. The Germans and *Kapos* are abruptly ordered to meet in the *Shreibestube*. They come out of the building wearing white armbands with the logo *Lager-Polizei*. Then the order is given to every prisoner not wearing a striped outfit to find one. We all have to have our heads shaved, leaving a swathe in the middle from the forehead to the nape of our neck. After first lining up on the inspection field, we are ordered to return to the blocks where we are given two blankets. "*Zwei Decken, nicht mehr!*" ("only two blankets, no more"), the *Kapos* shout. Then everyone gets a piece of bread. An air raid alert interrupts these procedures and they order us back to the blocks. While waiting we exchange comments. "Hey, Frenchman, finished. Germany is *kaput*. *Evacuieren*. Today!" the Polish doctor Antek tells me. Everyone is of the same opinion. We're being evacuated, but where to? The road from Zwickau to Flossenbürg by way of Weiden must surely be cut off by now. When the alert was over I managed to sneak into the *Blockmann's* room to save what was left of the flour I had received in my last package. We eat a few spoonfuls while the Russians swarm about us with hostile and gummy looks, trying to make off with some of it. My friends lose their patience and chase them away. "Away, Ruski, Move!" they shout. Chabert, who will accompany Robert Olivier and me, takes care of what's left of the flour and hides it under his shirt. We are fed again about 4 o'clock: a piece of bread and one rutabaga per person. The *Kapos* have organized us in groups according to nationalities, fortunately so, since this should cut down on the number of brawls. In the meantime, the SS have taken care of their personal baggage and food supplies. These are loaded onto a truck and some small carts. Some Russians and *Stubendienste* rush to perform the task. But the people in the *Revier* won't be leaving with us. Marcel Carrier waves to me through the window. I have only enough time to give him back his little missal and shout, "So long, see you in Paris at the JOC [headquarters] or back at home." A *Kapo* swooped down on us, brandishing his bludgeon.

About five o'clock the truck, now loaded down with food supplies, finally starts up and passes through the *Kommando* gate. Then follows a procession of Czechs, Russians, Poles, Frenchmen, Italians, Hungarians, Jews and Spaniards. The *Blockmann* and *Stubendienste* bring up the rear with their little carts and supplies. The column stretches out through the streets of the city between two lines of the

SS, all armed with machine guns. Goaded on by the *Lager-Altester* Alfred, the *Lager Polizei* come and go, shouting threats and beating those who lag behind or move out of line.

We break up into support groups as we proceed along the way. The stronger take care of the weak. Many, totally done in by the long afternoon roll calls, had slumped down on the cinders and have had to be to be propped up and carried forward as we left. Helped by Chabert and Olivier, I took hold of Chapellier who was suffering terribly from diarrhea and a phlegmon on his foot.

These human derelicts beat the pavement with their worn-out wooden clogs. They think that tomorrow they'll no doubt have to walk bare-foot and wonder where they'll sleep tonight. But this pitiful band still does not seem completely aware of the ultimate goal of this diabolical march.

Several times I relieve Chabert and Olivier as the three of us continue to hold up Chapellier: doing this, I have to go up and down the length of the column, despite the oaths and blows directed at me by the *Kapos*. We're now completely exhausted and I ask Willy to give our comrade a place on the truck. "*Verboten!*" he replies, "Walk with." But this soon becomes impossible as we halt when he is overcome with diarrhea. The column advances without us. While we help him to put his clothes back on alongside a ditch, two young SS who have remained behind come over, and one of them quietly asks: "What's the matter with your friend?" I show them his foot. "*So, Fuss kaput! Los!*" ("So his foot's given out, move on"). As we go back up on the road, he points to a field recently leveled by American bombs and says, "*Los Mensch! Weg.*" ("Come this way"). No doubt a short cut to join up with the column, we think. Olivier and I hold Chapellier by the arms and Chabert follows. Chapellier stumbles on every tuft of grass. The SS man swears and shouts out something that I can't understand. We advance to the edge of a bombed out hole. With a thrust of his body the officer shoves us behind him and then pushes Chapellier forward, shooting him twice in the back as he rolls to the bottom of the bomb hole. Chabert, who had understood what was going on before we did, screams out "He's going to kill him, he's killing him! But he's still able to walk." Chabert throws himself into the hole, but the other SS grabs him, pushes him aside, then takes his turn shooting at Chapellier's inert body.

Los! Weiter!—("Get going, straight ahead!") We get back to the road
where the column has just thrown itself into ditches, as American
fighter planes pock mark the soil of the surrounding fields with random machine gun fire. The air raid doesn't last long, and by the time
it ends, the SS have already informed the *Komandoführer* of their execution of Chapellier. Coming over to me, Willy asked: "Where is your
friend?" My silence told the story. Then he asked me if we still had the
dead man's bread. Chabert, who had already hidden it under his shirt,
said nothing. We shared it during the next road stop, remembering
our dead comrade while we consumed it. Our friends learned from
this incident that we now had either to be able to walk or die. Jean
Chapellier was the first and only one to be gunned down on that particular day's march, which went on until late in the night.

A little earlier, a truck and a trailer had passed us by at the bottom
of a hill. They were transporting the sick from the *Revier*. When they
stopped at the top of the hill before an entrance to a woods, the column came to a halt behind them, in the area near Kirchberg.

The SS, with rifles slung over their shoulders, encircle a field of green
wheat where we huddle together for the night. Chabert, Olivier, René
and a few others settle down around me to receive a few spoonfuls of
flour which I distribute on the sly from under our blankets, so as not
to have to confront the thieving and gluttonous Russians. Silence now
falls over this horde stretched out on the ground. We can distinctly
hear the canons, the crackling of machine guns, and the rumbling of
tanks. A battle was being waged in the vicinity to the west of Zwickau.
And here we were, lying supine and at the mercy of a single command
which could transform the area into an enormous open grave, victims
without honor at the very last moments of the war, jail bait whose
names would never grace any war memorial.

THE DEATH MARCH

Dawn, Saturday, April 14th. The "striped" ones painfully get up from
the ground. This is going to be a long session: during the entire day,
we'll have to play hide and seek with the Americans. The mountain
roads that the SS force us to take through the forests of Erzgebirge are
cut up by freshly dug zigzag-trenches guarded by the *Volksturm* and
Hitlerjugend, now that the *Luftwaffe* has been knocked out of the skies.
How long will we have to walk? Many of us already are without bread,
and we won't be given any until Monday, or so they say. Gradually our

column is falling apart: Up front the Czechs set the pace, leaning on each other's elbows. In the middle of the line, people stray in and out like sleep walkers. At the end they're shot down in batches of threes and fours. The first times we heard the volley of gun shots, we would turn around to see if we could believe what we were hearing. But we've long stopped doing this. Now it's all we can do to put one foot in front of the other. We mustn't use up whatever tiny ounce of strength we have left and not even think about what might be happening back there.

In fact, we're no longer even able to think at all; our brains have been cut out. We trot along like rabbits whose skulls are already filled with lead. We no longer have any feelings but live driven by only one instinct, to hold out, to survive at any price by putting one foot ahead of the other until evening falls. After that, we'll see. Now when the men bump up against each other out of fatigue, they no longer yell or curse but simply speak in whispers.

From time to time, one of the *Feldwebel* goes up and down the length of the column. We stiffen when he passes by because he is in the process of selecting other victims in addition to the ones who can no longer help themselves from falling down during the march. Anyone who is staggering a little too much has to step out of the lines; then if he still shakes too much, he is held up by two Russians while an SS man shoots him down alongside the road. This slaughter by selection slows down the progress of the march. Those who die allow the others to catch a second breath, since *their* time has not yet come.

We walk all day. Champing on his customary cigar, the Kommandoführer goes back and forth on his motorcycle always shouting the same words: "*Weiter! Los weiter! Immer weiter!*" ("Forward, faster, keep going, forward").

I've only eaten two slices of bread and I keep what's left against my chest under my shirt, along with the last letters from Zwickau bearing the handwriting of Jacques, André, and Pierre. These tattered scraps of paper, wet with sweat and clinging to my flesh, are the last remnants I have upon which to fasten my desire to live. I no longer have the strength to take out my rosary, and get dizzy when I lift my head high enough to see the crosses displayed on the roadsides.

After 5 o'clock we reach the mountain town of Schönheide. The SS pen us in for the night in a fairground for cattle, where we join up with two convoys of "striped ones"—men from Lengenfeld and women from Plauen. All the better if women are with us, we think: then perhaps we won't have to go so far or at least not walk as fast tomorrow.

The people from the *Revier*—cadavers looking like mummies in their blankets—are with us as well. René and some other friends take Marcel Carrier out of this living graveyard for the night, and under the cover of our blankets, we again share a few spoonfuls of flour. During this procedure, Chabert has his bread stolen from him during a scuffle provoked by the Russians, who had patiently been watching and waiting all around us. Our SS guards take great pleasure in observing the scene, while wolfing down slices of buttered bread. They obviously enjoy the systematic debasement of this frenzied herd of livestock that they're slowly and carefully pushing forward to extermination. One of them, who found Chabert's predicament particularly amusing, comes over to us pretending to want to be informed about what has happened. "I don't know," we all respond. And we draw back out of fear; no doubt he's going to play with his bludgeon. But not at all. He takes the cigarette butt that he's smoking and holds it up before the Russians, now standing stock still; then he throws it and, slightly bent over, his hands resting on his knees, watches with obvious enjoyment the fresh scuffle that breaks out among the group. He roughs up three or four of them and then leaves, roaring with laughter.

Frost has fallen during the night. At dawn we endure another interminable roll call. The *SS Führer* gives a pep talk to the older SS of his group who are not fanatics like their very young counterparts. We have to wait a very long time for those who have died during the night to be counted and stacked in a corner.

"Paul, warm me." I turned around, it's Chabert who has taken sick. I have neither the strength, energy, nor will power to rub his back in any effective way. Olivier and I squeeze him between our chests to give him a bit of warmth. Then taking from under my shirt the bit of bread that I still have left, I offer him a piece. "Eat!"

"You're crazy, I don't want to, I'd be taking your life away."

"Eat!" We had to force him. But not for long. "Eat and see what happens to you if you don't" we said; for at that very moment, the SS were rushing through the fairground, opening fire on all the human forms that were unable to stand up.

The column lurched forward at an accelerated pace on roads that had now become virtually impassable because of damage done to their surface by bombings and combat. This terrible "cleansing" process, repeated every morning, had succeeded in thinning out our ranks even somewhat sooner than planned. By ten o'clock, panic had peaked among those walking toward the rear of the column, and no one wanted to be found in the very last row. Then the firing ceased and we walked all day without anything to eat or drink. About two in the afternoon, I began to gnaw on my last small piece of bread. Chabert, who had resolutely refused my offer to share it with him, went off pretending he was going to the aid of a friend.

About four o'clock the column approaches a hill. "A friend, where can I find a friend to help me?" The man desperately begging for help had found no response from anyone as he came up the line. Now he was face to face with me. So tired that I could drop then and there, I pretend to be deaf. I had so often been called upon for help. This time it's a fellow countryman, Perret, a member of the Resistance and former railroad employee. Turning his feverish and gummy gaze on me, he gasps, "Paul, give me your arm."

"Man, I can't, I'll fall with you!"

"Paul, I've got no one to help me. They'll shoot me!" A crucifying dialogue between two human wrecks both on their last. My weak breathing can barely sustain my lungs as we start to ascend the hill. My arm doesn't move from my side. I barely feel Perret grabbing on to me. Then completely out of breath he mumbles, "Paul, I'm a Christian." He continues in a hoarse voice, "I'm going to say my act of contrition. Have mercy on me, my God, I'm dying for my wife, my kids, France and my friends. In the name of the Father, the Son, and the Holy Ghost. Amen." He slowly makes a big sign of the cross and lowers his hand, which I again feel clutching at my arm that is still sore from having held up others. His fingers cling to the fabric of my sleeve. "O.K. that's better,"

"Now keep going!"

"Paul, give me your arm."

"Keep going, make up your mind, yes or no."

"I can't go any farther."

"If you want to see your kids again, walk like me."

"No, I'm going to die."

"If I give you my arm I'll fall down with you."

"Paul give me your hand, I promise I won't have to be dragged." I take a hand that is soft and moist, as if of a dying man. I squeeze it very hard and it presses back. Later, without being hardly aware, I let go of it. When we ended the day's march that evening, Perret was still among the survivors.

Each time a companion fell to the ground during the march, I engaged in a terrible dialogue with myself: how can we leave the fallen behind as we move on? But it already required more courage than we could muster to continue this solitary march on our own. Also the temptation to end it all became stronger and stronger. Along the entire length of the column there were Russians who had given up. Leaning against the slope, with a funny, almost peaceful kind of look on their faces, they were waiting for the column to pass them by and for that moment when death would set them free. Death was this large glass of cool water that one drinks, even though knowing it is poison, because it slakes the thirst. Could such an act of cowardice be acceptable as an act of charity? I was too ashamed to give in to my suffering in front of my torturers. I would call that suicide. And how about the others living side by side with me? I must not be too quick to break the bond that I share with this wretched herd. What right do I have to put an end to my own sufferings when I feel an obligation to share the afflictions of the others? But what secret resources do I have to draw from to sustain my hunger for life? The man who attempts to surpass himself has to make a pact with the demands of the flesh: he will either give in to them, because the flesh is weak, or continue to resist because he still clings to life. Ultimately, no matter whatever the possibilities may be, the sacrifice of one's will starts in this state of absolute poverty and with this spirit of compromise for the sake of others, which perhaps accounts for the honor it is universally accorded.

We spent the night in Johangeorgenstadt, in a *Kommando* attached to Flossenbürg which had not yet been evacuated. Upon our arrival, Lacan,[2] a companion in the march, shared with us his last piece of bread: we were going to get soup and could savor the luxury of being able to share our food together.

At the morning roll call, some 650 of us (from the original 950) still survive and are preparing to go on. Bread is distributed. The Kommando's assembly field, transformed into a filthy bull pen. Once the Russians have either been satiated or beaten back, we spread out on the ground and enjoy the unfamiliar warmth of the April sun on

---

2   René Lacan was arrested at Nuremberg for his work as director of the Welcome Center and for being a Christian militant. He was sent to Dachau and Leitmeritz before joining us at Flossenbürg and Zwickau.

our famished bodies. In the meantime, a truck takes away the people from the *Revier* and, about an hour later, returns empty. These comings and goings continue unabated, and we interpret them to be a lucky sign telling us that we may not have to walk so far today. In fact we only progressed 16 kilometers on that Monday, April 16th but when we stopped, the truck from the *Revier* stood empty without any sick people to be seen any longer. That very morning, in fact, the officials had determined which of this group could still continue on. Marcel Carrier had been included among those allowed to go on, while the others had been "liberated" at some other location.

The following night was pure hell. The two convoys from Lengenfeld and Zwickau (numbering about 1500 men) were forced to pile together into one unlit room. It was impossible to stretch out and we had to remain standing or squatted down, swayed in all directions by the movement of the others, our bodies stiffened with anklyosis and heads dizzy from fever. Some Russians came in armed with heavy sticks. All night long we had to stave them off to save our bread. Chabert himself almost had stolen from him the supply of flour that we still had left, and he had to throttle the robber to get it back. The 17th of April was a very long day on the road. Willy told us that we had to reach Karlsberg[3] at all cost. We French banded together and the day passed without anyone dying in our midst—and without our exchanging even a word to one another or having anything to eat. When we arrived at Karlsberg, we had to oblique five kilometers further to the left and bed down in a *Kommando* of Russian POWs, who had just been evacuated during the bombing of the Karlsbad railroad station by the Americans.

Stuffed pell mell into the granary of this ugly barracks, 500 "pyjamas" wallow in their own excrement and the entrails of cattle slaughtered there the day before. The Russians and some others have already taken possession of the bunks. We have to be content with the filthy floor. Marcel, René, Olivier, Lacan and Chabert doze off side by side after having eaten the last spoonfuls of flour.

I was swarming with lice—I felt them running all over my body—but was content to be seated against a corner of the wall which wasn't too moldy or filthy. I still had had nothing to eat but it was rumored that we'd be given some potatoes tomorrow. I savored the simple joy of taking off my shoes after days on the road. The wooden soles of

3   Today Karlovy-Vary in the valley of the Eger.

my shoes, completely worn down, had caused large sores on my heels. Now I could put my feet up in the air without the risk of having my shoes stolen by my neighbors—what a luxury! Down below the SS and the *Kapos* were banqueting on roast pork and fried potatoes. Outside American planes were spitting death.

But I was still living—indeed very feebly—but alive, though detached from everything, and unable to get anything for myself, not even water. I could feel the beating of my heart—that song of the strange and singular life I had been living in a place where death was everywhere present. I now knew full well that I was still clinging to life because the Father personally willed it. That I was still alive seemed in itself to be rather incredible, given my lack of importance as well as the fact that death was closing in on us from all sides. What a tremendous gift to be allowed to live as a human being, even if barely recognizable as such, in this decaying and disgusting carcass that I now inhabited. Yet during the worst period of suffering, there comes a moment of angelic-like lucidity leading the spirit to consent to break away from the foul, sweating hold that the animal part of our nature exerts over us.

All of the following day was spent in this disgusting granary where we had to fight for water and a few potatoes which we then had to swallow whole and unpeeled before they could be stolen. We also hid some of them in our pants for food the next day.

On the 19th, we completed a 35-kilometer march along the way to Petschau (Becov) under a very hot sun. Chabert and I went to the back of the column to be near those being gunned down. At each stop, the SS and the *Kapos* gulp down *Schweinbrot* ("pork bread") under our noses, and the *Kommandoführer* throws pieces of bread to his little dog who yaps with glee. That evening, camped out on the grassy field of an abandoned stadium, we decide to respect each other's privacy as much as we can. So we retire to our own space to gnaw on raw potatoes before going to sleep. The next day, April 20th, we do another 25 kilometers and bivouac near Marienbad, in some damp fields behind a railroad embankment. Those in the best shape crawl about on their knees to graze on dandelions. Lacan, Chabert, Olivier and I still have enough strength to pick them as a team, and we stuff our stomachs with all these greens.

We had been walking for a week and had gone about two hundred kilometers. The column was now reduced to half its original size; every night we heard the muffled rumblings of Allied tanks. Tomorrow we'll have to keep going, falling into the trenches every time American fighter planes strafe the column, while at the same time having to avoid being shot down by the SS. This evening we're forced to attend the execution of some men who had volunteered to do kitchen duty for the SS and then tried to make away with bread from the supply wagons! Afterwards, we must once again spend the night on the soaking ground, squashed down in the mud because they shoot at any one who gets up; then we'll go on, leaving behind those poor buggers whose only burial shroud will be the snow freshly fallen during the night.

They still persist in giving us a crust of bread and a piece ... of soap! Why feed us anymore? What interest do they have in trailing this band of dying men while they themselves are being hounded by death? With one flick of the finger they could make us all collapse like puppets miming a massacre. But this they don't want to do. Much better to make us wait, to let our bodies decompose and our minds melt like wax under their gaze. For that's their entire aim—to be able to prowl around us till the very end, to count our bones, and to relish the extinction of every human trait that we may still possess. Time itself now becomes the bone of contention—the time during which the executioner confronts his victim, the former needing it to refine his taste for torture, the latter wishing to prolong it in the hope of deliverance. Which side will it favor? For which of the two will it prove more advantageous? Which of the two will end up being the stronger?

A miserable-looking fellow devastates me with the comment, "Paul you look at the end of your rope." So at last I resemble them and now have their pasty green color of meat that is going bad. Since I'm being told that these "end-of-the-rope" symptoms that I've noticed about others now can be applied to me, I probably won't last much longer. When you see others falling down around you while you can still stand, you feel privileged and develop a false sense of security.

I'm now suddenly seized with an absurd idea come to tempt me. Why not end it all in one grandiose action. Dropping out of the column, I would attempt to escape, then falling to the ground with my arms extended in a form of the cross—I even had prepared my words—I would say, "I am dying for Christ, France, and the working class." I don't know what held me back. It's possible that Olivier, who was silently walking at my side, might have spoken some trivial words out of the blue. In any case, what is the need for such an extravagant performance? After all, we're not on stage here! Lord, forgive me, You didn't engage in such theatrics when they crucified you at 3 o'clock in the afternoon. You were the one who never abandoned your group, Who died wracked with pain, naked as a worm, ludicrous, and at the very end exclaiming with marvelous lucidity, "Everything is consummated."

Up to the bitter end, the words that I guarded most deeply in my heart were those of the psalmist: "As for me, I am a worm, no longer a man..." (Ps. 12/7). Since *He* also experienced all of this, we can expect nothing worse. When one arrives at this stage of degradation, it may not be a sin of pride to compare oneself with Jesus Christ.

LIBERATION: MONDAY, APRIL 23RD, 1945

We continue on the road until Sunday evening, April 22nd and proceed through Marienbad, Kuttenplan, Plan, and Tachau, in short but back-breaking stages under very windy and rainy conditions.[4] The wind pressed down on the asphalt gliding over those emaciated figures desperately clinging to each other. Perret must have died during one of these last days. I could see him in his very weak condition only from a distance.

There are now only about 350 of us, soaked, foul-smelling and stinking like the exhausted dogs we see lying on damp straw in a barn located in the town of Schönwald, which they say is about 15 kilometers from Flossenbürg by way of the forest. Rumors, some of them sounding rather credible, abound on all sides: There's no food left, not even for the SS. We'll be shot here and now. By order of Himmler, we're to be incinerated by flame throwers upon our arrival. American troops have surrounded Flossenbürg.

The next morning the SS have not come to get us up. Olivier, Lacan and others are battling it out with the Russians, who now are trying to steal their shoes. Rain is trickling into the barn through the broken tiles. Rolled up in my blanket, I can hardly hear what Zeff, a former anti-Nazi journalist from Austria, is telling me: "Paul, *Kommandoführer* said, 'Liberation—! War finished.'"

Some kind of crazy hope takes hold of us, as if we're in a dream. When Chabert, sunk down on the ground next to me, hears this, he articulates sounds that I can hear through my blanket despite my weariness: "If only it were true!" We weep tears of joy and exhaustion.

---

4   Today, Marianske-Làzné, Chodova-Planà, Tachov, Lesna.

The news spread through the barn. Various groups coalesce around men who still are strong enough to sit upright. We hear more and more comments mechanically being repeated around us: "It's impossible!! An armistice has been announced!"—"Why do you say that? The Red Cross isn't here!" For us the Red Cross is the sign of the Resurrection, and with its absence everything remains in doubt.

"*Los!—Alles weg! Antreten zu fünf!* ("Everyone out! Form lines of five"). So we all stand in the courtyard and are regrouped according to nationalities. The Czechs must know something because there's a great deal of chatter in their corner. The *Kommandoführer* chews on on his cigar. We leave the dying behind, and as the column moves towards the forest, we hear a fresh outbreak of rifle fire at the back of the lines.

Now totally done in, Chabert, on whom so many had hung for support before they were shot down, begs me, weeping, to leave him behind. I resist. Using the last of his strength, he weakly pushes me away. I leave him without looking back.[5] Lacan has also suddenly disappeared from my side.[6] Now standing alone between the two groups, I feel what little strength I still have ebbing away as I proceed along the forest road. I think that I should get back with René or Marcel Carrier who must be walking up at the head of the lines. Barefoot, I continue on my swollen and bruised feet, feeling as if I'm passing through an ocean of glue which sticks to me up to my waist. With a slight shrug of the shoulders, I let my blanket fall behind me because it is now much too heavy to carry.

René has come back and we link arms. We've decided to be shot down together when our time comes, when everything has been consummated and events have taken their course. More resilient than I, René turns several times to look back and thinks that he sees "striped ones" moving in a separate group into the woods to the right. They are probably the Czechs. Suddenly an order is transmitted by the *Kapos* along the length of the lines: "*Alles die Hungaren heraus!*" ("All Hungarians step out"). Then a volley of machine gun fire—they were Jews. René and I manage to catch up with the Russians who have

---

5   After having been spared from extermination and abandoned by the SS in a delirious and totally exhausted condition, Pierre Chabert never left behind the slightest clues to indicate that he might have survived. (Testimony of R. Olivier)

6   René Lacan was in touch soon afterward. Spared by Alfred, he was taken in hand by French POWs at Schönwald.

remained at the head of the column, just to the rear of the SS wagon. At the back of the line they're now probably shooting stragglers and anyone else bringing up the rear. "Priest, what are you doing there with the Russians! Idiot, come over here!" I turn around and see Alfred, the *Lagerältester*, revolver in hand, beckoning me to join him. "Over here with the French, you moron!" We both catch up with Doctor Berjonneau's small group which is advancing behind him, surrounded by the SS. They're still shooting at the back of the line.

"What's going on?" Looking completely spent, the doctor responds with a vague gesture, saying, "Wait for the signal."

Meanwhile we proceed through a ditch, then stumble on for three meters more into a grove of tall heather, all the while expecting to feel something striking us at the nape of the neck or the spine. But nothing happened. Have the SS been shooting? The column has passed on. After some time we hear sustained rifle fire. It must be for the Russians near the wagon, and perhaps the people around Marcel Carrier. The manhunt in the forest continued for sometime, then everything became silent. It was now around 4 o'clock in the afternoon.

Lord, you had engraved our names on the palm of your hands.

René was the first to get up to say the Jocist prayer. Then limping along we went from farm to farm with a bit of bread in hand, because there was no place for us in any of the houses. We continued on until dusk and then spent the night sleeping on the straw floor of some hovel, together with some Poles who had also been liberated.[7]

✳✳✳

Tuesday, April 24th—In the early morning René and I leave the site where we have spent our first night as free men. When we prowl around the village church, the priest doesn't dare to put us up but gives us shoes. An old woman beckons to us from her window and, after having made us a large bowl of *café au lait* with bread soaked in it, she shows us the road to Tachau. A little farther along, a young woman

---

7   It is difficult to estimate the number of survivors of the Zwickau Kommando: 120, 150 perhaps. A monument has since been erected at Tachov to the memory of the victims of this last episode. The remains of most of them—229—have been buried together in a common grave under this monument thanks to the efforts of the Czechs, who now inhabit this region of the Sudetan.

taking care of her child in her home is frightened when we come into view; but she still gives us directions. In Tachau a few hours later, POWs, fellows from France, embrace us and then we are deloused and given a good bath. It's about time!

René becomes sick at his first contact with water. As for me, I can hardly hold myself up on my four paws over the bucket that we are using for our ablutions.

Friday, April 27th—Feast of St. Peter Canisius, Jesuit. Propped up by a POW, I manage to attend mass and receive communion in the church at Tachau.

May 2nd—That evening, after three hours of light bombing and military maneuvers, elements of the American army under the command of General Patton enter Tachau.

A French officer in an American military uniform comes to the POW shelter where we have taken refuge and we are officially liberated. It is now 10 p.m. The officer proceeds to collect our mail that we want to have sent to France. A letter I'm writing to my mother, dated the 3rd of May, will arrive at Lyons on the 10th, the feast of the Ascension.

Tuesday, May 8th—Armistice day. The Americans and Russians meet up on May 10th in the heart of Bohemia.

A few days later I go to get René Le Tonquèze at the hospital to which he had been taken. French military trucks are transporting French refugees to the neighboring city of Pilzen. The 16th, 17th, 18th of May—Days of joy and communal celebration by the Czech people at their new-found freedom. Then, still in military vehicles, we traverse a country whose roads are completely torn up and whose cities lie in ruins. We travel from Pilzen to Würzburg by way of Nüremberg in one single day.

Sunday, May 20th—feast of Pentecost. Five o'clock in the evening. I pencil these few lines:

> … In one of Hitler's barracks, which is now used to repatriate the French, on the day before we're to be transported in groups of 40 in the "8 horsepowers," I eagerly await my soul's return to life—and that of my entire being as well—after all these fierce and silent battles which I have had to undergo to remain alive. How passionately have I grown to love mankind since coming to Germany! Lord, you have known the times when I was at my lowest and will know the moment when I shall be able to raise myself up again! Only

one word can truthfully sum up the long period of wanderings that I have endured out of obedience and love for the greater glory of God, and that is, *Credo*, I believe.

May 23rd—Crossing the Rhine. May 24th, a Welcome Center in a Lorraine railroad station. Before we leave, a young mom hoists her little blond daughter up to the railway carriage to serve us. Handing me a bottle of wine, the little girl softly asks: "Mister, did those Germans hurt you very much?"

Friday May 25th—Paris. Gare de l'Est. Hotel Lutetia, the national welcoming center for returning deportés—where some of us once again find our own people and where we have our first contacts with the families of our brothers in misfortune and honor, who have not come back.

CHAPTER ELEVEN

WITNESSES FOR CHRIST

The following were condemned and put to death for following
Jesus Christ and for having come to the aid of their brothers:

THURINGIA

▶ Roger Vallée—Seminarian from the Diocese of Sées (Mortagne).
Deported to Flossenbürg, died at Mauthausen on October
30, 1944.

▶ André Vallée—Federal Jocist from Orne. Group Director at Gotha.
Deported to Flossenbürg, died at Leitmeritz on February 15,
1945.

▶ Jean Tinturier—Seminarian from the Diocese of Bourges (Vierzon),
Director at Schmalkalden. Deported to Flossenbürg, died at
Mauthausen, March 16, 1945.

▶ Marcel Callo—Federal Jocist from Rennes, Director at Zella-
Melhis. Deported to Flossenbürg, died at Mauthausen,
March 19, 1945.

▶ Henri Marannes—Federal Jocist from Paris-West, Director at
Gera. Deported to Flossenbürg, died at Zwickau, April 4,
1945.

▶ Camille Millet—Director of the Ivry-Centre section of the
JOC, Director at Erfurt. Deported to Flossenbürg, then to
Zwickau, died at Flossenbürg on April 15th, 1945.

▶ Louis Pourtois—Federal Jocist from Besançon, Director at
Eisenach. Deported to Flossenbürg, died at Mauthausen on
April 21, 1945.

▶ Marcel Carrier—Jocist Director from Paris-North, Regional
Director at Weimar. Deported to Flossenbürg-Zwickau, died
on May 6, 1945 at Neustadt-on-Tachau.

ROGER VALLÉE

Regarding the person whose identity you've asked me to recall, let me say that I've forgotten none of the details concerning Father Roger Vallée, who died on Octoer 30th, 1944 in the Mauthausen *Revier*. He had been sent here with another young priest who had also been arrested for having taken part in Catholic Action. The latter, whose brother was a Jesuit, was subsequently sent to a work *Kommando*.[1] Father Vallée had unfortunately become very sick and was thought to be suffering from infectious rhumatism. Doctor Peissel from Lyons, a very committed Christian and a skilled medical practitioner, was determined to try to save him; he managed to obtain sulfa drugs and thought for a brief period that the priest might recover. His heart gave out, however. All of this happened very quickly, in the course of only a few days.

As soon as I was aware that Roger Vallée was staying in block two of the *Revier*, I went to see him and heard his confession, which, by the way, he made very lucidly. I asked him to offer up his sufferings for his loved ones, his diocese, and for France. He did so with all his heart. I recall his having reproached himself for not praying often enough because he felt he didn't have the strength. I explained to him that the sufferings which he was enduring were the purest forms of prayer. The idea of dying before he had been ordained a priest was especially difficult for him to accept, and he worried a great deal about the pain that his family would have to bear. But he accepted all of this. The very last time that I saw him, he was in a very bad way, but he made me understand, by communicating with his eyes and giving me a broad smile, that he had resigned himself to everything. For quite a long time he pressed his lips to the crucifix I had hanging around my neck. He had a French friend at his side who was totally devoted to his care. He asked me to get him an aluminum bottle so that he would have something to drink during the night. I managed to do this and also got him some sugared tea, which I requested from one of the Poles working the kitchen. While he was drinking this and propped up by his friends, his heart abruptly gave out. His was not a painful death but more like the end of a lingering period of suffering which he accepted with Christian resignation; and he enjoyed the consolation of having a priest at his side to say the prayers for the dying and give absolution, which he

---

1   This is a reference to Jean Tinturier who left Mauthausen for the Kommando at Schwientschlowitz, near Oppein in Upper Silesia. His Jesuit brother, Jacques Tinturier, was a member of the Neumühle group at Wittenberg.

received while being held up in the arms of an attentive friend. Such were Roger Vallée's final moments. How I would like to be able to give equally precise and consoling details, as I have in his case, to so many other parents who often write me to request the details describing the final moments of their own children, at whose deaths I was unfortunately not able to be present. Immediately after he passed away, someone came to get me and I recited final prayers over his body; then back in my block, I said the prayers of the Requiem Mass for him. The following Sunday, during our block meeting, all of his comrades offered up their prayers for his intentions. Alas, we weren't able to have Mass or receive communion.

Given the motivation and circumstances for his arrest and deportation to Mauthausen, Roger Vallée died as a martyr for his faith and for Catholic Action, along with how many others!

- (Testimony of Father Michel Riquet, S.J., deported to Mauthausen, then to Dachau.) (Letter to Bishop Mercier, Vicar General of Sées.)

ANDRÉ VALLÉE

What became of him in the course of those harsh winter months after he had left his brother Roger and the entire team from Flossenbürg, in October of 1944, for the *Kommando* at Leitmeritz, in the Sudetan? He suffered and patiently bore the terrible mental and physical decline brought upon him by his life as a convict in a work prison, where he died alone with Christ. At the end of July (1945) a list sent to French officials of those who had died at Flossenbürg contained André's name and gave the date of his demise as February 15, 1945.

JEAN TINTURIER

Jean left Mauthausen for the *Kommando* at Schwientschlowitz, near Oppeln, a branch of Auschwitz, and spent the winter in the factory of this *Kommando* transporting pieces of metallic scrap in the haulage. January 23, 1945, on the only road still under German control, the "striped pyjamas," harnessed to sledges in the frigid cold and deep snow and escorted by SS soldiers armed with machine guns, were forced to evacuate in the face of the advancing Russian army. (According to the testimony of Jean Wis and René Chaumel, both Jocist STO workers at Schwientschlowitz.)

I met Jean Tinturier at the beginning of March, 1945 in what at Mauthausen was officially labeled the infirmary but what I call the slaughterhouse. Jean had been sent there for several days because of exhaustion and other maladies afflicting people living in these wretched places. From the day that I got to know this brave and courageous young man, I became more and more attracted to him because of his gentle gaze and constant words of comfort which endeared him to everyone. As soon it was possible, I came to the side of his pallet, and for that moment at least, we both were able to stop thinking about our sufferings. In the evenings we would pray together. He had fashioned a little rosary out of a piece of small board which he would often use to tell his beads. On certain days, I was able to pass on to him some of the soup that I had received for doing extra work. But he never wanted to take any, though from time to time I was able to persuade him to take some. About the 10th of May, I noticed a sudden change come over him—his face was drawn and he had become much weaker. I helped him to walk to the bandaging room. A few days later, on the 15th, at 7:30, his bedmate came to call me to his side. When I went back to where Jean was lying, I no longer recognized him as the person I had known, but rather someone else at death's door. I rushed to call Doctor Lapierre in Block 5, and he came immediately. After having examined him, he told me that Jean had a case of galloping meningitis. We sent for a priest; one came but was only able to say the prayers for the dying. We were very distressed at the sight of his poor lifeless body. God took him immediately away to be with Him, because Jean was a saint. A short time after his death, his body was placed at the end of the block where it would be thrown onto the pile of cadavers waiting to be incinerated.

(Testimony of Mr. Lundy from Aussonne,
a nurse at Mathausen, letter of Nov. 22, 1945.
)

MARCEL CALLO

When Marcel entered the infirmary in the Mauthausen Concentration Camp at the beginning of March, 1945, his strength was already greatly diminished by dysentery. Placed on the third level of a bedstead, he lay there completely naked and unattended for two days. At the end of this time, a Frenchman, Lieutenant Thibo from Rennes, happened to pass by. He tried to care for Marcel as best he could, providing him with pieces of oak bark to stem the dysentery; but Marcel expired without saying a word on March 19th at two o'clock in the morning, in a state of complete exhaustion without the presence of a priest.

Three days after the death of his sister, who died in a bomb attack, Marcel had left his mother as an STO conscript for Germany, telling her: "I'm not leaving as a worker, but as a missionary."
(Testimony of his brother, Jean Callo)

HENRI MARANNES

… Let's leave to the Divine Master what Henri must have experienced in the most secret depths of his soul. I got to appreciate him during the whole time we were working together at Gera. He loved his brothers from the working classes and wanted to win them over to Christ. He went out to meet the men wherever they could be found.

Several days before his arrest, knowing full well what awaited him, he had already completely accepted God's will. The goal that he sought for his spiritual life at this time was: "To be a redeemer like Christ; to offer oneself up for others as He had done."

(According to the testimony of Yves Rabourdin, clandestine priest and Chaplain at Gera)

CAMILLE MILLET

When we left the Kommando at Zwickau at the end of March, we were taken to the station and put into abominably packed train wagons. We traveled until noon the following day without having anything to eat. When they began to distribute bread, there wasn't enough for more than half of us: the Poles had swiped much of it. And you even risked being killed when you went up to get some from the person distributing it. There were even people who would stab you with their knives.

We remained holed up for the entire day in the rail cars. Many people died. Finally, we who were the most sick were piled together like packages into a truck and taken away to the Flossenbürg Concentration Camp. After making us take showers, they brought us to Block 17. At the end of a five-hour-wait out of doors, we got some soup while having to fend off bludgeon blows from all sides. The following day we were brought to Block 16, which housed the *Tubars*.

The four of us, Camille, Jean Duthu, another person, and myself, were placed in the same bedstead. It was at this point that poor

Camille began his death agony; and he suffered tremendously without uttering a word of complaint, saying only that God too had
suffered. Camille was afflicted with a very bad case of dysentery and
his body was covered with abscesses. It's impossible to relate how
many terrible things he had to endure! I was in somewhat better
shape and took care of the others, but every day I saw them growing more and more weak. One Saturday, as I was shaving the sick,
Camille called me over to ask if I would go with him: he had to
have an abscess opened but didn't have the strength to get there by
himself. They performed this procedure as if they were cutting up
a pig. Camille made no complaint, poor fellow, but kept clutching
my arm! The next day, Annette,[2] who worked in the *Revier*, came to
announce that, "The Americans are at Floss."[3] You can imagine how
happy we were! Camille said to me: "You know, old buddy, soon
we'll be taken care of in France.

The following day I was given an additional ration of the soup
specially prepared for the Germans as payment for some extra work
that I had done. I gave some to Camille, who insisted that I keep
it all for myself. As I was talking to him, his face went blank and
he seemed to be falling asleep. I tried to talk to him but he didn't
respond. I bent over and saw that he was dying. Then I heard the
very last words that he would ever speak: "I'm ready to do anything
for my God."

This is how Camille died…

(Testimony of a comrade who survived Zwickau and
Flossenbürg: Lucien Marié)[4]

LOUIS POURTOIS

… Your son, Louis Pourtois, died in the infirmary of the Mauthausen
concentration camp on April 20, 1945, at about 7 o'clock in the evening. He succumbed because of extreme exhaustion and depression
caused by lack of food, sleep, and rest. Just imagine that we were

---

2   Chief of the *Chantiers de la Jeunesse*, friend of Jean Chapellier, Pierre
     Chabert, and Jean Duthu. He died of exhaustion at the Flossenbürg infir-
     mary a few days after the camp had been liberated by the Americans.

3   Floss, located 13 kilometers from Flossenbürg, would be liberated on
     April 23rd.

4   This letter was addressed to us on the 18th of January, 1946. The text has
     been modified to include changes in spelling and style.

sleeping five to a bed measuring two meters in length and 0 meters 70 in width. We were literally being eaten alive by vermin and for our daily regimen received only a half liter of soup and two spoonfuls of liquid consisting of moldy flour in water. Some twenty or so of us shared 1500 grams of German ration bread. We were forbidden to go out to get anything to drink. Men were dying of hunger and thirst. Out of 1200 people, the normal population of a block, there were on average eighty to a hundred deaths every day, and not infrequently the number rose even higher. Louis did not die a painful death. I had been talking with him several minutes before and was stupefied to learn from a friend who had just come to look for me that he had died. During his last moments he was not in pain, his morale was high, and to the very end he held fast to his faith and maintained confidence in his country. Yours truly ... (Excerpt from a letter sent, on August 2, 1945, to Louis's family by Philip Freyre, a member of the Resistance deported to Mauthausen.)

What impressed me most about Louis was how his mind was so profoundly attuned to the supernatural. If he became as actively involved as indeed he was, this was not out of a strong preference for action—he was by nature somewhat timid and reserved—but rather stemmed from his love of Christ and a burning desire to lead his comrades to Him. This was all the more meritorious when one considers that he was physically not very strong and, from the very start, suffered tremendous fatigue from doing all kinds of work for which he was totally unaccustomed.

(Testimony of Father Dubois-Matra, S.J.,
Chaplain at Eisenach.)

MARCEL CARRIER

... Around the 23rd of April, when you lost track of him, Marcel and a comrade both went to Neustadt-am-Tachau and were taken in by the French POWs from the *Kommando* located there. The person from whom I received this information was also the same one who had taken care of both of them while they were there. But they had become completely done in as a result of the death march and dysentery from which they were both suffering. Marcel, however, had escaped being wounded by rifle fire (during the executions carried out during the death march). His friend died on May 5th and Marcel on the 6th. Two days before this, Marcel had announced that he was going to die and had requested a priest. He received the Last Sacraments and expired without saying a word. All my life I shall

regret not having been at his side during his last moments. Had
you been with him, he undoubtedly would have entrusted you with
messages that he would have wanted you to pass on to me. Because
I am sure that thoughts about me and our two daughters were uppermost in his mind during the period immediately preceding his
death. I would so very much like to see him again and my deepest
hope is to be able to rejoin him soon.

(Testimony of Mme. Marcel Carrier,
Paris, Saint-Ouen—Letter of August 1, 1946)

SAXONY[5]

The Halle Region

Several thousand French people lived in STO camps and worked in
factories in this area: about a thousand were in the camp connected
with Siebel Aviation which manufactured Junkers 88 air planes; farther South, there was labor camp supplying workers for several less
important factories; then there was another camp—whose hundred
or so inhabitants worked privately for a number of workshops scattered throughout the city of Halle. Jean Laroche from Nancy, who
perished in a bomb attack, was the Jocist Director of the Southern region; Marcel Regnault, from Belfort, was the Director for those working in the private sector; and Auguste Eveno was Director for Siebel
and the adjoining plants.

In the neighboring vicinity, at Schkopau about 15 kilometers distant, a camp has been organized to regroup workers from the Buna
synthetic rubber plant where the militants Joseph de Filippis, Jocist
from Lyons, and Father Pascal Vergez, from Lourdes, a POW
Chaplain transferred as civilian worker, and a number of others have
been very actively involved.

Some distance away at Merseburg, Colbert Lebeau from Poitiers is
the Director of the camp at Mülchen, to which workers from a factory
for synthetic gas have been relocated. Farther to the West, at Eisleben
where small factories for precision instruments have been set up,
André Parsy is the director of activities from Roubaix.

---

5   These testimonies were edited by Auguste Eveno, Julien van de Wiele,
and Roger Martins in October, 1988 for the new edition of *Mission en
Thuringe* ... with the intention of providing the reader with additional information regarding this region of Saxony.

One day when we asked the pastor of the church of Saint Elisabeth at Halle if he could lend us a room where a few of our men could meet, he said, "No, because Gestapo headquarters are located nearby and we're already being watched. But two of our priests who speak French are at your disposal for confessions. Also, for the major feasts, I'll repeat my sermon in French (which he did). Be careful. There are only five of us priests for 250,000 inhabitants, and they only put up with us because we've been taking care of the hospitals."

The priest in Ammendorf, ten kilometers distant from Halle and thus under less surveillance, provides a room and sometimes says special Masses for the French. They've all been wonderfully helpful.

When we arrived in December of 1942, we proceeded to meet up with several leaders. Each one is to take responsibility for a district. Clément Cotte, who first crisscrossed Thuringia and Saxony, helps us to organize our activities. Paul Léon, from Bitterfeld, serves as a liaison. A first regional meeting has been held at Leipzig, in the Dominican Convent of Wahren, on July 18, 1943.

My arrest at Halle—On September 6th, 1944, at two in the afternoon, a policeman comes to get me at the factory and takes me back to the camp to get my papers. Fortunately, a friend was in my dormitory at the time. Now completely certain that the policeman doesn't understand French, I slip some compromising documents that I want to have burned under my bedstead. The officer then takes me to Gestapo headquarters. When I am received there by Inspector Schade, he says to me: "So you're Eveno? You're the Jocist leader for Halle and receive your orders from Cardinal Suhard." Schade shows me a list of the names of several militants from the city. I'm now sure that we've been arrested because of our involvement in Catholic Action.

Initially I am the only occupant of my cell; then a Russian is placed there with me and stays until October 1st. Starting on the 6th I undergo several interrogations: one on the 6th, lasting for one hour, on the 8th, for four hours, and on the 24th, for only 10 minutes. On October 1st I change cells and find myself in one with Paul Léon, the lone Frenchman among some ten or so Russians. The oldest of them tells us: "This is the cell for people who have been condemned to death. Twelve of our comrades were hung last week." In a very depressed condition and feeling totally isolated from everyone, Paul and I say our prayers together before going to sleep. And what a man he was! At dawn I asked him, "Paul, what are you thinking about?" And he asked me the same question. For my part I had been reflecting upon what Cardijn had said on July 18, 1937 at the Tenth Anniversary Conference of the JOC at Paris.... "We'll need martyrs. You shall be martyrs." We were ready, but had not up to now had the opportunity to accept this honor.

On the 12th, the SS interpreter comes to get me. On the way from prison to Gestapo Headquarters, he keeps interrogating me. I guessed that he had checked out our cell assignments beforehand. "Do you know Léon?" he asks me. "I noticed that you were both sharing the same cell. That is strictly forbidden. How long have you been there with him?" "A few days." Upon his arrival at the office, the interpreter informs Schade of our cell assignment. This old thug, who was said to be very fearful of young Christians, had at his disposal a virtual arsenal of SS people who could annihilate them at any given moment.

Enraged by this information, Schade telephones the prison, and receiving no response to his first call, breaks the telephone stand when hanging up. When he calls a second time, he lashes out at the prison superintendent. At the end of my interrogation, which will last three hours, I am taken to another cell and would not see Paul Léon again.

On November 20th, we were sentenced to the *Arbeitslager* at Zöschen.

The Zoschön Camp

This disciplinary camp had replaced the one at Spergau, which, though destroyed during a bombing in 1944, still evoked fearful memories among the STO conscripts living in the area. Sentences meted out to those condemned to go there ranged from 4, 8, 12, and 16 weeks, though most prisoners died before being able to complete the longer periods of incarceration. Seven of us arrive in the same convoy at the camp on November 21st—where we meet Eugène Lemoine who arrived on the 16th, along with André Parsy, Julien Van de Wiele, Auguste Eveno, Louis Doumain, Roger Martins, Pascal Vergez and Colbert Lebeau; we are tattooed with the numbers 1195 to 1201.

Arriving in a driving rain storm under the escort of several SS guards, we find everything in darkness except for the central area of the camp. Here ten or more convicts in prison garb stand at attention while being bludgeoned by some "Kolifactors" (Kapos) who give no sign of letting up. The living conditions are virtually inhuman. There are thirty-two prisoners in each one of the bungalows—identical round wooden barracks measuring five meters in diameter. Water drips through the roof. We have neither heat nor blankets; and there are two to five of us on each mattress. The kinds of work performed by this *Kommando* are extremely taxing, especially the job of removing non-exploded bombs that have fallen on or around the factories in the area. The food is revolting, though we get slightly more of it than we did in prison. Theft is rampant among the prisoners. By the end of two weeks, all of us have fallen sick except Eveno, who still is managing to hold up rather well. In the infirmary, for no matter what ails them, the sick can expect to receive nothing more than one aspirin tablet per day. Ninety per cent of those in camp suffer from dysentery. It's in this kind of world that we witnessed the deaths of Pascal Vergez and Louis Doumain.

PASCAL VERGEZ—Priest from the Diocese of Lourdes, former POW, status changed to that of civilian worker, Chaplain at Schkopau. Arrested on September 12th and incarcerated in the prison at Halle, he died in the camp at Zöschen on the 19th of December, 1944.

LOUIS DOUMAIN—Priest from the Diocese of Viviers, STO Chaplain at Bitterfeld, arrested on the 19th of September. Incarcerated in the Halle Prison, he died in the camp at Zöschen on the 20th of December, 1944.

ANDRÉ PARSY—Federal Jocist Director from Roubaix. Director of Eisleben. Arrested and incarcerated in the prison at Halle on October 4th, he died in the hospital at Trebitz on the 26th of December, 1944, as a result of living conditions at Zöschen.

COLBERT LEBEAU—Federal Jocist Director from Poitiers. Director at Merseburg (the camp at Mülchen), he was arrested on September 13th. Incarcerated in the prison at Halle, he died in the infirmary at Zöschen on January 3rd, 1945.

EUGÈNE LEMOINE—Federal Jocist Director from Saint-Brieuc, Director at Wittenberg (the camp at Schleicher). Arrested on the 30th of September, released and then arrested and incarcerated in the prison at Halle, he died in the infirmary at Zöschen on February 8th, 1945.

COLBERT LEBEAU

As soon as he arrives in Germany in 1943, he seeks out comrades engaged in activities for Catholic Action. His own involvements takes shape very soon after the Halle—Merseberg federation is created. He organizes federal committees and arranges days for recollection and study groups. Scrupulously planned well in advance, these events take place in the true spirit of Jocist fraternity, that brand of brotherhood among conscripts—the sublime apostleship experienced by Jocists in Germany by which all are united in Christ. Colbert is always the one who takes charge of these activities. Whenever he speaks to his comrades, they become deeply moved by what he says. His great joy, the joy of the apostle seasoned by prayer and meditation, the joy he takes in accepting sacrifices that may include dangers not always foreseen but enthusiastically accepted beforehand, has profoundly affected everyone.

When he is arrested on September 13, 1944, he is already suffering from chronic rheumatism. Then began his way of the cross. He was taken to the prison at Halle, where he had to stay more than two months while awaiting his sentence. Assigned to extremely hard work, given barely enough food to sustain himself, and clothed in rags, he provides an example for all as he continues his apostolate of helping and caring for his comrades less strong than he. He is then sentenced to go to the camp at Zöschen. In this place—very much like Buchenwald and Dachau—where blows fall thick and fast and death reigns supreme, he constantly comes to the aid of his wretched comrades, thereby winning the admiration of all.

(Testimony of André Lefort, a Jocist friend,
Paris-18th Arrondissement.)

EUGÈNE LEMOINE

Eugène was arrested by the Gestapo on the same day as I— September 30, 1944. After having spent four days in the Prison at Wittenberg, he was taken to the central prison at Halle. After the interrogation, he was released and regained his freedom for the rest of the month of October. Returning to Wittenberg, he resumed his work in the camp at Schleicher. But the Gestapo still had him under surveillance.

In fact, sometime before our arrest, a man from Niort who had worked in Eugène's camp escaped from the disciplinary camp of Spergu and sought refuge, on September 16th in the camp at Neumühle. We took him in and Eugène, who has just come back, also establishes ties with this fellow. Then both are arrested by the Gestapo. I presume that Eugène placed total responsibility for the arrest on his own shoulders, because the Gestapo only interrogated me a single time about the entire matter. Once again Eugène was sent to prison at Halle, and on November 16th, he was incarcerated in the disciplinary camp at Zöschen, where I joined him on November 22nd. He had been sent there to serve out a twelve-week sentence, and I was to live in the same room with him for almost four weeks.

At Zöschen, Eugène was assigned to a terribly debilitating job which consisted of operating a water pump by hand for thirteen hours a day, while standing on the outside, without any protection from the frost and snow. When I left him, his health was already severely impaired—he was suffering from a very high fever and had a persistent cough. On December 21st, before our departure, Roger Martins, Auguste Eveno, and I gave him all our warm clothing, but we had no doubt about what would inevitably come to pass. He died February 8, 1945.

(Testimony of Julien de Wiele.)

PASCAL VERGIER

LOUIS DOUMAIN

ANDRÉ PARSY

... Two of our own expired at Zöschen while we were there; and two others, André Parsy and Colbert Lebeau, succumbed after our departure.

Father Pascal Vergez left us on December 19th, Louis Doumain on the 20th. Both had been more weakened than we by their stay in prison. They worked in our *Kommando* for a week, and we virtually had to carry them during the four kilometers we had to walk on our way back to camp every evening. For a while they managed not to attract attention. Then because a *Kolfactor*, who had been in the same prison with André Parsy and Vergez, took pity on them, they were allowed to stay in the barracks for two or three days. From that point on, they were given virtually nothing to eat and suffered terribly from thirst. Only after successfully fighting off the Russians and Poles did we manage to get a quarter liter of juice for each of them. During the day we lent them our blankets (two of them having to share one), and at night we all clung close together.

One morning we were ordered to transport them to the infirmary. I tremble whenever I think of these poor emaciated bodies that we carried away on one blanket.

We visited them in secret during the evenings, thus risking 25 blows of the bludgeon. In that infirmary, whose barracks were filthier than all the others and where there were poor wretches defecating in every corner, people were dying by inches. It was while being subjected to these conditions that our two chaplains met their death, as did Colbert Lebeau, who passed away three days after our departure, on January 4, 1945, as a result of pulmonary congestion. Suffering from dysentery, André Parsy had to reenter the hospital at Trebitz after we were both liberated on December 1944. He consummated his sacrifice on December 26, 1944."

(Testimony of Auguste Eveno)

"...*Happy are they who have died with this crowning achievement and in this obedience and humility.*" (Charles Péguy)

"*This much I know for certain, that I shall stay and stand by you, to encourage your advance and your joy in the faith, so that my return to be among you may increase to overflowing your pride in Jesus Christ on my account.*"

(Letter of St. Paul to the Phillipians 1 25/26)

THURINGIA

▸ JEAN LECOQ—Clandestine priest from the Diocese of Rennes, POW transformed as civilian worker, Chaplain for Gotha, deported to Dachau.

▸ PAUL BESCHET, Jesuit student at Mongré, in the Sonderhausen community, deported to Flossenbürg-Zwickau.

▸ RENÉ LE TONQUÈZE—Jocist from Tours, Director at Suhl, deported to Flossenbürg-Zwickau.

▸ FERNAND MORIN—Jocist from Flers de l'Orne, interpreter at Gotha, deported to Buchenwald.

▸ JEAN HAMÉON—Jocist from Tours, Director at Suhl, then at Eisenbach. Arrested and imprisoned at Suhl, sent to the prison at Eisenach, then set free.

arrested on March 2nd, 1944 and forcibly repatriated the following month.

TRANSLATOR'S NOTE

Father Beschet provides two Appendices in his work: 1) the Letter of Gestapo Head Ernst Kaltenbrunner concerning the activities of the JOC among French forced laborers in Germany and announcing the measures to be taken to eradicate them, and 2) the Letter of Father Jean Rodhain, Head of the French Chaplaincy for Workers in Foreign Countries (to priests, religious, seminarians, and militants). I believe it to be also useful for reasons of historical documentation to include two additional documents: the first, Reich Chancellor Martin Bormann's Secret Letter to all the *Gauleiter* describing the Third Reich's hatred for all the Christian Churches and declaring the Nazi objective to destroy them. This document first received public attention during the Nuremberg Trial and was printed in the publication of the daily court proceedings: *Trial of the Major War Criminals before the International Tribunal* vol. 35, Doc. 075-D, pp. 7-13. The second is an excerpt from Charles Molette's *La Mission Saint Paul traquée par la Gestapo*, pp. 186-191, which gives an historical overview of the entire operation of the JOC in Germany and more particularly presents the essential details of the "mission" as it was played out in Thuringia, thus substantiating Beschet's own narration of these events. The four Appendices are presented in the following order: 1) the Bormann Letter, 2) the Kaltenbrunner Decree of Persecution against the JOC, 3) Rodhain's Letter to the Missionaries, and 4) the excerpt from Mollete's *La Mission Saint Paul*.

APPENDICES

APPENDIX I

- Secret Circular Letter Sent to All *Gauleiters* by Reichsleiter M. Bormann
- Secret Decree of the Chancellor of the Party, signed by Reichsleiter M. Bormann
- Decree is dated June 6, 1941—addressed to Dr. Meyer at Munich and transmitted to all the other *Gauleiters* (without mention of its having been sent to Dr. Meyer) as Circular Letter n. 8/41 (classified as Secret)

THE RELATIONSHIP BETWEEN NATIONAL SOCIALISM AND CHRISTIANITY

The tenets of National Socialism and Christianity are irreconcilable. The Christian churches depend upon human ignorance and strive to keep as large a part of the population as possible in this state because this is the only way that these Christian churches can maintain their power. National Socialism, on the other hand, is based on scientific principles. Christianity is defined by precepts that have not changed in two thousand years and have become embedded in dogmas progressively more and more detached from reality. Conversely, if it is to complete its mission, National Socialism must constantly adapt itself to the most recent findings of scientific research.

The Christian Churches have always recognized the dangers stemming from discoveries made by the exact sciences, which strike at the heart of their existence. Thus they have done their utmost to promote their own dogma through the use of trickery and sham. The concepts explaining the world that have been provided by National Socialism are far superior to those contained in Christian beliefs, all of which originated with and have been drawn and adapted from Judaism. This is why we have no need of Christianity.

No person would have any idea about Christianity, if they had not been indoctrinated by priests during childhood. The so-called good God seems to have no interest whatsoever in transmitting knowledge of his own existence to young people as they start life; rather, though supposedly an absolutely powerful being, he mysteriously abandons this function to the priests. If in the years to come, young people no longer hear anything said about this Christianity, whose teachings are so enormously inferior to our own, Christianity will disappear automatically.

It is just as amazing that, before the beginning of our era, humanity as a whole knew nothing about this God of the Christians, and that since this time the largest number by far of the earth's inhabitants still have learned nothing at all, or very little at the most, about this Christianity; and for this reason they have been condemned without any recourse by the arrogant teachings of these same Christian churches.

When we National Socialists speak of faith in a God, we don't have in mind the God of these naïve Christians and their spiritual profiteers, who propose a God who resembles man but has his abode somewhere out in the celestial sphere. We must open men's eyes and make them understand that next to our little world—an extremely insignificant part of the universe—there exists an unimaginably large number of other celestial bodies which are encircled, like our sun, by other planets and these by smaller bodies, like our moon. This vital force which operates according to natural law and causes the planets to move, we call the Almighty, or God. The belief proclaiming that such a universal force is concerned with the destiny of every human being, every earthly bacillus and can even be influenced by so-called prayers, has remained in force because of the extreme naïveté existing among believers, but also by the cynical motives driving the actions of others who have profited enormously from its propagation.

In contrast, we National Socialists hold an absolutely natural view of life which conforms as closely as possible with the laws of nature. The more we get to know about the laws of nature and life, the more we scrupulously obey them, and hence, the more we are in harmony with the will of the Almighty. And to the extent that we accept the will of the Almighty, the greater shall be our successes.

From this impossibility of reconciling the concepts of National Socialism and Christianity, it follows that we must refuse to strengthen the existing Christian faith groups or encourage those in the process of developing. For this reason, the idea of eventually establishing a Church for the Reich, which would bring together the different Protestant groups, has been abandoned because the Protestant Church manifests as much hostility toward us as does the Catholic Church. Any support given to a national Protestant Church would therefore be detrimental to our interests.

[...] In the past, the control of people was left exclusively in the hands of the Church. The function of the State was limited to promulgating laws and decrees, and over-all administration. The control of the people was, generally speaking, not incumbent on the State but was left to the Churches. Through their intermediary, priests and pastors exercised a very strong influence over the lives of individuals, families and the entire community. Anything contrary to the interest of the Churches was stamped out with unparalleled brutality. Through the centuries, the State acceded in diverse ways to the control of the Church over its people. The Church had the power both to uphold or to combat the State. The State needed the help of the Church and was dependant on it. The battle of the German emperors against the popes could never have come to anything, either in the Middle Ages or in modern times, because it was not the emperors, but rather the Church which had ascendancy over the people.

The philosophical dependency of the State with regards to the Church and the relinquishing of its own powers over the people had become axiomatic and objected to by no one. For any leader about to assume power, not to consider this as a given would have been regarded as an absurd blunder.

For the first time in German history, the Führer holds the power of government consciously and totally in his own hands. By means of the Party, its divisions, sections, and affiliates, the Führer has created for himself, and hence for the German people, an instrument that can liberate him and make him independent of the Church. Any influences that might diminish his power or be damaging to the control of the people that the Führer exercises with the aid of the N.S.D.A.P. (National Socialist German Workers Party) must be eliminated. Greater and stronger efforts must be made to wrench the people from the hands of the Churches, their pastors and supporting organizations. It is to be expected that the Churches will and must defend themselves against this loss of authority. But we must never agree to allow the Churches to exercise the slightest influence in the control of the people. Such influence must be completely and definitively eradicated.

The Reich, along with the Party, its divisions and affiliated associations to which power has been mandated, is alone invested with the right to govern. Just as the nefarious influences of the astrologers, fortune-tellers, and other charlatans must be eliminated and crushed by the State, so also must the Church be made incapable of exerting even the slightest influence. Only when this objective becomes fully realized will the government be able to wield complete control over everyone of its citizens, and only then will the Reich and its people have their existence securely assured for all times.

If, after having fully taken into account the philosophical opposition of the various Christian groups against our Party, we should conclude that such an attitude emanates more particularly from one of these Churches than the others, we would then be committing the same errors that had proved to be particularly fatal for the German Empire in centuries past. For it is in the Reich's interests not to single out any one branch, but rather to maintain and reinforce the ecclesiastical divisions among the churches.

Signed, M. Bormann, *Reichsleiter*

NOTE

We include at the end of our narrative two documents of interest to the reader:

1. the Letter of Ernst Kaltenbrunner, Chief Security Officer for the Reich (Gestapo) dated December 3rd, 1943. This document was brought to our attention thanks to the consideration of Monsignor Charles Molette, postulator general for the collective cause of beatification for the martyrs of the apostolate conducted at the very core of the JOC. Though we had no idea of the existence of this document at the time, we nonetheless certainly suffered its effects.[1]

2. The Letter from the Chaplaincy Office to French Workers Abroad (Monsignor Rodhains Office in Paris), dated May 19th, 1944.[2]

---

1   Molette's, version of the Kaltenbrunner letter is a French translation of the original document found in the Bundesarchiv Berlin R 5B/030. (trans. note)

2   Beschet's text of this letter also appears in Molette, *En Haine de l'Evangile*, pp. 270-271. (trans. note)

APPENDIX II

GERMAN ARCHIVES

Order of Kaltenbrunner
    Head, Central Security Office of the Reich (Gestapo)
    Head Office of Security for the Reich Berlin, December 3rd, 1943

To all the administrative offices of the state police, the Heads of the security police and security operations.

To the agents of the Head Office of the security police and security operations.

At Brussels, to the Commanders of security police and security operations.

Special notice to: the inspectors of the security police and security operations.

For the groups referred to here: IV D 4, IV A 1, IV C 2, IV D—foreign workers—, III B, III D, and VI B

Concerning: The activities of French Catholic Action among French workers in the Reich.

Referral: None.

Because of the growing numbers of French civilian workers arriving in the Reich, the French Catholic Church has attempted to obtain, initially through diplomatic negotiations, legal moral assistance for its compatriots through the presence of French priests in Germany.

These requests have been rejected out of hand because of the anti-German sentiments displayed from the very beginning by French cardinals, bishops, and priests, and because of the constant sabotage conducted by the French workers presently residing in the Reich. Religious assistance for French, Belgian, Dutch, or other workers provided by churchmen from their respective countries has always been and remains strictly forbidden, and all such aid must be suppressed by all possible means.

Through numerous intelligence reports recently received, we have irrefutable proof that the French Catholic Church has launched a vast campaign not only to win these workers over to Catholic ideas through illegal means, but even to indoctrinate them with its own anti-German political biases and to try to bring them together in officially organized associations.

French Catholic Action seeks to attain its goals:

1) Through the involvement of certain numbers of French priests and seminarians who have come into the Reich disguised as volunteer civilian workers;

2) Through the Catholic association of young workers, *"Jeunesse ouvrière chrètienne"* (JOC), also called "Jocists."

Addendum I

At the beginning of this year, Cardinal Suhard of Paris invited all the French bishops to supply the names of 15 "qualified" priests from each one of their diocese who would be prepared to come to Germany, camouflaged as French civilian workers, in order to engage in the illegal practice of providing aid to their compatriots. At the end of this process, in the middle of April, Cardinal Suhard officially greeted before their departure those priests who had been selected for this function by their respective bishops and offered them the following directives concerning their future activities in the Reich:

"You are soldiers of God and will soon go into a country where the power of evil is very strong. You will leave illegally as civilian workers; you must not say Mass openly or tell anyone that you are priests, because we don't want to be involved in diplomatic conflicts with the Reich. The Vatican knows of your departure through the agency of a priest who is presently on special mission there. But I hope to obtain for certain ones among you official authorization to reside in Germany. Your mission is to make contact with the German Church. Once there, you must make strenuous efforts to provide us with information which we will be able to use once and for all to definitively refute the false ideas that are being circulated by these men. The people must understand to what an abyss they are being led by National Socialism. You must bring the French workers together, make them aware of one another and bring back to the Church those among them who have lost their way. Since French workers are totally isolated and are suffering a great deal, it should not be too difficult a task to bring them back into the fold."[1]

Several hundred French ecclesiastics, priests and seminarians especially trained for this mission have thus come into Germany. Concealing their real profession, some of them have skillfully been able to have themselves assigned to French civilian workers camps. Assuming leadership roles or other administrative responsibilities, they have managed to organize a vast enterprise of subversion under the cover of religion in line with their secret mission, and they have often received strong support from the German Catholic Clergy in carrying out their illegal practices.

Moreover, the organization of French social services under the direction of the social assistant La Morlais,[2] began when these French priests were being sent to Germany; and we have it from unimpeachable sources that these social services promote the aims of Catholic Action, as described above. From where she was operating in Germany, this certain de La Morlais was given the task of placing camouflaged ecclesiastics in the French civilian worker camps for the purpose of integrating them into her social service network and to enlist them as delegates for provincial administrative committees of the D.A.F. Once operating as such, they would therefore have greater freedom of movement and a freer rein in influencing the workers, according to the wishes of the Germanophobic French Cardinals. During the course

---

1   There is no proof whatsoever to indicate that this "letter" can be attributed in any way to Cardinal Suhard. See Molette, *La "Mission..."* #19, p. 308. (trans. note)

2   Anne Marie de La Morlais (1894-1967) offered her services as social worker for French workers deported to Germany while also engaged in the Resistance. She established as her residence and place of work the city of Essen where there were large numbers of STO conscripts. In her official capacity as counselor to the JOC members working there, she was able to provide documentation and means of escape for young workers and POWs at the Essen camp. She was also directly involved in Resistance networks that organized sabotage from within the factories of this area. Arrested on September 9th in Düsseldorf by the Gestapo, she was interrogated and tortured before being sent to the concentration camp for women at Ravensbrück. Surviving her captivity to the end of the War, she was liberated by American troops on April 30th 1945. She held the rank of Captain in the FFI (*Forces Françaises Intérieures*). For further details see, Molette, *La "Mission ..."*, pp. 289-292. (trans. note)

of their regular meetings at Düsseldorf, for example, some of these social delegates very openly attacked German National Socialism and introduced Gaullist propaganda.

2. The French organizations formed by the young workers of JOC in the civilian worker camps in the Reich are very closely allied with the illegal activities of French ecclesiastics, priests and seminarians. These ecclesiastics, disguised as civilian workers, who have been sent here with important propaganda devices and considerable financial resources, are very involved in the organization and ongoing support of JOC groups.

This association (JOC), which for reasons of its clearly anti-German activities has had to be banned in the French Occupied Zone as well as in Belgium (and which formerly had come under strong English influence, even to the extent of receiving financial support from English groups for recruitment purposes), is today still engaged in an active propaganda campaign among French workers. It also deliberately seeks out contact with Communists because, by definition, they are also radically opposed to the new German order, and it encourages them to join with the JOC to promote their own security and continue their clandestine activities.

As the number of young French people coming to work here has been on the rise, it has also become apparent that there has been a large and increasing influx of members of the JOC as well. They immediately organize into groups in their camps and carry on a vigorous program of recruitment. They take charge of regular meetings and of recreational activities, bringing to them a heavy, politically anti-German bias, and meet in sheltered outdoor places or in private rooms— often put at their disposal by the German clergy. They also hold meetings with other groups from camps and cities in the area. Moreover, they attempt in underhanded ways to win over the German workers. The following note from one of its members provides an instructive and typical comment on the JOC's agenda for Germany:

"We (the member of JOC) have already penetrated into 200 factories in the Reich and have thus organized 50 sections among French workers in Germany. To this end, moreover, we have established a number of contacts with the German clergy. German priests are very enthusiastic regarding this Catholic renewal which they didn't think was possible and which they were no longer expecting. However, it is our goal not only to promote religion but also to cause divisions within the German working class. Above all, we want to turn the workers against their Nazi leaders."

Finally, the JOC organizations have made common cause with the French Scouts who are animated by the same anti-German sentiments. According to a declaration made by the above-mentioned Madame de La Morlais, young French workers in Germany must be solidly integrated within groups such as these so as to be well positioned on the day that France will be liberated from under the German yoke.

It has been discovered that in many cases French ecclesiastics, camouflaged as civilian workers, and members of JOC have succeeded in transmitting important information of an anti-German nature to religious and civilian propaganda mills in France. In their reports, which they often make in response to special requests from French organizations, they don't limit themselves to their observations on the treatment of workers in Germany or on the social and economic conditions of the country, but also give descriptions of their work sites and other kinds of information that can be of important use to the enemy.

POLITICAL MEASURES

In order to put a stop to the corrupting influence exerted on French civilian workers in the Reich by the offices and organizations of the French Catholic Church, I order that the following measures be immediately put into effect:

1. All French and Belgian priests, seminarians and students of theology who have come into the Reich camouflaged as civilian workers must be identified by name and their present place of residence given; and this information must be sent to the Office of Security for the Reich.

2. The administration of the Bureau of Security, through the office of the General Director of Manpower, will then carry out the expulsion of the above to France and Belgium.

3. In the event that the French priests, seminarians, etc. should in any way demonstrate aggressive attitudes by word or deed, I ask that they be arrested and that a full report be sent to me concerning the matter.

4. French ecclesiastics, priests, seminarians, etc. who have acted as camp leaders or who have served in any other administrative roles must be immediately relieved of their positions and be employed in

the ranks of normal workers until their expulsion to France, which must carried out as quickly as possible.

5. I order that all of the groups associated with the JOC, that have been established in the camps of French workers, be immediately disbanded and that any subsequent activities by them be strictly forbidden under pain of severe measures to be put into effect by the police. In the case of French civilian workers who have given evidence of past support and are regarded as still being actively involved in the operations of the JOC, to the extent that their activities are recognized as being anti-German or conspiratorial, such persons must be placed in detention for 21 days, without necessarily requiring that they be sent to a concentration camp; then after being given a severe warning upon their release, they must be assigned and relocated to a site as far as possible from their original place of employment.

6. Rigorous and appropriate measures must be initiated against German Catholic ecclesiastics who have supported the JOC or the illegal activities of the French clergy, according to the circumstances of each particular case and also taking into account any criminal charges that may previously have been leveled against them.

7. To assure that these orders are effectively carried out, I request that operations of all branches of national security be informed and their forces placed in operational mode so as to deal actively with this matter.

Signed: Dr. KALTENBRUNNER
Reich Chancellor

APPENDIX III

Letter of Father Jean Rodhain, Head of the Chaplaincy for French Workers in Foreign Countries

Paris, May 19th, 1944

My Dear Friend,

On the eve of my departure for another journey to Germany, whose itinerary will not, alas, allow me to be in your area, I wish to reply personally to the most recent letters we have received at the Chaplaincy Office.

All of the very numerous messages you have sent to us bear testimony to the many acts and works of friendship that you have been able to accomplish while in that country. One can examine each one of your letters and cards without finding one single sentence alluding to politics, all of which proves conclusively that you're obeying the orders given you by your religious superiors. In analyzing your letters it is also abundantly clear that you have provided your comrades with many kinds of aid and charitable assistance that are completely beyond reproach. Indeed, how many times have mothers or fiancées come into our Office to thank us personally for the help you have given their loved ones over there?

In the name of so many families, let me congratulate you and tell you that all of France feels united with you.

- Only a very few of the thousands of letters received from you give even the slightest hints of weariness. You'll be able to overcome this, in spite of the very real difficulties you are encountering, once you'll have better understood how many families back here are depending upon you. Despite repeated requests by the Episcopacy, the German authorities have not as yet authorized, as they have for our POWs, that French chaplains be allowed to be with you there. Thus up to the present time, you members of the laity have had to bear upon your own shoulders the major responsibilities for carrying out religious observances. Indeed the Church has officially entrusted you with this task, and in empowering you, she prizes what you are doing and values you "as the apple of her eye."

A few days ago, His Excellency Monsignor Valerio Valeri, Nuncio of the Sovereign Pontiff, even came to our offices here; he visited our headquarters and thumbed through your letters to show what great interest the Pope has for you. His Eminence Cardinal Suhard, who is the real head of the Chaplaincy, and for whom I serve merely as a delegate, constantly asks me about the religious activities in which you are engaged for your comrades. Even more significantly, when informed that I was going to write you, His Eminence immediately insisted on sending you his blessing—see the attached document to this effect that I am honored to transmit in this same letter. And if this surprises anyone of those around you, show them this letter; because what I'm sending you can in no way be construed as a clandestine command—nothing would be more contrary to the way that I operate. My purpose in writing is to state what I have endlessly been repeating to all the German authorities from Paris to Berlin, during the more than three and one half years and over 150,000 kilometers that I've spent travelling throughout the work camps in Germany, and that is simply to express how much confidence the living Church from top to bottom has in its lay members. What I'm saying to you is only a resume of what has been written in numerous books sent out from our Chaplaincy Headquarters—you must have noticed on everyone of your packages containing them the authorization stamped by the German censors, because we regularly must have the titles of each one of books formally approved by the Office of Propaganda. Thus the urgent requests which we receive from factories in every area asking us to send more of the same kinds of reading material clearly indicates how well our intentions have been understood, as well as the great demand and appreciation there have been for your labors among a large segment of French workers.

Finally for some time now many of you have been repeating in your letters a request similar to the one we've received so many times in the past from those writing from the POW camps: it seems that like them, your gaze also instinctively turns more and more toward Lourdes as the site you desire for making a pilgrimage after your return. Yes, indeed, let me announce here and now, that on a still-undetermined date, the Chaplaincy Headquarters will lead all of you to the Grotto of Lourdes. It won't be a trip for tourists: starting now, prepare for it by fulfilling the promises you have made and carrying out your efforts to come to the aid of others: thus you won't arrive at Lourdes with empty hands! It won't be a pilgrimage for people who are cut off from one another; so starting now, prepare your team, get recruits, and you won't arrive at Lourdes all alone.

This won't be a pilgrimage in the distant future: to make it a reality soon, we ourselves are already praying and preparing for it from here where we are in union with you and all your friends. Shall we not then start to build together that cathedral from which our gaze even now can almost catch a glimpse of that triumphal dawn, when God will see his people returning to Him?

Head Chaplain
Jean Rodhain

My Dear Friend,

"I thank you for all the good your have done for your comrades. I bless your efforts and pray for you."

Emmanuel Cardinal Suhard
Archbishop of Paris

APPENDIX IV

Excerpt from Charles Molette, *La Mission "Saint Paul" traquée par la Gestapo*, pp. 186-191.

"The Catholic apostolate in Thuringia gradually took shape during the summer of 1943. It was at this time that the various teams of Catholic Action—those that had already been organized, those in the process of being developed, as well as the STO groups that had already been set up beforehand in the labor camps and cities of Thuringia—established close contacts among themselves. Frequent communication (realized either through trips taken back and forth, meetings, and correspondence by mail) provided the means to establish a supple and efficient network not only on the local level, but also for an effective regional organization. Yet this organization and the many displacements required for it to function, as well the postal system that it relied upon for communication, soon brought its members under the suspicion of the Nazi police who, in the course of several days, proceeded to arrest and put in prison their leaders ("the pillars of the Church"), and eventually convicted them for their "Catholic Action" carried out for their comrades in the STO. They were finally sent to concentrations camps, where eight (out of ten) of them met their death before the camps were liberated.

"Though operatives—'pillars of the Church'—had been functioning among the work conscripts sent to Thuringia before 1942, these initiatives took on formal structure when the first Jocists to come to the region arrived in November of that year, thus providing an initial surge in apostolic activities during the Christmas season: Henri Marannes (1923-1945) in Gera; André Vallée (1919-1944) in Gotha; in December, Louis Pourtois (1919-1945) in Eisenach; then Camille Millet (1922-1945) in Erfurt. René Le Tonquèze arrived soon after in Suhl in February, 1943; Marcel Callo (1921-1945) who was beatified in 1987, comes to Zella-Mehlis; at the beginning of August,

Marcel Carrier (1922-1945) whose two daughters had been warned by what might happen to them in the future if he did not accept his draft notice, was sent to Weimar; then two seminarians were sent to Southern Thuringia: Roger Vallée (1920-1944) who joined his brother in August, 1943 and Jean Tinturier (1921-1945), sent to Schmalkalden in September of 1943 (along with two other students for the priesthood from the Seminary of the Carmelites, Paris): Louis Kuhn, future bishop of Meaux and François Donati; at the same time the Jesuit Scholastics Paul Beschet, André Yverneau and others arrive at Sonderhausen; other young militants are scattered in the Leipzig or Halle regions to the West of Saxony.

"The transformation of priest POWs to civilian work status (zivils)—Abbé Jean Lecoq in Gotha in June of 1943 and Abbé Rabourdin at Gera in July—and the arrival of a number of seminarians at the end of the academic year—gave structure to this apostolate: André Vallée reports that there were seven autonomous federations existing in Gotha at the beginning of December, 1943; and in Northern Thuringia, Emile Picaud, Federal Jocist from Paris, in collaboration with Paul Léon, a National STO Director arriving at Halle as an STO worker, establishes apostolic links with Saxony.

"But starting in October, 1943, the apostolic activities and frequent trips taken by the militants come under increasing police surveillance. Soon even without having clear knowledge of the Kaltenbrunner Edict of Persecution by Kaltenbrunner (3rd of December), the leaders of Catholic Action groups feel the vice of police security tightening around them and, by the beginning of 1944, are persuaded that they have to reduce the number of regional meetings and downsize the scope and numbers participating in meetings at the local level, thus having to go more and more underground in conducting Catholic Action at the various regional locations.

"Beginning in the month of April, some of the 'pillars of the Church' are arrested and sent to prison. On April 17th, Marcel Carrier is arrested (turned in, it seems, by an interpreter, for having come back late from an overnight trip). He joins the two Vallée brothers (themselves arrested on April 1st the Vigil of Palm Sunday) in the local jail at Gotha: Roger the seminarian had just received from the Vicar General of Sées the text of Cardinal Suhard's official protest against the campaign of the Occupation authorities directed against Catholic Action, and he also had on his person a small notebook sent to him by his brother containing notes about study groups, places where retreats had taken place, and names of comrades. Targeted mail and other information coming in from France, as well as whatever else found on the spot, especially information provided by a Flemish female volunteer worker in the pay of the police, conclusively supported the charges that had already appeared in dossiers the authorities had prepared concerning them. On April 4th, Jean Lecoq was also taken in at Gotha; and after Marcel Carrier's arrest, a veritable dragnet was set on April 19th: Louis Pourtois was arrested at Eisenbach; Henri Marannes at Gera; Jean Tinturier (but not the two other seminarians who, though sharing his living quarters, were not participating in the same apostolic activities) at Schmalkalden. Not surprisingly, Camille Millet was arrested at Erfurt; Marcel Callo, whom on the preceding 14th of November Jean Tinturier had gone to meet and, as a result of this visit, had decided to become part of the apostolic movement he saw taking shape, was seized at Zella-Mahlis; the arrests of still two others who had arrived from France and would survive as witnesses to report on the outcome of these events: René Tonquèze at Suhl, and Paul Beschet, were taken in at Sonderhausen. Thus on the following day, Thursday, the 20th of April, they all learn, when once brought together in the prison at Gotha, that they have been incarcerated out of hatred for their faith and their apostolate, for being "too Catholic," and for attempting "to reinstate the kind of society that has been forbidden in Germany," etc.

[...] "The interrogations that they are forced to undergo at the hands of Inspector Wincklers, a specialist in religious matters, make them realize that the police have not brought them in to be questioned about incidents of sabotage, in which some of them could possibly be implicated. Almost immediately the police also are forced to renounce their manufactured myth 'that Quiclet and the Chaplaincy had given them orders to enter into contact with political resistance movements in Germany.' Even after beating Henri Marannes 'like a dog' to try to back up this charge, his interrogators aren't able to find anything in their dossiers which substantiates this. But what they do have are lists of the 'leaders' (Fernand Morin, the interpreter at Gotha, saw on the table one that had been sent from France), as well as reports on activities of Catholic Action, support groups, contacts that had been made, trips taken, meetings, and clandestine Masses said. And if anyone of them cannot deny the evidence contained in the mail that had fallen into the hands of the police, he would assume total responsibility for all of the charges in order to clear the others. These interrogations, which usually lasted a whole day and sometimes even went on far into the night, proceed with a revolver (which seems not to have been used) and a bludgeon (employed with great frequency) lying on the desk in full view for all to see. The seminarians were particularly badgered and attacked for matters concerning the Eucharist: In between two sessions of being beaten with the "*gummi*" on Holy Thursday, April 6th, Roger Vallée was forced to dress up in his priestly vestments and was then boisterously mocked by all present; on April 20th, Jean Tinturier had to drink from a chalice containing beer; and we should add that on the following day, Camille Millet had been made to swallow unconsecrated hosts contained in the chapel-valise kit that had been used for saying Mass at Erfurt, found by the police among his possessions.

"After this they spend five months (April-October, 1944) in detention in the city jail at Gotha where they had been transferred at the end of April. Sometimes their work on the outside afforded one or another of them the opportunity to go down the Alexandrinenstrasse with their guards and, when they pass by the window of the sisters' convent and are recognized, some of the nuns get down on their knees and begin to pray to show how spiritually united they are with them; or during their work they sometimes make contact with comrades outside the prison: on July 16th, with two of the latter acting as intermediaries, the men who were being taken from prison to work on the outside were able to receive fragments of consecrated hosts that had been collected by Abbé Dansette (from the Lille Diocese), a POW priest at Sonderhausen, who had been trying for two weeks to get these to them.

"Their time spent in the Gotha Prison gradually becomes a kind of "novitiate for martyrdom," a sort of long spiritual retreat interspersed with novenas and petitions. First, novenas for the feast of Pentecost (March 28th), then for the feast of Corpus Christi (June 16th). At the moment when they accept the fact that they must go beyond the demands of 'an apostolate of action to one of redemption,' they begin a novena on the feast of Saint Ignatius of Loyola (July 31st) 'to ask him for additional spiritual strength so that we may endure our imprisononment.' They accepted the changes that were then occurring in their lives as an answer to their prayers. At the beginning of August, the increasing number of prisoners having to be housed led to a decision by the prison head to put these French Catholic militants together in the same area: a large cell on the uppermost level of the prison called the "*Kirche*" because, in the past, the Protestant minister had used it as the site to minister to his flock; in entering there on August 9th, Roger Vallée, the seminarian from Sées, names it the " upper room" (after Acts I, 14), and Camille Millet makes a cross out of everlastings blessed by Jean Lecoq, which they hang on the wall for all to see. From this point on, these young apostles live the authentic life of a community, starting with the sign of the cross when they get up, to evening prayers, the reading of the Mass on Sundays by Jean Lecoq, meditation led by a seminarian on Thursdays, and for their daily readings in common, passages from the work *France, pays de mission?* ('Is France a Mission Country?', Henri Godin and Yves Daniel, 1943).

[…] "Thus for everyone of them, the Gotha prison will have served as a novitiate for martyrdom marked by periods spent praying together. After the novena begun on the feast of Saint Ignatius, they made two more: one on August 15th to learn from the example of Mary, who had accomplished her own eternity by accepting God's will for her on earth and finally, a novena begun on the 24th of September to Saint Theresa of Lisieux 'to ask her for the necessary patience to endure these final days of our imprisonment because, let me tell you, with what we're going through, we'll need it.' The following day, each one was found guilty of the following charges (and forced to sign the statement): '*Because of the Catholic Action he has provided for his comrades in the STO, he has posed a danger to the State and the German People.*' The day after, Camille Millet writes: "All of us are happy about the reasons for our having been convicted. We are certain that we're doing God's will. During all this time that we've been imprisoned for Christ, He has never abandoned us. […] So our morale can only be high."

"Then they leave for the concentration camps. Flossenbürg is the first stop for these men distinguished by their zeal and their labors in maintaining close rapport among the groups comprising the Catholic community of Thuringia. At the selection center, Jean Lecoq is separated from the little group and sent to Dachau to live with the hundreds of other priests interned there. The remaining ten become part of the convoy which crosses the threshold of the Flossenbürg camp (near the Czech border) murmuring the *Our Father*. During the registration they are tattooed with the numbers 28901 to 28910.

"But if they were all classified as 'Zivilarbeiter' ('civilian laborers'), four of them were also designated as 'Schutzhaft' ('prisoners detained while awaiting trial'), thus solely under the jurisdiction of the Office of Security of the Reich (Gestapo): they were two seminarians, Jean Tinturier and Roger Vallée, as well as the recently beatified STO conscript Marcel Callo, and Louis Pourtois, 'a strong and dependable fellow' (as he was described by Jean Tinturier in a letter sent by him to Louis's family). The four are transferred from the 23rd to the 25th of October to the Mauthausen Concentation Camp. Roger Vallée dies there on October 30th virtually in the arms of Father Riquet, S.J., who says in his testimony: 'Roger Vallée died as a martyr for his faith and for Catholic Action.' From Mauthausen Jean Tinturier is sent at the beginning of December 1944, to the camp at Auschwitz. Arriving there less than a week after the destruction of the gas chambers at Birkenau (Auschwitz II), he is dispatched to the Kommando at Schwientochlowitz, from which, at the end of January, 1945 (the last roll call at the camp was held on January 17th, before the advancing Russians), he is sent back to Mauthausen. He dies on March 16th in transit while traveling in a convoy of open sledges, with the temperature less than -20 centigrade, three days before the demise of Marcel Callo—both of whom offered up their final moments to the Virgin Mary. The last of the four, Louis Pourtois, would die on April 21st.

"Only two of the six who had remained in the Flossenbürg Kommandos would return: Two died in a Kommando: André Vallée, on February 15th in Leitmeritz; and Henri Marannes at the Zwickau Kommando on April 4th, 1945, where he was beaten to death by wooden planks. Camille Millet, who had also been in the Zwickau Kommando, dies not there but in the infirmary at Flossenbürg, where he had been transported in the same convoy (March 27/29) as Jean Duthu, a seminarian from Clermont Ferrand.

"Finally, Marcel Carrier collapses in the death march and is shot to death on one of the highways where the Germans are continuing to evacuate and exterminate the deportés."

From La "Mission Saint Paul" traquée par la Gestapo, by Charles Molette. First published by François-Xavier de Guibert, Paris, France. ©2003 by François-Xavier de Guibert Groupe DDB / Editions Desclée de Brouwer. Used by permission of the publisher. All rights reserved.

SELECTED BIBLIOGRAPHY

Amouroux Henri, *La vie des Français sous l'occupation*. Paris: De Borré. 2011.

Bédarida, Renée, *Les armes de l'esprit. Témoignage Chrétien*. Paris: Les Éditions ouvrières, 1977.

————. *Les catholiques dans la guerre 1939-1945*. Paris: Hachette, 1998.

Bernadac, Christian, *Les sorciers du ciel*. Paris: Éditions France Empire, 1969.

Beschet, Paul, *Mission in Thüringen in des Zeit des Nationalozialismus*, trans. Mittelmeyer, Hans and Pabel, Rosmarie. Erlangen, Germany, 2005.

Bourdais, Henri, *La J.O.C.sous l'occupation allemande*. Paris: Les Éditions de l'Atelier, 1995.

Christophe, Paul, *Les catholiques devant la guerre, 1939-1940*. Paris: Éditions ouvrières, 1989.

Collaboration and Resistance: Images of Life in France, 1940-1944. trans. Lory Frankel. New York: Harry N. Abram, Inc., 1989.

Chaunu, Jean, *Esquisse d'un jugement chrétien du Nazisme. Paris:* F.-X. de Guibert, 2007.

Comte, Bernard, *L'honneur de la conscience, Catholiques français en résistance 1940-1944*. Paris: Les Éditions de l'Atelier, 1998.

de Gaulle-Anthonioz, Geneviève. *La traversée de la nuit*, Editions du Seuil, Paris, 1998.

Duquesne, Jacques, *Les catholiques sous l'occupation*. Paris: Grasset, 1966, rpt. 1986.

Evrard, Jacques. *La déportation des travailleurs français dans le troisième Reich*. Paris: Fayard, 1971.

Fouilloux, Étienne, *Les chrétiens français entre crise et libération 1937-1947*. Paris: Seuil, 1997.

Gildea, Robert, *Marianne in Chains*. New York: Picador, 2002.

Godin , Henri and Daniel, Yvan, *La France, pays de mission?*, Lyons: Éditions de l'Abeille, 1943.

Halls, W.D., Politics, *Society and Christianity in Vichy France*. Oxford and Providence, USA: 1995.

Haas, Rheimund and Tillman, Elizabeth, *51 Französische Märtyrer im Nazi-Reich 51 Martyrs français dans le Reich Nazi*. Dortmund/Cologne: Initiativkreis Französische, 2005.

Kammerer, Jean, *La baraque des prêtres à Dachau*. Paris: Éditions Brepols, 1995.

Klein, Charles, *Le diocèse des barbelés*. Paris: Fayard, 1973.

Levi, Primo, *Survival in Auschwitz*. New York: Touchstone Books-Simon and Schuster, 1996.

Lubac, Henri de, *Résistance chrétienne à l'antisémitisme Souvenirs 1940-1944*. Paris: Fayard, 1988.

Molette, Charles, *"En haine de l'Évangile" Victimes du décret de persécution nazie du 3 décembre, 1943*. Paris: Fayard, 1993.

————. *Martyrs de la Résistance spirituelle Victimes de la persécution nazie décrétée le 3 décembre, 1943 contre l'apostolat français à l'oeuvre parmi les travailleurs requis en Allemagne*. 2 vols. Paris: F.X. de Guibert, 1999 .

————. *La "Mission Saint Paul" traquée par la Gestapo*. Paris: F.X. de Guibert, 2003.

————. *Prêtres, Religieux et Religieuses dans la résistance au Nazisme, 1940-1945*. Paris, Fayard, 1995.

Morvannou, Fanch, *Marcel Callo 1921-1945*. Brest: Fanch Morvannou, 2007.

Paxton, Robert, *Vichy France 1940-1944: Old Guard and New Order*. New York: Alfred K. Knopf, 1972.

Pélissier, Jean, *Prêtres et religieux victimes des Nazis*. Dijon and Paris: L'Échelle de Jacob, 2009.

Perrin, Henri, *Journal d'un prêtre ouvrier en Allemagne*. Paris: Seuil, 1945.

Poulat, Émile, *Naissance des Prêtres-Ouvriers*. Paris: Casterman, 1965.

La Résistance Spirituelle 1941-1944 Les cahiers clandestins du Témoignage Chrétien. ed. Bédarida, François and Bédarida, Renée. Paris: Albin Michel, 2001.

Simon, Albert, *Dieu à Buchenwald*. Paris: Les Éditions de l'Atelier, 2000.

Sommet, Jacques, *Liberté démesure de la foi*. Paris: Éditions du Cerf, 1983.

Sweets, John F., *The Politics of Resistance in France, 1940-1944*. De Kalb, Illinois : Northern Illinois University Press, 1976.

Tournet, André, *Montluçon 1940-1944 La mémoire retrouvée*. Nonette, France: Editions Créer, 2001.

Trial of the Major War Criminals before the International Military Tribunal 42 vols. Nuremberg, Germany, 1945-1949.

Tusa, Anne and Tusa, John, *The Nuremberg Trial.* New York: Skyhorse Publishers, 2010.

Vergnet, Paul, *Les catholiques dans la Résistance.* Dijon and Paris: L'Échelle de Jacob, 2009.

Verrier, Philippe, *Le P. Victor Dillard, jésuite, mort à Dachau en 1945 "l'un des Cinquante."* Magny-les-Hameaux, France: Socéval Éditions, 2005.

Vinen, Richard, *The Unfree French Life Under the Occupation.* New Haven and London, 2006.

Vittari, Jean-Pierre, *Eux les S.T.O.* Paris: Ramsay, 2007.

Zaretsy, Robert, *Politics and Public Opinion in the Gard 1938-1944.* University Park: Penn State Press, 1995.

INDEX